Education and
Anthropology

# Education and Anthropology

## Other Cultures and the Teacher

**Frank Musgrove**
*Victoria University of Manchester*

**JOHN WILEY & SONS**

Chichester · New York · Brisbane · Toronto · Singapore

Copyright © 1982 by John Wiley & Sons Ltd

**Library of Congress Cataloging in Publication Data:**
Musgrove, Frank
   Education and anthropology.

   Includes index.
   1. Educational anthropology.   I. Title.
LB45.M87            370.19            81–16241
                                     AACR2
ISBN 0 471 10143 5


**British Library Cataloguing in Publication Data:**
Musgrove, Frank
   Education and anthropology
   1. Educational anthropology
   I. Title
   370.19            LB45

   ISBN 0 471 10143 5

Photoset by Paston Press, Norwich
Printed by Pitman Press Limited, Bath, Avon

# *Contents*

# CHAPTER 1

# *Introduction*

## 1. THE SAVAGE AS MODEL

The savage is a potent image in Western educational thought. He has been a model for reformers—especially reformers of upper-class education—since the middle of the eighteenth century when Rousseau wrote *Émile*. This was an enormously popular work, but it is almost equalled in our own times by the anthropological writings of Ruth Benedict and Margaret Mead. Primitive man has been a powerful symbol of courage, independence, strength, virility, and intelligence. He has stood for nature and purity against the artificial and corrupt.

He has also been a symbol of hope. In the seventeenth century John Locke used anthropological data to show that moral ideas varied among mankind and therefore could not be innate (Locke, 1690). Since that time the variability of mankind has been an argument for liberation and reform. Anthropologists showed that the characteristics of men—whether moral, intellectual, or temperamental—were not immutable or fixed: they varied radically and profoundly with circumstances. Vice and stupidity were not, perhaps, ineradicable. All things were possible. The savage in his infinite variety has been the great hope of Western education for three centuries. This has been especially true in the past 50 years.

Rousseau, Mead, and Benedict drew explicit lessons for Western education from their picture of primitive life. So does this book, What have studies of other cultures to tell the teacher in England about the nature of children and the process of growing up? About the way children learn, remember, and think? About the conditions in which rational thought prospers? This book attempts to answer these questions.

It will also have something to say about an especially difficult educational problem of our times—the teaching of children from 'other cultures' who are now in large numbers in our own British schools. But it would be folly to treat Pakistanis, West Indians, and Africans who are settled in Britain, out of respect for their native cultures, as if they were still in their overseas communities of origin. In Britain they are new people, they present a new cultural reality which cannot simply be extrapolated from abroad. A major point of this book is that the immigrant must be seen and treated *in situ*. He is not an African, a West Indian, or a Pakistani who has merely changed his location: he has changed his nature. It is this new nature, and not the old, that we must understand and which must guide the way we teach him in our multicultural schools.

1

Rousseau drew a clear distinction between the peasant (who was dull) and the savage (who was sharp): 'Speaking generally, there is nothing duller than a peasant or sharper than a savage.' The peasant, said Rousseau, lived by tradition and under authority, but the savage was tied to no one place and had no prescribed task: he lived by constant improvization and by reason rather than tradition and habit. (This contrast is not wholly out of line with recent highly sophisticated research—which is fully discussed in chapter 5—on the personality characteristics of agriculturalists in nonliterate societies on the one hand, and pastoralists and hunters on the other.) It was the sharp savage and not the dull peasant whom education should take as its model; and the clear lesson from the life of savages was that education should be based not on words but on things. Modern anthropologists (like Goody and Leach) have arrived at a similar conclusion.

Systematic knowledge of savages (and peasants) has enormously increased since Rousseau's day, and with particular speed in the past two or three decades. We know much more about a wide range of issues which have a direct bearing on education, for instance the way memory is organized and aided in societies which do not know how to write and the way social relationships are affected in societies that do; the conditions under which people in traditional societies will develop a capacity for abstract thinking and for rational belief; the way the language people learn influences the manner in which they look at and sort out the world.

But what we get from these studies is not only new knowledge of old cultures but new ways of seeing our own. What was formerly taken for granted about children, school, and society may become problematic, no longer inevitable and in the nature of things. In our own world we are like Schutz's phenomenological stranger for whom the culture pattern is 'not a shelter but a field of adventure' (Schutz, 1964): recipe knowledge becomes suspect, typifications lose their typicality, and the society's proverbs, wise saws and instances lose their authority.

For the student of another culture there may be a sense of new possibilities in his own. Submerged or little-regarded aspects of life and work may take on a heightened significance: 'empty' rituals and symbols of school life may be reappraised and filled with new meaning. The significance of schooling itself may be seen in a new light. In the small-scale world of preliterate man, as Lévi-Strauss has shown, the social order has often rested on the exchange of sisters for wives (Lévi-Strauss, 1969); in our own the provision of free schooling, like other charities, may be part of a system of social exchange on which the social order stands.

## 2. SUSPICION OF PSYCHOLOGY

Anthropologists are the experts on other cultures. In recent years economists and sociologists who are interested in the modernization of 'Third World' countries and psychologists who study children's thinking have made their specialist contributions. Anthropologists with the notable exception of Hallpike (1979) commonly view cross-cultural psychological work with suspicion, largely on technical, methodological grounds; but the tradition of psychological inquiry in primitive societies is now well established.

Seventy years ago Lucien Levy-Bruhl did psychology great harm. It only slowly recovered. From what was then known about primitive beliefs he argued that the primitive mind was mystical and prelogical (Levy-Bruhl, 1910). Today he is being reinstated, but for more than half a century his work seemed to discredit psychology and deter psychological work.

Psychologists are today highly sensitive to the criticisms of anthropological colleagues and respect their misgivings about 'parasitic research conducted on a hit-and-run basis' which neglects the meaning of the social context (Doob, 1957). They are now quite properly extraordinarily cautious not only about the cultural equivalence of their tests but of the social contexts in which they are administered (Cole and Bruner, 1971; Cole and Scribner, 1974; pp. 172–174). The English psychologist Vernon, like the American psychologist Doob, counters criticism not only with a perceptive intelligence but with a robust and impressive technical competence (Vernon, 1965; Vernon, 1969; p. 98).

The new experimental psychology had already been put to effective cross-cultural use before Levy-Bruhl published his speculative accounts of the primitive mind. At the close of the nineteenth century the Cambridge anthropological expedition to the Torres Straits, which was led by A. C. Haddon, included several well-trained psychologists who devoted themselves to studies of perception. Their work under the direction of W. H. R. Rivers cast doubt on any notion that primitive man was endowed by nature with superior powers of observation and perception, although his mode of life might give rise to close attention to and mastery of detail (Rivers, 1901).

In the interwar years psychological investigation of primitive peoples continued to make some headway. The distinguished Cambridge psychologist Sir Frederick Bartlett worked in the tradition of the Torres Straits expedition and made notable studies of memory among Swazi herdsmen. Like Rivers he brought seriously into question a widely held view that preliterates have a natural superiority (Bartlett, 1932, pp. 248–250). In the meantime Margaret Mead was making her celebrated 'cultural' studies in Samoa and New Guinea. These were essentially psychological in character, focusing on personality development.

They were the prelude to an extensive literature on child rearing and growing up in various tribes. They enlarged our understanding of child development and education in the widest sense. The English anthropologist Margaret Mead made studies in the 1930s of growing to manhood as a member of the Ngoni tribe in Nyasaland which earned here a Chair of Education in the University of London (1940–1955).

Psychologists' research on child-rearing practices and culture and personality became extensive, ambitious, and over-complicated; but in the past 15 years or so more focused and limited psychological studies of primitive thinking have been made. Attention has shifted from personality in the South Seas to problem solving in West Africa, and the Wolofs of Senegal, the Kpelle of Liberia, and the Tiv of Nigeria are almost as well known today as were the Manus, the Tchambuli, and the Arapesh to an earlier generation of education students.

We know when they achieve 'conservation'. Cross-cultural Piagetian research on concept development—of considerable technical difficulty but carefully and expertly conducted—has underpinned programmes of curriculum reform and development especially for the poor (the 'disadvantaged') in Britain and America. This work in the cognitive field—much of it associated with Bruner's Center for Cognitive Studies at Harvard—will receive particular attention in this book.

## 3. KNOW-IT-ALL FOLK

Attempts to pinpoint the defining characteristics of primitive societies are legion. What is incontrovertible is that by our standards they are poor. In recent years economists have turned their attention to the countries which are held to constitute a 'Third World'. They belong neither to the rich capitalist West nor to the equally rich communist East. They are mainly in tropical countries in Africa, Asia, the Pacific Islands, and Central America. It is in this Third World that the 'other cultures' of this book are to be found.

In the rich industrial countries of the world more than 40 per cent of the population live in cities of 100 000 inhabitants or more, in Third World countries only some 10 per cent do so; in the rich countries there are only some 17 births per thousand of population per year, in the Third World countries there are 30. In rich countries the proportion of normal diet from animal sources is usually between 30 and 40 per cent, in Third World countries as little as 5 per cent (Goldthorpe, 1975, pp. 78–79). Third World countries are often trapped in a 'culture of poverty'.

Poverty does not necessarily breed what Oscar Lewis has called the 'culture of poverty', but some sociologists have argued that it will tend to do so if it is experienced in an emerging cash economy with low-wage, semi-skilled labour and a wealthy and propertied upper class. This is increasingly the situation in many 'modernizing', former tropical dependencies. Oscar Lewis (1966) argued that the culture of poverty implied a similar way of life wherever it was found, cutting across or transcending regional and national boundaries. That is not the view taken in this book. 'Other cultures' in tropical Africa, Pacific Islands, and Central America today no less than in the past differ profoundly among themselves in ways of thinking and forms of social life in spite of life at near-subsistence level for most of their members.

But the 'other cultures' of this book are not simply poor: they are preliterate. Today there is usually a minority of people who can read and write, and small Westernized elites have usually succeeded to political power. But these cultures are still essentially oral cultures; in an intellectual sense they experience, in Robin Horton's term, a 'closed' rather than an 'open predicament'. The people do not live in uncertainty and bewilderment oppressed by a sense of inadequacy and ignorance: they have an answer for everything. These are not humble cultures; they are know-it-all cultures. Within the closed intellectual world of oral tradition they can explain everything. 'What the anthropologist almost never finds is a confession of ignorance about the answer to some question which the people themselves consider important. Scarcely ever, for instance, does he come across a common disease or crop failure whose cause and cure people say they just do now know' (Horton, 1967). In the 'other cultures' of this book there is nothing of note that the people concede they cannot understand.

## 4. 'COLD' SOCIETIES: POLYGYNY, WITCHCRAFT, AND BRICOLAGE

There is no single blueprint for a primitive society. 'Primitive' and 'preliterate' refer to a range. The societies which fall within this range include 'precontact' tribes with zero modernization, and small-scale, partially modernized societies of the present day.

The range encompasses at its more primitive end what Robert Redfield (1947) called a 'folk society': 'small, isolated, nonliterate, and homogeneous, with a strong sense of group solidarity'. Folk societies, said Redfield, are enclosed and unself-critical; 'there is no money and nothing is measured by any such common denominator of value'; the sacred prevails over the secular; and the family group is the unit of action. The folk society was the polar opposite of the society of the modern city.

Few 'preliterate' societies are today wholly nonliterate: most enjoy at least restricted literacy. (In these circumstances nonliterates become illiterates.) Few of these societies live with near-zero external relationships and subsistence economies: limited cash crops, external trade, and a 'dual economy' mark them off from the self-contained and perhaps internally coherent societies of precontact times. Few are now without a city, and many have an international airport. Nevertheless, there is a major discontinuity between the small-scale societies within this 'primitive' range and the advanced industrial nations of the 'developed' world.

Some anthropologists and sociologists have argued that the discontinuity is so great that meaningful comparisons cannot be made. Among American sociologists Robert Bierstedt held such a 'Great Gap' theory (Bierstedt, 1948); among English anthropologists John Beattie has shown extreme caution (Beattie, 1966, pp. 46–48). This book rests on the assumption that comparison and extrapolation are not only possible but highly instructive. But the very real difficulties of comparison and extrapolation (in what is often rather loosely called 'cross-cultural' research) are not minimized.

There are large and even fundamental differences between modern and primitive societies. Lévi-Strauss distinguishes sharply between societies that are 'hot' and those that are 'cold'. Hot societies have history and science, cold sciences have myth and 'bricolage' (Lévi-Strauss, 1962, pp. 16–36, 233–234). Hot societies have scientists who work with abstract theories, cold societies have bricoleurs who work with and reconstitute the leftovers to hand: material odds and ends. Lévi-Strauss's admiration is unreservedly for bricoleurs and myth makers (who are a kind of intellectual bricoleur). Bricoleurs, like myth makers, can be ingenious and devious in their work: what they intricately cobble together is often 'brilliant and unforeseen', highly imaginative and even poetic in quality. But theirs is essentially a 'science of the concrete', operating 'half-way between percept and concept'. Although hot societies still have their bricolage, their distinctive science is highly theoretical and abstract: it is not so embedded in the here and now.

A further far-reaching distinction is this: cold societies do not have social classes. The social order of modern societies rests principally on occupation and class, that of primitive societies on kinship and age (Lloyd, 1966). But although primitive societies do not have 'classes', today they mostly have small, Westernized elites who may conceivably so look after the interests of their children that they solidify into classes as we understand them.

Primitive societies are highly personal, partly because of their 'smallness of scale'. Evans-Pritchard said smallness of scale was their defining characteristic (Evans-Pritchard, 1951, p. 8). A small-scale primitive society might number a million or more members, like the Tiv of Nigeria or the Nuer of the Sudan, and the territory occupied might be vast; but 'In a small-scale society the individual interacts over and over again with the same individuals in virtually all social relations' (Benedict, 1966, p. 27). No one can be anonymous. Life is regulated in face-to-face encounters rather than through remote and abstract rules. In Mary Douglas's terms, it is the difference between 'small-group' societies and 'strong grid' (Douglas, 1973, pp. 77–92).

These small-scale, highly personal, primitive societies are polite where we are abrupt, ritualistic where we are unceremonious, and helpful to relatives to the point we should consider corrupt. They are usually polygynous; like us they say whom you may not marry, but unlike us they often say whom you should. Cross-cousin marriage in particular may be not only preferred but prescribed.

Primitive societies have a tradition of witchcraft practice and belief. Our own relatively recent past saw similar widespread beliefs. The crucial difference is this: whereas witchcraft practices and beliefs among primitive peoples are 'normal', with us they are not.

This point was emphasized by Evans-Pritchard when he wrote his classic study of witchcraft and oracles among the Zande almost 50 years ago: 'To us supernatural means very much the same as abnormal or extraordinary. Zande certainly have no such notions of reality. They have no conception of "natural" as we understand it, and therefore neither of the "supernatural" as we understand it.' Witchcraft was an everyday matter, taken for granted, scarcely worthy of comment, ordinary: 'It is a normal and not abnormal happening' (Evans-Pritchard, 1976, p. 30).

Beattie underscores the same point: 'To an African or Melanesian peasant it is just as "natural" for a rainmaker to make rain, or for a witch to bewitch his enemy, as it is for a woman to bear children, or for a man to harvest the crop he plants' (Beattie, 1966, p. 203).

Beidelman raises the problem of comparing witchcraft in 'modern' and 'primitive' settings when the meaning for the people involved is so different: 'to what extent can we speak of such Zande beliefs as being comparable to those in other societies where suspected witches may be lynched?' (Beidelman, 1970). Primitive peoples do not generally divide the world as we do into two mutually exclusive zones labelled 'natural' and 'supernatural' (although, as Beattie points out, they usually dichotomize it in other ways). This illustrates one of the fundamental problems of comparative studies: the extent to which our own taken-for-granted categories and labels can be applied to societies markedly different from our own. Does our very terminology falsify or seriously distort the comparisons we make?

## 5. CAN WE COMPARE PRIMITIVE AND MODERN SOCIETIES?

Margaret Mead never hesitated to compare primitive societies and modern America. She drew confident lessons for American education and family life. Comparative studies taught us, for example, that fatherhood is a social invention. Margaret Mead concluded that America could and should 'rephrase the incest taboo' so that men would compete less and cooperate more (Mead, 1962, p. 191). Robert Bierstedt was appalled by her methods. He considered her book, *And Keep Your Powder Dry*, a particularly 'stunning example of the inadequacy of anthropological methods' in studying a complex society (Bierstedt, 1948).

'Incest taboo', 'ritual rebellion', and 'rites of passage' are now part of our everyday vocabulary. These specialized technical terms originated as tools for the analysis of primitive societies. They are now applied loosely and almost indiscriminately in the social (and historical) analysis of our own society. Stone's recent study of the family and marriage in sixteenth- and seventeenth-century England, for example, is embarrassingly larded with the anthropologist's (and psychoanalyst's) technical vocabulary, and even sixteenth-century apprenticeship, which took most young men away from home, is interpreted as a manifestation of the incest taboo (Stone 1979, p. 84). The problem is usually the other way round—taking terms which have precise and exact meaning for us (like 'wife' and 'king') and exporting them to primitive societies which we then recreate in our own image.

The African woman who is married like an English or American woman is not a wife but a whore. No bride-price has been paid. Christian missions have converted wives into whores throughout tropical Africa. In Britain in the 1950s and 1960s we discovered that scarcely remembered uncles and cousins were an 'extended family'. Anthropologists warned us against the pretensions of this technical terminology (Firth, 1961; Lancaster, 1961) which created an often misleading illusion of similarity.

Radcliffe-Brown and Gluckman had always insisted that the study of primitive societies was simply a branch of comparative sociology. Both stridently asserted the 'scientific' and generalizing character of social anthropology. Radcliffe-Brown said the anthropologist's methods and aims were the same as the physicist's, and although he discussed the problem of 'meaning' for the people involved, he decided rather plaintively that you couldn't trust what they told you (Radcliffe-Brown, 1952, pp. 142–147). But his Huxley Memorial Lecture in 1951 was an impressive illustration of the comparative method. From a consideration of Australian aboriginal social groups (endogamous moieties) referred to respectively as Eaglehawk and Crow, he proceeded to show through comparative materials how binary opposition was a universal feature of social structure. He was satisfied that 'A study of the system of moieties in Australia can give us results that should have considerable value for the theory of human society' (Radcliffe-Brown, 1951).

Max Gluckman always played down the difference between primitive and advanced societies and readily make comparisons across cultures. 'The "primitive" African today is part of modern industrial civilization,' he wrote in 1944; 'he works in its mines and factories and he consumes their products. Therefore I shall speak of sociology rather than of social anthropology' (Gluckman, 1944). He was always over-impressed by van Gennep's concept of 'rites of passage' as one of 'the broad generalizations that have emerged in the history of our science (Gluckman, 1949), and readily applied his notion of ritual rebellion to British parliamentary institutions (Gluckman, 1954, p. 30).

Gluckman was delighted with Evans-Pritchard's study of witchcraft among the Zande because, he said in 1944, a historian had told him that it was like witchcraft in sixteenth-century Europe: 'That is, it established relationships between types of events, not specific events: and that is scientific (Gluckman, 1944). By the 1960s historians of European witchcraft also had high hopes of a comparative, anthropological approach (Thomas, 1963); but the comparisons with Africa that eventually emerged were more tentative, provisional, and partial than had been hoped. Richard Kieckhefer, the historian of European witch trials in the fourteenth and fifteenth centuries, was very doubtful of the relevance of anthropological studies because European society even in the fourteenth century was so different from an African or American Indian tribe. But he conceded that phenomena of witchcraft in early Europe were 'analogous to such phenomena in primitive societies whether one thinks they should be or not' (Kieckhefer, 1976, p. 1).

The problem of terms and categories remains unresolved. Our terms 'witchcraft' (internal, unseen forces) and 'sorcery' (material potions) do not necessarily correspond to the different magical practices of primitive peoples—although Evans-Pritchard said they did in the case of the Zande (Evans-Pritchard, 1935). Beidelman thinks we produce gross distortions by using these terms on a cross-cultural, comparative level (Beidelman, 1970); Leach conducted an illuminating sociological analysis of magic by designating two mystical forms of influence simply 'x' and 'y' (Leach, 1961, pp. 23–27). Mary Douglas thinks that no fixed terminology should be used: 'I suggest it would be far better to let the traditional European terms be freely applied according to the whim of the ethnographer' (Douglas, 1967).

And yet both Leach and Mary Douglas are among those who make the boldest and most far-reaching cross-cultural comparisons. Leach points out that even our words 'consanguinity' (blood relations) and 'affinity' (in-laws) are not absolute technical terms with the same meaning for all societies; but he argues strenuously for large comparative generalizations (Leach, 1961). Even Beattie, who is more wary, is prepared to compare such far-flung gift-exchange institutions as the 'potlatch' of North American Indian tribes, the 'kula' of Melanesia, and 'bridewealth' of Africa (Beattie, 1966, p. 44). But his preference is for comparisons 'between institutions in very similar (and therefore probably contiguous) societies'.

This book is based on the assumption that comparisons among primitive societies and between modern and primitive societies, when made with a full awareness of the technical and conceptual difficulties, are not only possible in principle but profitable in practice. 'Idealist' strains of thought both in sociology and philosophy have made us perhaps unduly cautious. In sociology this 'idealism' stems from Max Weber, in philosophy from Wittgenstein: it emphasizes the inwardness of experience and the inaccessibility of its meaning to outsiders. For this reason Lévi-Strauss dismissed it contemptuously ((Lévi-Strauss, 1976, pp. 71–72).

Even the famous Wittgensteinian philosopher Peter Winch conceded that we can learn from primitive societies. He is preeminent among those who have emphasized the difficulty of doing so. In a famous paper (Winch, 1964) he castigated Evans-Pritchard for imposing Western standards and criteria of rationality and truth on a primitive people. But even Winch concluded that we are able to understand and learn from primitive societies, although we must first enter into their ways of thinking. Members of sophisticated societies may have to jettison their sophistication to achieve this, 'a process which is itself perhaps the ultimate in sophistication'. This is clearly difficult and the method obscure, but not in principle, it seems, impossible. To succeed in the attempt, says Winch, brings not simply comprehension but wisdom.

This book has a much more modest aim: it hopes to throw some light for teachers on critical influences on the development of thinking and rationality. To do this it is not enough vaguely to compare 'cultures', but the behaviour of individuals (including their thinking) in different social contexts. The aim is neither wisdom nor general laws but simply to discover what works.

Anthropologists compare institutions. They do not compare societies—Beattie has warned us that to treat societies as 'things' is to be guilty of the 'fallacy of misplaced concreteness' (Beattie, 1966, p. 34). They do not compare cultures either, says Evans-Pritchard: they compare 'systems of relations' (Evans-Pritchard, 1951, pp. 91–98). Malinowski argued that institutions were comparable ('commensurable') across the dividing line of culture, and even his sternest critic, Max Gluckman, agreed with him (Gluckman, 1949). Institutions are simply regular and established relationships, for instance between husband and wife and ruler and ruled. These are the prime concern of anthropologists.

They must also be our concern. But we are also interested in the kinds of comparison that psychologists are able to make. We are interested in values, beliefs, and customs ('culture') as well as institutions, and we are interested (with Strodbeck) in cultures as 'treatments'. It is useless, says Strodbeck, to demand 'culture-free' instruments for cross-cultural (psychological) research; they do not exist. But culturally appropriate instruments can and should be used. It should be possible to show the effect of 'treatment' (culture) A compared with 'treatment' (culture) B.

This book will show particular interest in the effect of the following on children's learning, rationality of beliefs, and cognitive growth: the city, literacy, the school, tight groups, and pastoral compared with agricultural life. In this story the small tight group is the villain and the city is the hero.

## 6. USING ANTHROPOLOGY TO ATTACK THE MIDDLE CLASS

Modern anthropology has upgraded primitive man; modern psychology has done the opposite. The work of such anthropologists as Robin Horton, Thomas Gladwin and Claude Lévi-Strauss (and linguists with anthropological interests like Edward Sapir, William Labov, and Benjamin Lee Whorf) has strongly indicated the subtlety and complexity of primitive thought; the work of present-day psychologists like Philip Vernon and Leonard Doob has underlined its limitations. This is so even in areas—like spatial-perceptual abilities—where we might have expected at least equivalence with ourselves if not superiority. The work of the anthropologists has been deployed by sociologists of education to attack the middle class of Britain and America, to cast doubt on their 'real' intellectual and verbal ability, and to question the abstract, literary school curriculum which allegedly expresses their values and ensures their continuing 'hegemony'.

White middle-class language, culture, and school curricula were traduced in the Inglis Lecture at Harvard University in 1948. The lecture was given by Allison Davis, Professor of Education at Chicago University. Primitive language and thought were compared with white middle-class language and thought to the detriment of the latter. The authority cited was Edward Sapir.

Allison Davis recalled Sapir's low regard for 'so-called "advanced" European languages' and observed:

> It is very doubtful, in fact, that the refinements, as we consider them, of middle-class English indicate any higher degree of mental capacity than the complexities of lower-class dialects or of primitive languages. (Davis, 1949, p. 83)

The Harvard audience was informed with obvious relish that Sapir had maintained:

> The lowliest South African Bushman speaks in the forms of a rich symbolic system in essence perfectly comparable to the speech of the cultivated Frenchman. . . . Many primitive languages have a formal richness, a latent luxuriance of expression, that eclipses anything known to the languages of modern civilization.

Much of the debate has revolved around the issue of concrete versus abstract thought. Considerations of language were formerly central to this debate; in the 1970s language was eclipsed by navigation. The writings of Thomas Gladwin on Polynesian canoe navigators (Gladwin, 1971) have been extensively cited by sociologists of education in their sustained attack upon the middle class.

The attack through anthropology became shrill in the 1970s. Three influential 'readers' appeared addressed primarily to teachers interested in the sociology of knowledge and of the school curriculum. The first was *Knowledge and Control* (Young, 1971) which brought the specialized anthropological papers of Robin Horton to a wider public of educationalists. (Horton claimed that traditional religious thought in Africa was 'theoretical' and comparable to Western science.) The second 'reader' appeared two years later: *Tinker, Tailor . . . The Myth of Cultural Deprivation* (Keddie, 1973). This included an article by Gladwin on Trukese navigation, on the diagnosis of disease among the pagan Subanum of the southern Philippines, and William Labov's celebration of 'the logic of nonstandard English'. The third 'reader' in this genre was *Worlds Apart* (Beck *et al.*, 1976). This included articles on childhood among the Chaga of Tanzania, on arithmetic among the Kpelle of Liberia, further papers on the Subanum, and more of Gladwin's work on Polynesian navigation.

All these issues—of abstract versus concrete thought, primitive versus 'advanced' languages, the cognitive skills involved in navigation—will be considered closely later in this book (especially in chapter 2 which deals with literacy, in chapter 3 which deals with cognitive abilities, and in chapter 4 which deals with rationality and belief). At this point I would merely underline the polemical uses to which social and cultural anthropology have recently been put.

The cross-cultural investigations of modern psychologists powerfully suggest the cognitive inequalities of men (that is not to say that these inequalities are innate or ineradicable); the work of modern anthropologists—at least since Kroeber—has tended to minimize differences. Kroeber asserted the 'psychic unity' of mankind, Lévi-Strauss and the structuralists see a universal mentality beneath the diversity of cultures.

In the 1920s Evans-Pritchard showed how eminently sensible, logical, and practical was Zande witchcraft, and what a constructive role in the social system it had. As Mary Douglas observes: 'Evans-Pritchard's Azande study minimizes the gulf between European and primitive cultures' and so finds sympathy with liberal and progressive opinion in the West (Douglas, 1970). What is new is the use of such anthropological work in polemics which claim that white middle-class culture is actually inferior.

This is quite explicit in Allison Davis's Inglis Lecture that has already been cited; it is explicit in Labov and in Gladwin; it is explicit in the editorial comments which preface and interleave the 'readers'.

The high power of abstraction which Gladwin sees in Puluwat canoe navigation (abstract thinking is its 'pervasive characteristic') is apparently matched in the West in relatively plebeian and 'uneducated' occupations such as big-city taxi driving. Gladwin is explicitly concerned to counter the view that the school-educated middle classes have superior powers of abstract thought. Taxi driving, says Labov, is an occupation which 'frequently engages people who are poor, have dropped out of school, and presumably cannot handle the kind of thinking usually required in intelligence tests'. But big-city taxi drivers work with an image of the city on which they superimpose the flux of traffic as this is governed by the time of day and day of the week. The Puluwat canoe navigator and the New York taxi driver work with a minimum of conscious deliberation, but 'What is so obvious in both is that they are dealing constantly in complex abstractions' (Gladwin, 1971, pp. 224–225).

Labov considers lower-class Negro speech and concludes that in comparison the standard English of the middle class is verbose, 'words take the place of thought and nothing can be found behind them'. Middle-class speakers are 'enmeshed in verbiage' and the 'elaborated code' which Bernstein says they speak is 'turgid, redundant, and empty'. But barely literate lower-class Negroes who do badly in all school subjects (and intelligence tests) are often 'more effective narrators, reasoners and debaters than many middle-class speakers who temporize, qualify, and lose their argument in a mass of irrelevant detail' (Labov, 1973).

And so a careful selection from contemporary studies of other cultures is now deployed to show that they are not simply equal but superior to ourselves, and a 'middle-class' school curriculum is as personally disabling as it is (unfairly) socially advantageous. Some of the selected authors themselves draw such conclusions from their studies; if they do not, the editors do. Thus in the Introduction to *Knowledge and Control* Young tells us:

> Formal education is based on the assumption that thought systems organized in curricula are in some sense 'superior' to the thought systems of those who are to be (or have not been) educated. It is just this implicit 'superiority' that Horton is questioning when he compares Western and African 'theoretical' thought in his paper.

But Horton is at pains to emphasize here and elsewhere that African religious thought is not a variety of scientific thought, from which it is different in crucial respects. Scientific thought is more successful in establishing causal connections. And it does not let us suppose that a person can change the world simply by thinking or talking about it. The scientific view may not be 'superior', but it is certainly, says Horton, less 'horrific'.

## 7. PERSONAL VIEW

My essential qualification for writing this book is my experience of teaching and research while serving in the Colonial Education Service in Uganda in the 1950s. I argued then what Gellner has argued since, that there is no real alternative for primitive societies to the scientific rationality of Western civilization which is in any case, in Gellner's phrase, 'manifestly superior' (Gellner, 1968; Musgrove, 1951). I also argued, as Nettl did later, that this Western civilization is best mediated by small, highly selected and educated native elites (Nettl and Robertson, 1966; Musgrove, 1952c).

These arguments were contrary to powerful influences of the day. These influences had three sources: the reports of the Phelps-Stokes commission on African education, published in the 1920s and still widely heeded 30 years later, and whose advocacy of 'local bias' I questioned (Musgrove, 1952a, 1952d); the effect of 'cultural' anthropologists, notably Malinowski, on a few univerity educated and politically well-placed Africans; and the policies of Unesco which promoted 'fundamental' (or 'mass') education rather than selective, high-level schooling—a thin smattering of Westernization widely spread.

The traditional culture or way of life that I encountered among the Bakonjo, Batoro, Banyankole, Ba'amba, Bachiga, and Banyoro tribes of western Uganda was characterized by a belief in pervasive witchcraft and the malign influence of ancestral spirits, the 'Bachwezi' by slash-and-burn subsistence farming (and cultivation of the arts of rain making and rain stopping as an essential part of agricultural technology); forced labour for chiefs; polygyny and the bride-price; and heavy kinship obligations—including the inheritance of deceased brothers' widows—in the absence of any other form of social welfare services. Life in this remote interior region of Africa was isolated from the wider world except through missionary activity which communicated not contemporary Western values but an archaic theology and morality redolent of Victorian England. Grotesque myths of the outer world proliferated: white men in distant Kampala were cannibals: they had few children because they ate them. They used a red vehicle with a bell to make predatory raids on villages and red buckets contained the blood of victims (Musgrove, 1952b).

My experience of living among these people, of teaching their children in a government college, and of conducting research into educational aspects of 'cultural change', led me to the following conclusion about Westernization and cultural adaptations:

> The African seeks the strange new knowledge of the West which many fear to offer in case he becomes less African and an 'imitation European'. And because, at the moment, they are being given something less, Africans openly complain that they are receiving an inferior brand of education designed to handicap them in competition with the European and confirm them in a subordinate condition.

They were right to resent a specially tailored 'African' education, I argued, but not only or principally for political reasons:

> Occupying a central place in Africa's new learning must be the history of our own most characteristic tradition, the scientific tradition. Perhaps the most valuable thing recovered by Western Europe from the ancient civilizations was the scientific attitude, developed in Iona in the sixth century B.C., which first sought explanations of nature in and not beyond nature. It is an understanding of this attitude that Africa most needs: a conception of the rule of law in nature and in human affairs, of orderly processes rather than arbitrary forces at play. A secondary education should stand four-square on this attitude. An education which begins and ends with instruction in supernatural events scarcely more credible, for the most part, than the animistic beliefs they replace, is open to serious doubts. (Musgrove, 1951)

On the subject of elites and their strategic role in social change my evidence was clear: the highly educated young were not cut off from their families in the bush. They were models:

> The people at home are willing to learn from them They [college boys] realize that the old must be respected and their counsels heeded; they know that if they speak English at home they may be in actual physical danger. . . . But they are always anxious to return home and their parents treat them as honoured guests. . . . The educated man is accorded a high status by the villagers: the chiefs respect him and will not require of him the customary services (such as attending the weekly hunt or acting as an unpaid porter to an official safari) which the peasant must perform. The educated man is an admired type. (Musgrove, 1952c)

My experience as a teacher of boys and young men from a score of remote and relatively untouched African tribes made me very doubtful of the wisdom, and above all the efficacy, of cultural adaptations and in-context learning. This was patently socially conservative and personally stultifying: it did not promote cognitive development but inhibited it.

In the interwar years anthropologists' studies of primitive education—for instance by Mead in Samoa (Mead, 1929) and by Fortes in Taleland (Fortes, 1938)—had suggested great virtues in 'embedded', contexted learning closely related to the real-life concerns of adults. They had even suggested that these traditional primitive methods of teaching and learning should be the model for everyone. They are, in fact, a disaster, if our interest is in science rather than bricolage—or even if the humble, and with us taken-for-granted, ability to multiply five by seven (as distinct from adding five to five seven times). The crucial importance of out-of-context learning for the young in any culture is the central argument of this book.

## REFERENCES

Bartlett, F. C. (1932), *Remembering*, Cambridge University Press, Cambridge.
Beattie, John (1966), *Other Cultures*, Routledge & Kegan Paul, London.
Beck, J., Jenks, C., Keddie, N., and Young, M. F. D. (1976), *Worlds Apart*, Collier-Macmillan, London.
Beidelman, T. O. (1970), 'Towards more open theoretical interpretations', in Mary Douglas (ed.), *Witchcraft Confessions and Accusations*, Tavistock, London.
Benedict, Burton (1966), 'Sociological characteristics of small territories and their implications for economic development', in M. Banton (ed.), *The Social Anthropology of Complex Societies*, Tavistock, London.
Bierstedt, Robert (1948), 'The limitations of anthropological methods in sociology', *American Journal of Sociology*, **54**.
Cole, M., and Bruner, J. S. (1971), 'Cultural differences and inferences about psychological processes', *American Psychologist*, **26**.
Cole, M., and Scribner, S. (1974), *Culture and Thought*, Wiley, New York.
Davis, Allison (1949), *Social-Class Influences upon Learning*, Harvard University Press, Cambridge, Mass.
Doob, L. W. (1957), 'Psychological research in nonliterate societies', *American Psychologist*, **12**.
Douglas, Mary (1967), 'Witch beliefs in Central Africa', *Africa*, **37**.
Douglas, Mary (1970), 'Thirty years after Witchcraft, Oracles and Magic', in Mary Douglas (ed.), *Witchcraft Confessions and Accusations*, Tavistock, London.
Douglas Mary (1973), *Natural Symbols*, Penguin, Harmondsworth, Middx.
Evans-Pritchard, E. E. (1935), 'Witchcraft', *Africa*, **8**.
Evans-Pritchard, E. E. (1951), *Social Anthropology*, Routledge & Kegan Paul, London.
Evans-Pritchard, E. E. (1976), *Witchcraft, Oracles and Magic Among the Azande*, Clarendon Press, Oxford.
Firth, R. (1961), 'Family and kin ties in Britain and their social implications', *British Journal of Sociology*, **12**.
Fortes, Meyer (1938), *Social and Psychological Aspects of Education in Taleland*, Oxford University Press, London.
Gellner, E. (1968), 'The new idealism—cause and meaning in the social sciences', in I. Lakatos and A. Musgrave (eds), *Problems in the Philosophy of Science. Proceedings of the International Colloquium, London 1965*, **13**, North Holland Press, London.
Gladwin, T. (1971), *East is a Big Bird*, Harvard University Press, Cambridge, Mass.
Gluckman, M. (1944), 'The difficulties, achievements, and limitations of social anthropology', *Rhodes-Livingstone Institute Journal*, no. 1.
Gluckman, M. (1949), 'An analysis of the sociological theories of Bronislaw Malinowski', *Rhodes-Livingstone Paper*, no. 16, Oxford University Press.
Gluckman, M. (1954), *Rituals of Rebellion in South-East Africa*, Manchester University Press, Manchester.
Goldthorpe, J. E. (1975), *The Sociology of the Third World*, Cambridge University Press, Cambridge.
Hallpike, C. R. (1979), *The Foundations of Primitive Thought*, Clarendon Press, Oxford.
Horton, R. (1967), 'African traditional thought and Western science', *Africa*, **37**; reprinted in Young (1971).

16

Keddie, Nell (1973), *Tinker, Tailor . . . The Myth of Cultural Deprivation*, Penguin, Harmondsworth, Middx.
Kieckhefer, R. (1976), *European Witch Trials. Their Foundations in Popular and Learned Culture, 1300–1500*, Routledge & Kegan Paul, London.
Labov, W, (1973), 'The logic of nonstandard English', in Keddie (1973).
Lancaster, Lorraine (1961), 'Some conceptual problems in the study of family and kin ties in the British Isles', *British Journal of Sociology*, **12**.
Leach, E. R. (1961), *Rethinking Anthropology*, Athlone Press, London.
Lévi-Strauss, C. (1962), *The Savage Mind*, Weidenfeld & Nicolson, London.
Lévi-Strauss, C. (1969), *The Elementary Structures of Kinship* (ed. R. Needham), Beacon Press, Boston, Mass.
Lévi-Strauss, C. (1976), *Tristes Tropiques*, Penguin Harmondsworth, Middx.
Levy-Bruhl, Lucien (1910), *Les Fonctions mentales dans les societés inférieures*, Paris.
Lewis, Oscar (1966), 'The culture of poverty', *Scientific American*, **215**.
Lloyd, P. C. (1966), 'Introduction' in P. C. Lloyd (ed.). *The New Elites of Tropical Africa*, Oxford University Press, London.
Locke, John (1690), *Essay Concerning Human Understanding:* Book I, 'Of innate ideas', London.
Mead, Margaret (1920), *Coming of Age in Samoa*, Cape, London.
Mead, Margaret (1962), *Male and Female*, Penguin, Harmondsworth, Middx.
Musgrove, F. (1951), 'History teaching in African secondary schools', *Overseas Education*, **23**.
Musgrove, F. (1952a), 'What sort of facts?', *African Affairs*, **51**.
Musgrove, F. (1952b), 'A Uganda secondary school as a field of culture change', *Africa*, **22**.
Musgrove, F. (1952c), 'The sociology of African education', *African Studies*, **11**.
Musgrove, F. (1952d), ' "Bias" in the African secondary school', *Corona: Journal of Her Majesty's Colonial Service*, **4**.
Nettl, J. P., and Robertson, R. (1966), 'Industrialization, development or modernization', *British Journal of Sociology*, **17**.
Radcliffe-Brown, A. R. (1951), 'The comparative method in social anthropology', *Journal of the Royal Anthropological Institute*, **81**.
Radcliffe-Brown, A. R. (1952), *Structure and Function in Primitive Society*, Routledge & Kegan Paul, London.
Redfield, Robert (1947), 'The folk society', *American Journal of Sociology*, **52**.
Rivers, W. H. R. (1901), 'Introduction and vision', in A. C. Haddon (ed.), *Reports of the Cambridge Anthropological Expedition to the Torres Straits*, vol. 2, Cambridge University Press, Cambridge.
Schultz, A. (1964), 'The stranger', in *Studies in Social Theory* (ed. A. Brodersen), Martinus Nijhoff, The Hague.
Stone, L. (1979), *The Family, Sex and Marriage in England 1500–1800*, Penguin, Harmondsworth, Middx.
Strodbeck, F. (1964), 'Considerations of meta-methods in cross-cultural studies', *American Anthropologist*, **66**.
Thomas, K. (1963), 'History and anthropology', *Past and Present*, no. 24.
Vernon, P. E. (1965), 'Environmental handicaps and mental development: part II', *British Journal of Educational Psychology*, **35**.
Vernon, P. E. (1969), *Intelligence and Cultural Environment*, Methuen, London.
Winch, P. (1964), 'Understanding a primitive society', *American Philosophical Quarterly*, **1**.
Young, M. F. D. (1971), *Knowledge and Control*, Collier-Macmillan, London.

# CHAPTER 2

# *The Importance of Literacy*

Literacy has been discredited by anthropologists. Few people would now equate literacy with education, although some quite sophisticated historians of education have recently done so. They have been suitably rebuked (Clanchy, 1979, p. 8). Far from equating literacy with education, some contemporary anthropologists think it subverts it.

So did both Plato and Rousseau. The latter took an 'anthropological' view. The only book he was inclined to allow Émile to read described life in a state of nature:

> Since we must have books, there is one book which, to my thinking, supplies the best treatise on education according to nature. This is the first book Émile will read; for a long time it will form his whole library. . . . What is this wonderful book? Is it Aristotle? Pliny? Buffon? No; it is *Robinson Crusoe*. (Rousseau, 1911, p. 147)

Rousseau wanted the growing boy to experience the world directly and not through symbolic representations. Contemporary anthropologists are similarly concerned about the thinning of experience that comes with the printed word. One principal consequence of literacy in the remote village of Birifu in northern Ghana has been that instead of their former 'palavers' and face-to-face dealings people nowadays send notes (Goody, 1972).

Today two Professors of Social Anthropology at Cambridge University are among literacy's foremost critics. They are Jack Goody and Edmund Leach. Leach is more extreme and uncompromising than Goody and draws explicit conclusions for the school curriculum: although literacy should not be wholly excluded, it should retreat from its present centrality. The Professor of Social Anthropology at the Collège de France, Claude Lévi-Strauss, is even more severe in his strictures. The general conclusion seems to be that literacy has had calamitous social and personal consequences and should be de-emphasized in our schools. This chapter maintains that this view is not simply wrong but perverse. It will examine first the influence of literacy on society, then on individuals' mental capabilities, and finally on truthfulness. For one of the age-old charges against literacy (recently reiterated by Leach) is that it cannot tell the truth.

# 1. LITERACY AND DOMINATION

Many anthropologists and some historians have linked literacy very closely with power. The extreme view is that literacy brings enslavement. More moderate views emphasize its socially conservative influence and support for the *status quo*. Literacy is preeminently the possession of the dominant classes which they use to legitimize and maintain their position: it is cultural capital which they invest to 'reproduce' themselves (Bourdieu, 1971; Bourdieu *et al.*, 1977).

'No difference could be more fundamental than that between peoples who can read and write and those who cannot' (Bierstedt, 1948). The latter, says Robert Bierstedt, have customs but no laws, techniques but no science, religion but no theology. But it is important to make other distinctions than this gross one between literate societies on the one hand and wholly oral or nonliterate cultures on the other. Literacy when everyone can read and write does not have the same meaning, or potential for social differentiation, as in a society with partial or restricted literacy. In the latter circumstances literacy may be profoundly socially divisive, even within families. As Hardy said of Tess, who had reached Standard Six:

> Between the mother, with her fast-perishing lumber of superstitions, folk-lore, dialect, and orally transmitted ballads, and the daughter, with her trained National teachings and Standard knowledge under an infinitely Revised Code, there was a gap of two hundred years as ordinarily understood. When they were together the Jacobean and the Victorian ages were juxtaposed. (Hardy, 1974, pp. 50–51)

Another crucial distinction is between ideographic and alphabetic cultures. The former came into existence first in China, Sumeria, and Egypt perhaps around 4000 BC, the latter arose relatively recently, around 700 BC, with the parsimonious Greek alphabet of 24 simple characters. The alphabetic culture was big with implications for power: it was from its sheer simplicity potentially democratic, within virtually everybody's grasp. The 'print-culture' which followed Gutenberg's fifteenth-century invention of a press with infinitely repeatable type again had its distinctive features and unique power implications. This was not simply a literate culture nor more specifically an alphabet culture: it was a book culture with enormous potential as a social solvent. It nourished inwardness, privacy and individualism, undermined tradition, communal wisdom, communal myth, and communal authority (Bantock, 1980). The gross distinction between literate and oral cultures is a crude first step in social analysis.

It is the only distinction that Lévi-Strauss makes. As a social anthropologist his subject is 'cold' societies which include the neolithic cultures of the past and nonliterate primitive cultures of today: they have art but no writing, myth but no history. Lévi-Strauss concluded from his contemplation of these 'cold' societies and the 'hot' societies that followed them that 'the primary function of written communication is to facilitate slavery' (Lévi-Strauss, 1976, p. 393).

Lévi-Strauss concedes that modern science would have been impossible without literacy, but his emphasis is on the impressive social and intellectual achievements of nonliterate societies in the past. No intellectual transformation accompanied the invention of writing, he says: one of the most creative periods in the history of mankind occurred in the early stages of the neolithic age. Technical and artistic (including architectural) advances were possible— 'gigantic strides'—because 'for thousands of years, small communities had been observing, experimenting and handing on their findings'. Accurate transmission of knowledge, skills, and techniques had occurred although writing was unknown. Writing was a consequence, not a cause, of the neolithic revolution; and for long its principal result was stagnation where formerly there was spectacular advance.

But above all there was now exploitation and oppression of ordinary people and great concentrations of power:

> The only phenomena with which writing has always been concomitant is the creation of cities and empires, that is the integration of large numbers of individuals into a political system, and their grading into castes or classes. (Lévi-Strauss, 1976, p. 392)

Lévi-Strauss's direct observation of the effect of writing on a primitive people is extraordinarily fleeting and fugitive. He travelled for a short time through the remote villages of the illiterate Nambwikara Indians of South America and for some obscure reason handed out paper and pencils to their 'Stone Age' inhabitants. Because the chief imitated Lévi-Strauss writing without in the least understanding what this (highly precarious and vulnerable) white man was doing, Lévi-Strauss reached the remarkable conclusion that the chief had a deep, intuitive understanding of literacy as a source of power: 'I could not help admiring their chief's genius in instantly recognizing that writing would increase his authority.' Ironically, it seems that the chief was deposed for precisely this reason: 'after my visit he was abandoned by most of his people'.

Goody's observations in West Africa were more prolonged and systematic. He, too, concluded that literacy was a major means of oppression by colonial powers: 'Once they had locked away the Maxim guns in their armoury, it was the pen and telegraph that took over' (Goody, 1972). In northern Ghana the first schools were established by the British army and the sons of chiefs and headmen were educated so that they could be messengers between district headquarters. Independence strengthened the link between literacy and power. Throughout Africa elementary school teachers became prime ministers almost overnight. Like Lévi-Strauss's writing on this subject, Goody's has an elegiac quality. He laments: 'They [the nonliterates] are at the mercy of a hostile world, geared to the man who can read and write. That is what development, modernization, is all about.'

Historians of Western societies have taken up this theme, in some cases acknowledging their debt to anthropologists (Clanchy, 1979, pp. 7–8). Some have focused on the effects of printing rather than on literacy itself. Books, says Eisenstein (1970), meant more authoritarian families (with the Bible to buttress the father's power), more despotic schools now that children had to be kept to their books instead of participating in the life of workshops and fields. Class distinctions were enhanced through printed symbols, notably heraldic devices, and a new, subservient concept of 'childhood' owed much 'to the widened gap between literate and oral cultures'.

An important function of the teaching of reading, says another historian, 'is to make students accessible to political and historical myth.' Printing may have had revolutionary implications at the outset, but

> For us print is the technology of convention. We have accommodated our senses to it. We have routinized and even ritualized our responses to it. . . . By maintaining the printed word as the keystone of education, we are therefore opting for political and social stasis. (Postman, 1970)

Literacy, the anthropologists tell us, has produced elites and classes. 'The art of writing', says Edmund Leach, 'started out as a secret code through which a literate élite exercised bureaucratic control over the illiterate masses' (Leach, 1977). For Leach writing as an 'antiquated fetish' which was given a new lease of life in the service of industrial capitalism and colonial expansion.

In an influential paper Goody and Watt similarly argued that literacy was an important cause of human inequality. Protoliterate cultures in particular, with their difficult systems of writing, gave rise to sharp social distinctions. The Chinese had a minimum of 3000 characters to learn, and a repertoire of 50 000 finally to be mastered. Becoming fully literate might take 20 years. In these circumstances a small, literate elite enjoyed great power. Even the easier Greek alphabet contributed in turn to the formation of modern elites and classes: 'Achievement in handling the tools of reading and writing is obviously one of the most important axes of social differentiation in modern societies' (Goody and Watt, 1968).

This is the point picked up by M. F. D. Young to support his attack on literary knowledge and skills as the basis of the 'middle-class curriculum' and middle-class status and power. Young's well-known 'stratification of knowledge' thesis draws heavily on Goody and Watt's characterization of literacy as the root of social stratification (Young, 1971). It is a curiously naive (and non-Marxist) interpretation of power. As Kathleen Gough more convincingly says in rebutting this view:

> I would argue that classes, whether modern or ancient, are based primarily on division of labour and means of production, and that difference in levels of literacy and reading habits tend to spring from these arrangements rather than giving rise to them. (Gough, 1968)

There are other compelling reasons for thinking that the literacy-and-domination thesis is not simply wrong but the opposite of the truth. These will be examined below.

## 2. LITERACY AND LIBERATION

The argument about literacy and power as it has been advanced by anthropologists is extremely confused. Literacy in the hands of the dominant classes, it seems, makes them more powerful; but literacy in the hands of the subordinate classes makes them weaker and more vulnerable. In fact, the main sources of power are elsewhere. But in general literacy will give some protection to the weak: codes, rules, treaties, contracts, and charters are written down and taken away from the personal caprice of rulers and the uncertainties of memory. The 'Queen's Regulations' do not diminish the private soldier's power: they increase it. A written code enables him to verify his rights and cite them if he thinks they have been infringed.

The long-term consequence of modern literacy is certainly to remove its special, exclusive benefits from any particular social group. The simple Greek alphabet allied with mass schooling conducted in the vernacular is an extraordinarily potent force for equality (Havelock, 1976, p. 45). Universal schooling, as Marx foresaw, means the proletarianization of middle-class, white-collar workers. Various restrictive devices have been used to ration literacy and schooling and so delay these effects: these include selective and 'qualifying' examinations and a strategic use of Latin and Greek. But as these restrictive and rationing devices give way before popular pressure, the special advantages of even a higher education rapidly diminish—except, perhaps, in some of its more esoteric mathematical areas which relatively few will ever master.

My own experience of working in a 'preliterate' society in transition to 'restricted literacy' led me to see a very weak connection between literacy and power. But I saw clearly the protective potential of literacy. The most powerful (and capricious) tyrants in the past had been illiterate chiefs ruling illiterate subjects. The new masters—the Colonial Government—had written codes and sometimes contracts and agreements. The subjects were protected when they could read them.

Literacy gave protection against superiors; it did not confer power over subordinates. In Uganda in the 1950s it could hardly be imagined that elementary school teachers would everywhere and overnight become prime ministers; a School Certificate could not even ensure a Mutoro an eventual chief cashier's job in a Kampala bank—such jobs were effectively reserved for Asians. Commonly a School Certificate meant less power, a lower status, then enjoyed, say, by one's cattle-owning father (Kelley and Perlman, 1971). Literacy often carried serious disabilities and there were real difficulties in interpreting the 'function' of literacy and (entirely voluntary and fee-paying) schooling in terms of a fashionable (and essentially hedonistic) sociological functionalism (Musgrove, 1952a).

It is quite false to say that primitive peoples have wanted to read and write because they saw literacy as an art of the powerful white man. They often wanted to read and write when they knew the white man only as pitiably weak and defenceless.

The tyrannical and illiterate Kabaka Mwanga slaughtered the African readers in Buganda in 1886. The martyrs had not learned their dangerous skill because they saw that imperial rulers—or even white traders—were literate. There were neither white rulers nor traders: only highly precarious missionaries. There were no jobs in imperial or mercantile bureaucracies for which literate skills would qualify them.

The British East Africa Company was not even chartered until two years after the massacre of readers; Captain Lugard, the company's first administrator, did not reach Uganda till 1890; theUganda Protectorate was not established until 1894. The white men the Baganda had known were, in spite of their ability to read, manifestly impotent. They were constantly humiliated and belittled by capricious chiefs; and one of their leaders, Bishop Hannington, was imprisoned, put on show in his abject humiliation, and finally, in 1885, speared to death before his bearers.

The missionary Robert Ashe, who survived these troubled events, wrote bitterly in 1886 that 'the Baganda imagined that Englishmen might be killed with impunity in Africa' (Ashe, 1889, p. 239). But Baganda at all social levels wanted to read (with the notable exception of the king)—not only the downtrodden and lowly, but great chiefs and those at the centre of power in the royal household. Ashe recounted the events which he witnessed in May 1886. His friend Nyoni Entono, a senior court official who had learned to read, was mutilated on the orders of the king:

> He recovered, and afterwards actually became katikiro, or chief judge, in place of the haughty chancellor. That functionary killed two of his pages who had been seen reading. The same day Kagwa (Apolo) was called into the king's presence with another youth; a stormy scene ensued. The king, acting on an impulse of uncontrollable fury, attacked the other lad with a spear, gashing him frightfully, and he was hurried away to be murdered by the executioners. Then the king turned to Apolo: 'Are you a reader?' he cried, trembling with passion. 'Nsoma Mukamawange,' 'I read, my Lord,' was the brave reply. 'Then I'll teach you to read!' shouted the angry king, and gashed him too with the spear, and then took the wooden handle and broke it over his back.

Literacy assumed a new significance under the conditions of colonial government. The literate were able to protect themselves and their fellows by questioning written rules and agreements. Illiterate chiefs were felt to be useless because they could not do this: as one of my educated informants from the remote and backward Lango tribe said to me in 1952: 'The chiefs are mostly uneducated, and some are even unable to read and write. Most chiefs think they are working for Europeans and not for the good of their country. They work simply to please the District Commissioner and other officials' (Musgrove, 1952b). In 1949 the rebel leader Mulumba challenged the Uganda Agreement of 1900—generally held to have stolen the people's land and minerals—because it was concluded with illiterate peasants (Kingdon, 1951, p. 91). Literacy would have protected them from exploitation and oppression.

The same protective use of literacy can be seen in its rapid spread in England in the twelfth and thirteenth centuries—long before the printing press was invented. Clanchy has recently detailed the massive shift that occurred at this time from sacred scripts to practical literacy. There occurred a 'production and retention of records on an unprecedented scale'. This was a time of charters which curbed superior power as well as exacting obligations—the Magna Carta of 1215 is only the most celebrated. Royal writs made writing familiar throughout the countryside:

> Similarly the use of charters as titles to property made its way down the social hierarchy—from the royal court and monasteries (in the eleventh century and earlier) to secular clerks and knights (in the twelfth century), reaching the laity in general by the reign of Edward I. (Clanchy, 1979, p. 2)

The rights as well as the obligations of serfs, who used charters for conveying property to each other, were being regularly recorded in manorial rolls.

Gellner (1980) has made much of the point that 'writing fixes and freezes things'. One consequence may be conservatism in the working of ecclesiastical and political bureaucracies. But it fixes and freezes rules and agreements outside the influence of personal power: it makes them publicly accessible and open to verification. The illiterate man who cannot read and make reference to his rights is a highly vulnerable man even—perhaps especially—in an electronic age of computers which some have said makes literacy superfluous.

## 3. CELEBRATING ILLITERACY

In recent years American anthropologists have celebrated a 'culture of poverty' and the virtues of illiteracy. They appear to be vindicated by Marshall McLuhan whose *Gutenberg Galaxy* they frequently cite: an illiterate culture of poverty is appropriate to a post-literate electronic age which is making print obsolete. It is not simply irrelevant but impertinent to provide 'compensatory education' for poor and barely literate North American (or West Indian) Negroes: their culture is not pathological or deficient (or even derivative), but a positive and adaptive affirmation of an alternative way of life.

These views gained influential support among social scientists in the 1960s and 1970s. Previously lower-class culture (and even working-class culture) had often been regarded as seriouly defective and an educational handicap. Prewar studies talked of lack of self-discipline; postwar studies of 'cognitive poverty'.

In 1963 Glazer and Moynihan published a famous study of America's ethnic minorities and characterized the culture of urban Negroes as deficient, even pathological, with disorganized and inadequate families at the heart of the problem. The American Negro had no distinctive culture, he was simply an inferior American: 'the Negro is only an American and nothing else' (Glazer and Moynihan, 1963, p. 53). This picture of a seriously defective and still deteriorating American Negro culture was reinforced two years later in the influential *Moynihan Report* (Moynihan, 1965).

Yorkshire miners also appeared to be merely inferior Englishmen in the sociologists' accounts of the 1950s. The general level of literacy was low, there were no books in the working men's clubs but 'several copies of the papers which specialize in horse-racing' (Klein, 1965, p. 88). Thinking was concrete and personal and people were ill at ease with general ideas:

> There is the interest in personal detail as contrasted with an interest in wider and more abstract issues, concern with which is felt to be incomprehensible as well as slightly ridiculous. . . . There is the dislike of the unfamiliar, the abstract, the not here-and-now-factual, as well as an inability to keep ideas at this level in mind or rehearse them intellectually. (Klein, 1965, pp. 95–96)

They were in the grip, says Josephine Klein, of cognitive poverty.

Since 1965, when the Moynihan Report was published in America and Josephine Klein published *Samples from English Cultures* in England, there has been a massive upgrading of nonliterate primitive peoples and ethnic minorities and a corresponding demotion of the white middle class. 'Cultural deprivation' has been pronounced a myth, and literate cultures, it seems, may be cognitively impaired.

'Compensatory education' is dismissed contemptuously along with 'deficit views' of ethnic minority and lower-class cultures (Reissman, 1967). The culture of poverty is weak on literacy but strong on intellectual abilities which would enable men 'in other social circles to become successful stockbrokers' (Bonney, 1975). Linguistic abilities are preeminent in this barely literate culture: people are 'cool' and 'smart' and notable for quick and very clever repartee.

This is also the picture that Labov painted of Negro urban ghetto life. Although young Negroes were very poor readers (the street groups Labov studied were virtually illiterate), they 'participate fully in a high verbal culture'. In the streets the child is 'bathed in verbal stimulation from morning to night. We see many speech events which depend upon the competitive exhibition of verbal skills . . . a whole range of activities in which the individual gains status through his use of language' (Labov, 1973).

Oscar Lewis's 'culture of poverty' served a 'significant adaptive function' but nevertheless had weaknesses—it often entailed feelings of helplessness, inferiority, and dependence (Lewis, 1966); but the culture of poverty in Rodman's 'Coconut Village' in Trinidad was essentially healthy and positive (Rodman, 1971, 1977). The 'culture of poverty' has been powerfully attacked for its conceptual inadequacies and lack of empirical support (Harrison, 1976; Irelan *et al.*, 1968–1969; Roach and Gursslin, 1966–1967). Few would now support its more ambitious and comprehensive formulations. But the sheer cleverness of the scarcely literate Negro is an image that emerged and remains powerful.

This cleverness was the hallmark of the culture-hero, the hustler. Card-games were an opportunity to outwit and outsmart, to show both cleverness and courage. In the Negro urban ghetto the exchange of insults was an elaborate art form: 'a very high premium is placed on ingenuity, hair-trigger responsiveness, inventiveness, and the acute exercise of mental faculties' (Miller, 1958).

Perhaps the most powerful, certainly the most evocative, celebration of the barely literate Negro is Charles Keil's book, *Urban Blues*. This articulate book scathingly attacks Moynihan's deficit view of Negro culture and programmes of compensatory education that it inspired ('a misguided effort by white men to make Negroes into their own ugly image'). Negro education should give only a minor role to print and centre on the skills and rituals of the entertainer.

Keil strongly contests the view that the Negro is 'only an American' and claims that highly prized features of African life survived the experience of slavery: although the family and economic organization were obliterated, 'predispositions governing religion and aesthetics not only survived slavery but were reshaped, nurtured, and magnified . . .'. Aesthetics and religion are the distinctive ingredients of Negro culture: they are not merely debased variants of white culture. Even an ostensible Protestantism is really much more, with accretions of possession, frenzied dancing, healing and trance.

These key values of aesthetics and religion are subsumed in the concept of 'entertainer'. He is the repository of Negro culture. 'Entertainers' include singers, musicians, preachers, comedians, and some athletes. The 'bluesman' is not a drunken bum: he is the custodian of a long and varied cultural tradition. 'Entertainers' will be even more important to Negroes in the future as their conditions improve: 'Unwilling to cast them aside in a quest for homogeneous middle-class anonymity, they will rebuild and revitalize a culture that will give these figures the profound and unambivalent respect that is their due' (Keil, 1966, p. 192).

Theirs is not a print culture: it is an aural–oral culture. Print should play little part in the education of the American Negro: what is required is 'A thorough revamping of slum schools along revitalized and rhetorical lines'. The wrong things are being taught (and that includes Negro history and 'the Negro contribution'); but above all they are being taught by the wrong means: 'What is being taught to Negro children is certainly demoralizing enough, but the typographic manner in which it is being taught is even more destructive.' Keil is quite clear that the aural–oral Negroes are the natural heirs of Marshall McLuhan's postliterate future. It is they, and not our literate, middle-class whites, who will inherit the electronic age.

## 4. LITERACY AND THINKING

In fact literacy is a powerful help to thinking. To reduce or limit literacy is to impair the ability to think. In particular literacy supports three things: abstract thinking, logical thinking, and memory.

Belittling and perhaps even discouraging literacy and the programmes of compensatory education that promote it is folly. It is true that we have underestimated the difficulty of making compensatory education work; but if we want people to have an understanding which is not highly restricted and context-bound a high level of literacy is crucial.

Basil Bernstein fully realized this. He is often credited with the view that 'education cannot compensate for society'. That is not surprising because he once wrote an extensively cited article with that title. But in the actual article he said the opposite. He maintained that any true education, for anyone, must give access to 'the universalistic meanings of public forms of thought' and he knew that lower-class culture would not in itself provide this. (It is because he acknowledged this that he was so severely rebuked by William Labov.) Bernstein made the unremarkable point, which simply restates traditional wisdom, that the teacher must start from where the child is, and if necessary keep going back there. But his job is to get the lower-class child out. Bernstein does not say this cannot or should not be done. But it is difficult. His article is about how to do it. The teacher must first get the lower-class child on his side and he will not do this if he simply belittles the child's past experience and the lower-class way of life (Bernstein, 1970).

Literacy helps individuals directly with abstract thinking, logic, and memory; it also helps indirectly, because its effects in the past have been institutionalized. The past influence of literacy gave rise to prepackaged answers which the individual does not have to discover all over again for himself.

This distinction between literacy's direct and indirect effects is important. If they are confused, we give the individual credit which should really go to institutions. We say that he has engaged in abstract thinking when his language has done it for him. (Some of the early anthropological linguists like Sapir and Whorf were particularly prone to this fallacy.) As Eleanor Leacock says, 'the simplest act of naming involves abstracting certain features of an object' (Leacock, 1976). The very words our language puts at our disposal have already done a great deal of abstracting for us.

A language may provide only one word for 'cow' where formerly it provided one word for white cow and a different words for black cow: the language now abstracts the notion of cow for the language user. Similarly the member of a literate culture does not have to invent the multiplication table all over again. This highly sophisticated product of literacy is a prepackaged commodity, ready for use. So is a system of numbers separate from things numbered. In nonliterate societies goats may be numbered differently from sheep: detachable numbers may not be available for transfer and attachment as circumstances require. A number is fixed to its context.

Individuals will learn to 'abstract' over and above what their language does for them when they go to school and learn to read and write. Then they do not simply classify: they show the ability to *re*classify. This is one definition of abstract thinking (but by no means the only one: 'abstractness' also depends on the criterion for classification that is used.)

Alexander Luria of the State University of Moscow made studies of the effects of literacy in the 1930s in remote villages in Tadzhikistan and Uzbekhistan. There had been moves towards farming collectives, but above all 'a large network of schools designed to liquidate illiteracy was introduced'. Luria gave illiterates and the newly literate a simple test of abstract thinking: they were asked to pick 'the three which go together' out of four pictures—of a saw, an axe, a shovel, and a log. Classification by illiterates was generally context-bound, by literates context-free. The illiterates usually put the saw, axe and log together and excluded the shovel: these 'went together' in the specific, concrete situation of felling trees and cutting up wood. The literates, on the other hand, usually excluded the log and put the three implements together. They were seen in relation to no particular situation or task but grouped according to a general criterion, 'tool' (Luria, 1971).

Vygotsky argues that writing facilitates remoteness of reference: it is an activity independent of immediate context. Compared with speaking, it is removed from immediateness (Vygotsky, 1962, p. 99). Literacy is far more than a 'mere' training in the use of words: thus literates are commonly better than illiterates at grouping relationships that do not involve, or are not presented in words (for instance the psychologist's 'performance tests'). The superiority of literate over illiterate Indians in non-verbal intelligence tests led Bhatia to suggest that becoming literate involves learning to pay attention to essentially abstract situations for appreciable periods of time. Giving sustained attention to abstract situations is a skill which 'is essentially the result of formal school practice and the demands of civilization' (Bhatia, 1955, p. 92).

We still have no developed experimental ethnology of learning: we know far more about what primitive people believe than the way they think. (Inferences about the way they think are often drawn quite improperly from what they believe.) But on the question of counting and measuring we have Goody's useful account of the LoDagaa tribe of northern Ghana and more detailed and systematic inquiries by Michael Cole and his colleagues among the Kpelle of Liberia. Both deal with the problem of embedded (or non-independent) numbers; both see literacy as an influence that gets numbers disengaged; but Goody tends to see literacy simply as an intellectual technology that helps thinking; Cole has a better grasp of the importance of literacy in influencing thought processes themselves.

'When I first asked someone to count for me,' says Goody, 'the answer was "count what?" For different procedures are used for counting different objects. Counting cows is different from counting cowries' (Goody, 1973). In fact, the LoDagaa have a numerical system that applies to both cowries and cows, but the way it is used is 'embedded in daily living'. A shift from these highly concrete procedures to the more abstract ability simply to count comes with reading and writing: 'Literacy and the accompanying process of classroom education brings a shift towards greater abstractness. . . .' Goody is properly cautious about too sharp a contrast between abstract and concrete thought; but the procedural changes that literacy apparently facilitates seem clear.

Cole and his colleagues gave a strikingly similar account of the use of numbers and measurements among the Kpelle of Liberia. But they saw more difficulty in bringing about change. They actually taught arithmetic in the schools and were impressed above all by the restrictive and stultifying effects of the strong nonliterate tradition of rote memory. This was the principal reason for the Kpelle child's inability to take knowledge out of context and transfer it from one area to another—and why, when puzzled, he relied on shrewd guesswork rather than reason.

The illiterate Kpelle were superior to American university graduates in judging the number of measuring cups in a bowl of rice; but they could not separate numbers from the things numbered; they were incapable of division and multiplication; and they had great difficulty in handling numbers larger than 30 or 40.

The Kpelle could add two stones and three stones to make five stones; they could not add two to three to make five: 'the abstract statement, "two and three is five," is not permissible in the language'. Objects are counted, but there are no independent abstract numerals; multiplication and division exist only as repeated addition and subtraction:

> The Kpelle recognize no abstract arithmetic operations as such . . .
> they have no occasion to work with pure numerals, nor can they speak
> of pure numerals. All arithmetical activity is tied to concrete situations. (Gay and Cole, 1967, P. 50).

The (Western-type) school is in difficulty in teaching transferable skills and intellectual processes, to be deployed as required, but that is its job: 'By contrast [with Kpelle practice], when the school child is asked to learn numbers the operation has changed. He is no longer using numbers for the purpose of manipulating particular things; he is manipulating numbers qua numbers; they are themselves the things' (Scribner and Cole, 1973).

The multiplication table is a product of literacy *par excellence*. Multiplication and division are 'literate', addition and subtraction are 'oral'. Ready-made multiplication tables, says Goody, are essentially a written aid to 'oral' arithmetic (Goody, 1973). Gay and Cole refer to the difficulties of Kpelle market women in pricing different quantities of goods: they 'use simple repeated additions, although they have trouble with complicated problems'. The arithmetical skills of the women of Ghana's Cape Coast fish markets have been closely studied. They cannot do the proportion sums involved in simple pricing operations: they have achieved the remarkable feat of memorizing all possible quantities: a gigantic memory bank is handed down from mother to daughter:

> It appears, however, that these relations [of price and quantity] are not calculated by each woman but memorized in form handed down by mother to daughter, which takes account of every price relation. Clearly, someone at some time worked out these calculations, but the basic stability of the market system and the limited range of the problem allowed the solution to be codified and transmitted by memory alone. (Hallpike, 1979, p. 101)

This is a good illustration of the clumsy, inelegant and enormously burdensome intellectual operations of an oral culture, massively dependent on memory rather than reasoning and deduction. (A similar situation will be examined in chapter 3 in the case of Polynesian navigation.) Literacy (including multiplication tables) is not simply a technical aid to thinking: it shapes the conceptual development of those who acquire it. Multiplication is conceptually different from addition, and division from subtraction. Multiplication and division require a mastery of more complex logical relationships between classes. Without literacy and its effects, says Hallpike, there is indeed a 'primitive mentality' (Hallpike, 1976).

Goody would by no means wholly disagree. He sees logic itself as the product of literacy: and the preliterate are probably as 'prelogical' as Levy-Bruhl said, but perhaps for rather different reasons.

Goody has regretted various alleged social consequences of literacy: social differentiatioin and stratification, social 'distancing', social and intellectual conservatism (except in Classical Greece); but he is clear that the consequences for the individual's intellectual functioning are of enormous benefit. Literacy promotes logic, consistency and scepticism. The prerequisite of logic is the list.

The kind of analysis involved in the syllogism, say Goody and Watt, is clearly dependent on writings: verbal statements can be set out clearly and dissected. With the alphabet came the idea of logic as 'an immutable and impersonal mode of discourse' (Goody and Watt, 1968). The alphabet made possible sophisticated lists which relied on discontinuity of presentation in contrast to the continuity and connectedness of ordinary speech, which could be read in different directions—up and down as well as right and left; which facilitated the hierarchical ordering of information, and in general provided a potent instrument for chopping and changing reality and for ordering and reordering the world of the mind. The list brought a sense of order, system, and control, for it 'alters not only the world out there but the psyche in here' (Goody, 1977, p. 108).

In his account of primitive 'prelogical' mentality Levy-Bruhl emphasizes indifference to contradiction. Many contemporary studies (including those of the

Kpelle) are consistent with this picture. Goody points out that it is easier to perceive contradictions in writing than in speech. He is careful not to agree wholly with Levy-Bruhl's analysis but cautiously concedes that 'there is some element of justification behind Levy-Bruhl's distinction between logical and pre-logical mentality, as well as behind his discussion of the law of contradiction' (Goody, 1977, p. 12). Literacy itself is not enough: a willingness to question 'authorities' is also important (and religious authorities commonly signal their status and power by propounding contradictions). But it is valuable in moving a closed society towards an awareness of alternatives, as well as in pinning down contradictory statements for leisurely inspection.

## 5. MEMORY

In Plato's *Phaedrus* Socrates is critical of writing because it is supposed to help memory but actually subverts it. It is true that oral cultures must depend heavily on memory. But there is good evidence that members of literate cultures are better, not worse, at remembering.

Poetry was the great invention of oral cultures for the support of memory and the accurate and reliable transmission of technical knowledge. Modern historical scholarship has discovered what was clear to Thomas Love Peacock when he reproved the 'Lake Poets': poets at their highest peak, at the time of Homer, said Peacock, were 'depositories of all the knowledge of their age' (Peacock, 1921, p. 5). Shelley in his reply said the opposite: 'Poetry is a sword of lightning, ever unsheathed, which consumes the scabbard that would contain it' (Shelley, 1921).

Early poetry, says a modern scholar, was 'preserved communication': in oral societies it handed down recipe knowledge. Important safeguards were that poetry should be standardized, codified, and avoid any tincture of 'originality'; that it should be publicly performed on ceremonial occasions so that the entire community learned from it and checked its accuracy; and that it should be constantly reiterated. The Homeric epic was an encyclopedia in which the tale was the vehicle for a vast weight of technical detail including instruction in navigation and sailing. Poetry was of critical importance for maintaining and transmitting an oral culture: 'The only possible verbal technology available to guarantee the preservation and fixity of transmission was that of the rhythmic word organized cunningly in verbal and metrical patterns which were unique enough to retain their shape' (Havelock, 1963, p. 42).

It was above all the Greek alphabet that liberated thought from the tyranny of memory and robbed originality of its danger. There is no need to think about or consciously recall our modern (Greek) alphabet once you have learned it. This was not so with earlier, pictorial 'alphabets'. The letters of our modern alphabet are in themselves meaningless: they are not a set of pictures to be interpreted but are 'robbed of any independent meaning whatsoever, in order to become convertible into a mechanical mnemonic device' (Havelock, 1976, p. 47).

With the invention of the Greek alphabet there was no longer any need for rhythm as a 'prompt', filling out the sense and telling the reader (or hearer) what the meaning was. Novel and unexpected statements could now be made without putting the apparatus of transmission at risk. There was no need to remember what poems or records said: the meaning could easily be retrieved afresh. 'The mental energies thus released by this economy of memory', argues Havelock, 'have probably been extensive, contributing to an immense expansion of knowledge available to the human mind' (Havelock, 1976, p. 49).

But this does not mean that in alphabetic culture memory is in any way impaired. Levy-Bruhl seemed to imply that it was. He pointed, quite correctly, to the enormous importance of memory in the mental operations of primitive peoples and argued that memory had to do for them what logic and reasoning do (more economically) for us; our mental operations are 'condensed' because we use 'a hierarchy of concepts which co-ordinate with, or are subordinate to each other'; but primitive peoples tend to memorize rather than think (Levy-Bruhl, 1926, p. 109). 'We must therefore expect to find the memory extremely well developed in primitives, and this is, in fact, reported by observers.'

This is a myth. Bartlett told how the Swazi herdsman had 'an accurate and prodigiously retentive capacity to recall the individual characteristics of his beasts'; he also gave instances of illiterate herdsmen recalling the intricate detail of the purchase and sale of cattle after more than a year. But he discounted any general superiority in powers of memory. He attributed apparently good memories to a generally boring life which encouraged a tendency to ramble on at inordinate length even in native councils and courts: there was no coordination of interests, 'everything that happens is about as interesting as everything else', recall was 'relatively effortless' but in 'a recitative, copying manner' and there was no reason to highlight some issues and subordinate others (Bartlett, 1932, pp. 248–266).

This is precisely why their memories are bad. Their recall is chaotic, indiscriminate, unorganized. Becoming literate helps, but only a high school education is likely to bring about approximate parity with ourselves.

This seems to be the inescapable conclusion from the careful, elaborate (even ingenious) and inordinately cautious cross-cultural work of Michael Cole and his colleagues with Californian and Kpelle children. The Kpelle children were certainly highly 'trained' by traditional methods in memorizing (even with material they did not understand): their reliance on rote memory was the despair of their teachers in Western-style schools. But in tests which asked for the free recall of words (the names of objects) and others which asked for the recall of objects which had been shown to the testees, Americans were superior to illiterate Kpelle, and certainly Kpelle children schooled below high school level were inferior to similarly schooled Americans (Cole and Scribner, 1974, pp. 126–140).

The first Kpelle studies compared illiterate adults and white American college students. A list of 20 items in common use in both countries was used—clothing, foodstuffs, cooking utensils and tools. The Americans were markedly superior: their scores ranged from 13 to 19, the Kpelle scores from 9 to 11. Cole refused to draw any conclusions: 'there is little or nothing we can infer from this mini experiment'. The Americans recalled items in clusters that 'went together', the Kpelle did not; the Americans improved in successive trials, the Kpelle did not:

> From the data . . . what do we want to conclude? Are Americans better memorizers than tribal Africans? Does the lack of clustering indicate that Africans are indeed rote learners? What about the lack of improvement across trials—does that indicate that Africans are slow learners? (Cole and Gay, 1972)

The experimenters concluded that they had demonstrated nothing of interest or profundity.

'Clustering'—organizing and grouping items in some meaningful way— seemed to be at the heart of the process of free recall. Perhaps the Kpelle were handicapped because the items, although familiar, were not in the same 'clusters' in their culture: items which we see as 'cooking utensils' or 'tools' were not cooking utensils or tools for the Kpelle. But further investigation showed that they were.

The experimenters were highly sensitive to the various problems of equivalence in American and Kpelle test situations and took appropriate measures. When the testing was extended to schoolchildren both non-clusterable and clusterable lists of items were used, in case clusterable lists were unfair to the Kpelle. In fact Kpelle did better on clusterable than unclusterable lists (without actually clustering the items), but in both accuracy and pattern of response they were inferior to Americans: 'Americans seemed to take much greater advantage of such supposed aids to learning as organizing according to semantic category' (Cole and Gay, 1972).

Literate Kpelle were superior to illiterate Kpelle of the same age. 'This result is just the opposite of what we would expect if lack of literacy fostered memory' (Cole and Scribner, 1974, p. 129). Cole is immensely cautious; there are inexplicable features of the results; they are limited in many senses, not least in the 'kinds' of memory investigated. But Cole and his colleagues are reasonably certain that the ability to search for and impose 'structures' is crucial for efficient short-term recall, and 'it appears that people who attend Westernstyle schools learn to provide structures, which organize their recall of arbitrary material, while noneducated people do not' (Cole et al., 1971, p. 230). But there is only a 'patch-work of education-related changes in Kpelleland'. Nevertheless, Cole and his colleagues feel able to state firmly, at least for children below high-school level (and it is not altogether clear what happens above that level):

> Nonliterate Kpelle, as well as elementary school children, show no evidence that they are imposing structure of the sort familiar among American children. Over a wide variety of presentation conditions,

the recall of our pre-high-school Kpelle subjects failed to improve markedly with practice or show marked organizational structure, despite a repeated search for organization in terms of order properties of the list or semantic categories. (Cole *et al.*, 1971, p. 223)

There are still large questions to be answered and more extensive research to be done; but two common beliefs have been seriously challenged—that primitive peoples have a natural superiority in powers of memory, and that memory is enfeebled when literacy is acquired. The indications are that the opposite is the case.

## 6. LITERACY AND WORD-MAGIC

In oral cultures words are mixed up with things. Literacy extricates them. In preliterate societies names are not sharply separated from things named: they do not vary independently. When the name changes so does the thing. That is magic. It seems that with the rise of literacy—and perhaps especially with the rise of print—words were effectively separated from things. Descartes effected the final separation. Words and things now achieve their proper autonomy.

The word-magic of primitive peoples has often been described; Ogden and Richards have pointed to its influence on Greek philosophy in general and Platonic Idealism in particular. In early Greek thought the name of a class of things was its soul, and 'to know their names is to have power over souls'. The structure of speech was intimately tied up with the structure of the world and to change one was to change the other. For early Greek philosophers 'Language itself is a duplicate, a shadow-soul, of the whole structure of reality' (Ogden and Richards, 1969, p. 31).

The anthropologist Robin Horton has put African word-magic on a par with post-Cartesian philosophical Idealism in Western Europe. He points out that throughout traditional Africa there is a common assumption that words, uttered under appropriate circumstances, are able 'to bring about the events or states they stand for'. He seriously compares this with modern philosophical Idealism. He concedes that Idealism does not say that words have power over what they represent: 'Rather, it says that material things are "in the mind". That is, the mind creates, sustains and has power over matter. But the second view is little more than a post-Cartesian transposition of the first' (Horton, 1967).

But even passionate Idealists in the West do not, like the boys I taught in Africa, think that by uttering a name they can change the thing named. Incantations and spells have disappeared, 'swearing' has become a meaningless impropriety, and oaths have a restricted significance in legal formalities. Vestiges of the old beliefs are to be found in highly restricted spheres: in the case of a blessing (which will change the state of a person from damned to saved) and in the case of exorcism (in which words used in a ritual context change a person from 'possessed' to normal). But in general we do not behave as if words, even in ritual contexts, did something as opposed to saying something.

Today we hold the highly eccentric view that words should normally say something. In the past they have often had the contrary job—to hide the truth rather than reveal it. Special languages (notably Latin, Pali, Arabic, and Hebrew) have been used—and kept in use—precisely because practically nobody could understand them. As Tambiah puts it: 'In ritual, language appears to be used in ways that violate the communications function' (Tambiah, 1968).

Levy-Bruhl made essentially the same analysis as Tambiah more than 50 years before. He dealt perceptively with the use of special languages and the importance of unintelligibility in primitive word-magic. Non-communication—'using songs and formulas which are unintelligible to those who hear them, and sometimes even to those who utter them'—was the basis of ritual power. To translate the songs and make them intelligible would simply render them impotent (Levy-Bruhl, 1926, pp. 177–180).

When I taught in Africa I had to face this ancient problem of words and things head-on: for instance, how to account for rainstorms without reference to the rites and spells of rain makers. My pupils learned to write about condensation, convection currents, and temperature lapse-rates, but when there was drought or torrential rain and floods they went with their fathers and brothers for the help of the *omwigi w'e njura*.

I investigated the rites of rain makers and rain stoppers in Ankole and also among the Bakonjo in the foothills of the Ruwenzori Mountains (Musgrove, 1952c). In Ankole plants and grasses were used in rain-stopping rites, and the names of the grasses, which were intoned, were also verbs which mean 'prevent' or 'stop'. Thus the plant 'omubuza' (*Dichrocephala integrifolia*) has a verbal counterpart, 'okabura', to disappear; the plant 'omwetango' (*Chenopodium album*) has the verbal counterpart, 'okutanga', to stop or prevent; the plant 'rwahera' (*Olderlandia corymbosa*) has a counterpart 'okuhera', to get out of sight; and the plant 'orubingo' (*Pennisetum purpureum*) has a counterpart 'okubinga', to go away for good.

The *omwigi* made a bundle of these plants and grasses and placed them on dry earth near the fire. (If they were put in water or touched by a person who had recently washed they would not stop rain but bring more.) The *omwigi* then uttered incantations which began as follows:

*Ninkwita ninkwita orubingo nirukububinga* (infinitive: *okubinga*) *omunsi omu ninkumiza obutaka* (I will kill you with elephant grass and drive you away from here; I will make you disappear into the ground).

and so on, with the plant name and a verb-counterpart in each spell.

The rain makers in the Bakonjo tribe similarly made use of a correspondence between words and things. The rain maker blew through a wooden pipe on to a white stone. The name of the stone is 'embulla' and this is also the name for rain.

I had rather impressionistic evidence that literacy and a high school education went some way towards undermining faith in the *omwigi w'e njura*. Old and new explanations could happily coexist—as one boy said to me: 'I agree that there can be a person who can make rain. And on the education idea, I agree that rain comes from evaporation and then comes down as rain.' But as boys progressed through four or five years of senior schooling the *omwigi w'e njura* became something of a figure of fun and his incantations were regarded more cautiously if not with open scepticism.

It is impossible to relate this changing outlook tightly to particular features of a Western-style education. Direct instruction, even when perfectly understood, does not necessarily lead to the downfall and displacement of old and incompatible ideas. But literacy gave words a separate and independent existence as black marks on pieces of paper and the general history of word-magic suggests that this has been important in undermining it.

By the fourteenth and fifteenth centuries word-magic as a separate procedure seldom occurred in European sorcery (although incantation over herbs or wax images was common). Kieckhefer contrasts this with the common use of verbal spells in European antiquity and suggests that the difference is related to the isolated social position of the late-medieval sorcerer (Kieckhefer, 1976, p. 104). But the decline in verbal incantations tightly parallels the dramatic increase in written documents which culminated in the invention of printing.

Two processes dislodged names from the things named and set them apart, separate: the first was writing itself, the second was the (surprisingly late) practice of 'silent reading'. Gellner regards as 'the great moment in history' the externalization and disembodiment of thought in writing. The great achievement of writing was to take an idea or thought out of context and give it a separate existence: 'Writing engendered faith in the independent existence of objects of thought' (Gellner, 1980).

Gilbert Ryle made a famous onslaught on the Cartesian 'dogma of the ghost in the machine'. He objected to the polar opposition that Descartes had made between Mind and Matter (Ryle, 1963). But it is precisely this 'ghost in the machine'—our reflections, within ourselves, on the external world—that has saved us from magic. Ryle referred contemptuously to belief in thinking as an internal, private, hidden affair as belief in 'occult episodes'. But it is by taking thought (and the words that express it) into ourselves that we have extricated it from matter and ourselves from magic.

A print or book culture, argues Bantock, requires and encourages privacy and inwardness of experience: it is, *par excellence*, the culture of the inner consciousness (Bantock, 1980). This inwardness had been implicit in the vast multiplication of printed papers and books after the fifteenth century, but for long 'oracy' and literacy had happily coexisted. In medieval England even public documents were usually read aloud and charters were publicly proclaimed.

Silence did not yet surround reading and writing: indeed writing, always held in some suspicion, still needed the spoken word to validate and authenticate it. Even accounts were 'audited'—checked by hearing them read out. 'Because the pre-literate emphasis on the spoken word persisted, the change from oral to

literate modes could occur slowly and almost imperceptibly over many generations' (Clanchy, 1979, p. 219). Silent reading and the final death of the oral
tradition came at last with mass elementary schools and public libraries in the
nineteenth century.

Ryle shrewdly levelled his attack against silent reading for keeping the ghost
in the machine:

> Much or our ordinary thinking is conducted in internal monologue or
> silent sililoquy. . . . [But] The trick of talking to oneself in silence is
> acquired neither quickly nor without effort. . . . Keeping our
> thoughts to ourselves is a sophisticated accomplishment. It was not
> until the Middle Ages that people learned to read without reading
> aloud. (Ryle, 1963, p. 28)

But whereas Ryle seems to find in these (belated) effects of literacy a triumph
for occult beliefs, the argument here is that it was a signal triumph for rationality.

## 7. CONCLUSION

Hilaire Belloc paid tribute to the truth-telling character of a seafaring friend:
'He was a man who observed closely; and never said a thing because he had
read it' (Belloc, 1906, p. 227). The view that writing is untrustworthy as a vehicle for truth has a long history from Plato to Edmund Leach; it underlies the unwillingness of our courts of law to admit written evidence from witnesses instead of their oral testimony; in the twelfth century it gave rise to the development and widespread use of the seal as some added assurance of writing's truthfulness (Clanchy, 1979, p. 299). In oral cultures the vehicle for truth is the oath:
the witness establishes the truth precisely because no 'verification' is possible.
The test of truth is the form of words in a particular social context rather than
logical consistency or independent empirical evidence—as Steiner brilliantly
shows us in the case of the Chagga (Steiner, 1954). Written statements of truth
were held as inferior to oral statements (swearing) until the later Middle Ages
(Clanchy, 1979, pp. 203–211). The truths of Christianity before the Protestant
Reformation were statements by popes rather than biblical quotes. Luther's 95
theses were revolutionary less from their content than their widespread dis-
semination by German printers. This was print truth—a new and for many a
deeply inferior truth.

In Plato's *Phaedrus* Socrates is critical of writing because it cannot answer
back: it is inert, it cannot answer questions, it gives one unvarying answer, it is
helpless, at the mercy of circumstances. This in essence is Leach's view today—
literacy falsifies:

> Written texts, whether in books or in documents, tend to be valued
> because they can be made unambiguous. But this specious clarity is

achieved only at great cost. Since the real world of experience is not one-dimensional and linear, it follows that by gearing our whole educational system to the written word we automatically teach the young to misrepresent their environment. (Leach, 1977)

This is part of a sustained attack on literacy which has continued over the centuries and has found a particular virulence in the past decade. The reasons for this recrudescence are varied: it is part of renewed class warfare conducted by well-heeled intellectuals who have done handsomely out of literacy and oppose it for the lower classes in their own best interest; it is also a response to a 'cyberculture' based on electronic communication. All the evidence is that electronic forms of communication are far less trustworthy and much more open to manipulation than old-fashioned print.

The argument of this chapter is that the attack on literacy is profoundly misguided and commonly based on error. The charge of social conservatism—even the claim for intellectual innovation—must be considered in context. It matters greatly whether the context is full or partial literacy, and whether the uses of writing are primarily religious or secular.

Much has been made of the fact that literacy 'fixes and freezes things' whereas in oral cultures constant adaptation is possible with no sense of breaking with the past. Goody and Watt (1968) talk of 'structural amnesia' whereby knowledge and ideas which lose their utility and relevance quietly drop out of use; Horton (1967) similarly talks of 'selective recall' which is possible when there is no reference back to what is 'frozen' in the historical record. Goody and Watt say that literate societies cannot discard, absorb, or transmute the past in the same way. This is profoundly to misunderstand the most powerful inner dynamic of modern societies—at least since they developed a sophisticated historical consciousness from the end of the eighteenth century. Modern societies engage in a constant and highly conscious dialectical relationship with their own recorded history: their thrust today is a deliberate, calculated, and highpowered response to their (frequently revised and updated) record of the past.

Even the scribes are no longer a conservative force. Formerly they often had great power: when the script was ideographic, when writing was principally of sacred texts, and when literacy was highly restricted. The scribes of the New Testament were men of great consequence although presented in an unflattering light as sticklers for tradition and the letter of the law. But North Semitic systems of writing needed scribes as interpreters, not as literal readers: 'The "scribe" at the time of Christ was still the required and recognized exponent of scripture, because the script used was precisely of the kind which required the services of an interpreter. That is to say, the Palestinian culture, even at that date, was . . . only craft-literate' (Havelock, 1976, p. 38).

When scribes were literati, guardians of recondite knowledge, custodians of the sacred, their influence was restrictive, conservative (Wilson, 1962). Goody interprets the highly conservative effects of literacy in the western Sudan as the outcome of its essentially religious (Islamic) uses (Goody, 1968). Literacy has also served other socially disciplined interests like the bureaucratic rationality of large-scale industrial production. Today the context is changing rapidly. In Western societies literacy is secular and it is unrestricted, but increasingly it serves consumption rather than production. As Gellner has cogently and perceptively argued, since the Californian 'counter culture' of the 1960s, advanced literacy has been linked ever less with discipline and restraint, ever more with unconventional experience. If the influence of literacy was formerly conservative, its future is perhaps revolutionary (Gellner, 1980).

## REFERENCES

Ashe, Robert P. (1889), *Two Kings of Uganda*, Sampson, Low, Marston, Searle, and Rivington, London.

Bantock, G. H. (1980), 'The implications of literacy', in Peter Gordon (ed.), *The Study of Education*, vol. 2, Woburn Press, London.

Bartlett, F. C. (1932), *Remembering*, Cambridge University Press, Cambridge.

Belloc, Hilaire (1906), *Hills and the Sea*, Methuen, London.

Bernstein, B. (1970), 'Education cannot compensate for society', *New Society*, 26 February.

Bhatia, C. M. (1955), *Performance Tests of Intelligence under Indian Conditions*, Oxford University Press, Bombay.

Bierstedt, Robert (1948). 'The limitations of anthropological methods in sociology', *American Journal of Sociology*, **54**.

Bonney, Norman (1975), 'Work and ghetto culture', *British Journal of Sociology*, **26**.

Bourdieu, Pierre (1971), 'The thinkable and the unthinkable', *The Times Literary Supplement*, 15 October.

Bourdieu, Pierre, and Passeron, Jean-Claude (1977), *Reproduction in Education, Society and Culture*, Sage, London.

Clanchy, M. T. (1979), *From Memory to Written Record. England 1066–1307*, Arnold, London.

Cole, Michael, and Gay, John (1972), 'Culture and memory', *American Anthropologist*, **74**.

Cole, M., Gay, J., Glick, J., and Sharp, D. W. (1971), *The Cultural Context of Learning and Thinking*, Methuen, London.

Cole, M., and Scribner, S. (1974), *Culture and Thought*, Wiley, New York.

Eisenstein, E. L. (1970), 'The impact of printing on European education', in P. W. Musgrave (ed.), *Sociology, History and Education*, Methuen, London.

Gay, J., and Cole, M. (1967), *The New Mathematics and an Old Culture*, Holt, Rinehart & Winston, New York.

Gellner, Ernest (1980), 'Breaking through the bars of the rubber cage', *The Times Higher Education Supplement*, 9 May.

Glazer, Nathan, and Moynihan, Patrick Daniel (1963), *Beyond the Melting Pot*, MIT Press, Cambridge, Mass.

Goody, J. (1968), 'Restricted literacy in northern Ghana', in J. Goody (ed.), *Literacy in Traditional Societies*, Cambridge University Press, Cambridge.

Goody, J. (1972), 'Literacy and the non-literate', *The Times Literary Supplement*, 12 May.

Goody, J. (1973), 'Evolution and communication', *British Journal of Sociology*, **24**.

Goody, J. (1977), *The Domestication of the Savage Mind*, Cambridge University Press, Cambridge.

Goody, J., and Watt, I. (1968), 'The consequences of literacy', in J. Goody (ed.), *Literacy in Traditional Societies*, Cambridge University Press, Cambridge.

Gough, Kathleen (1968), 'Implications of literacy in traditional China and India', in J. Goody (ed.), *Literacy in Traditional Societies*, Cambridge University Press, Cambridge.

Hallpike, C. R. (1976), 'Is there a primitive mentlity?' *Man*, **11**.

Hallpike, C. R. (1979), *The Foundations of Primitive Thought*, Clarendon Press, Oxford.

Hardy, Thomas, (1974), *Tess of the d'Urbervilles*, Macmillan, London.

Harrison, D. (1976), 'The culture of poverty in Coconut Village, Trinidad', *Sociological Review*, **24**.

Havelock, Eric A. (1963), *Preface to Plato*, Blackwell, Oxford.

Havelock, Eric A. (1976), *Origins of Western Literacy*, Ontario Institute of Studies in Education, Toronto.

Horton, R. (1967), 'African traditional thought and Western science', *Africa*, **37**.

Irelan, L. M., Moles, O. C., and O'Shea, R. M. (1968–1969), 'Ethnicity, poverty and selected attitudes: A test of the "culture of poverty" hypothesis', *Social Forces*, **47**.

Keil, Charles (1966), *Urban Blues*, University of Chicago Press, Chicago.

Kelley, J., and Perlman, M. L. (1971), 'Social mobility in Toro: Some preliminary results from western Uganda', *Economic Development and Cultural Change*, **19**.

Kieckhefer, R. (1976), *European Witch Trials. Their Foundations in Popular and Learned Culture, 1300–1500*, Routledge & Kegan Paul, London.

Kingdon, A. (1951), *Report of the Commission of Inquiry into the Disturbances in Uganda during April 1949*, Uganda Government, Entebbe.

Klein, J. (1965), *Samples from English Cultures*, Routledge & Kegan Paul, London.

Labov, William (1973), 'The logic of nonstandard English', in Nell Keddie (ed.), *Tinker, Tailor . . . The Myth of Cultural Deprivation*, Penguin, Harmondsworth, Middx.

Leach, Edmund (1977), 'Literacy be damned', *Observer*, 20 February.

Leacock, Eleanor (1976), 'Abstract versus concrete speech: A false dichotomy', in J. Beck *et al.* (eds), *Worlds Apart*, Collier-Macmillan, London.

Lévi-Strauss, C. (1976), *Tristes Tropiques*, Penguin, Harmondsworth, Middx.

Levy-Bruhl, L. (1926), *How Natives Think*, Allen & Unwin, London.

Lewis, Oscar (1966), 'The culture of poverty', *Scientific American*, **215**.

Luria, Alexander K. (1971), 'Towards the problem of the historical nature of psychological processes', *International Journal of Psychology*, **6**.

Miller, Walter B. (1958), 'Lower class culture as a generating milieu of gang delinquency', *Journal of Social Issues*, **14**.

Moynihan, P. D. (1965), *The Negro Family: The Case for National Action*, Office of Policy Planning and Research, United States Department of Labor, Washington D.C.

Musgrove, F. (1952a), 'A Uganda secondary school as a field of culture change', *Africa*, **22**.

Musgrove, F. (1952b), 'The sociology of African education', *African Studies*, **11**.

Musgrove, F. (1952c), 'Teaching geography to the peoples of western Uganda', *African Studies*, **11**.

Ogden, C. K., and Richards, I. A. (1969), *The Meaning of Meaning*, Routledge & Kegan Paul, London.

Peacock, Thomas Love (1921), 'The four ages of poetry', in H. F. B. Brett-Smith (ed.), *Peacock's Four Ages of Poetry etc.*, Blackwell, Oxford.

Postman, Niel (1970), 'The politics of reading', *Harvard Educational Review*, **40**.

Riessman, F. (1967), 'In defense of the Negro family', in Lee Rainwater and William L. Yancey, *The Moynihan Report and the Politics of Controversy*, MIT Press, Cambridge, Mass.

Roach, J. L., and Gursslin, O. R. (1966–1967), 'An evaluation of the concept "culture of poverty"', *Social Forces*, **45**.

Rodman, H. (1971), *Lower-Class Families: The Culture of Poverty in Negro Trinidad*, Oxford University Press, London.

Rodman, H. (1977), 'The culture of poverty: The rise and fall of a concept', *Sociological Review*, **25**.

Rousseau, J.-J. (1911), *Émile*, Dent, London.

Ryle, Gilbert (1963), *The Concept of Mind*, Penguin, Harmondsworth, Middx.

Scribner, S., and Cole, M. (1973), 'Cognitive consequences of formal and informal education', *Science*, **182**.

Shelley, Percy Bysshe (1921), 'A defence of poetry', in H. F. B. Brett-Smith (ed.), *Peacock's Four Ages of Poetry etc.*, Blackwell, Oxford.

Steiner, F. B. (1954), 'Chagga truth', *Africa*, **24**.

Tambiah, J. S. (1968), 'The magical power of words', *Man*, **3**.

Vygotsky, L. S. (1962), *Thought and Language*, MIT Press, Cambridge, Mass.

Wilson, B. R. (1962), 'The teacher's role—a sociological analysis', *British Journal of Sociology*, **13**.

Young, M. F. D. (1971), 'Curricula as socially organized knowledge', in M. F. D. Young (ed.), *Knowledge and Control*, Collier-Macmillan, London.

# CHAPTER 3

# *Culture and Thinking*

People in the different cultures of the world differ greatly in their ability to think. In some societies the skills of thinking are much more developed than in others. The difference between people living in primitive societies and those in advanced societies is particularly marked. The advantage is undoubtedly with the latter.

The gap narrows if the children in primitive societies go to school and live in cities. It also helps if they have been free to play, explore, and manipulate material objects in their early years. But of critical importance is learning to learn out of context and developing the ability to shift knowledge learned in one situation to another.

This is an emotionally highly charged subject. To point to differences among culture groups, especially in cognitive abilities, is to invite the charge of 'racism'. There may be inborn and ineradicable differences between culture groups. That is no concern of this chapter. Here the interest is in observed differences and the ways in which they can be at least in part eliminated.

Ethnocentrism in the approach to primitive thinking has come under spirited and sustained attack. One focus in recent years has been the connection between language and thought. The complexities of primitive languages have led some linguists and anthropologists to argue that primitive thinking is not more limited and restricted but more subtle and sophisticated than our own. Language shapes thought (rather than the other way round); and the language and thought of advanced societies are a decline from an earlier elegance and rigour.

The superiority of primitive thinking has recently been claimed on other grounds: on the one hand, it is better than ours in our own terms, for instance it is not less and is perhaps more abstract and 'theoretical'; on the other, it has its own distinctive mode which is not logical–scientific like ours but symbolic and 'literary' (Beattie, 1966a, p. 69). This should not be evaluated by irrelevant 'scientific' criteria.

Scribner and Cole, who are among the most ardent opponents of ethnocentric psychology, conclude that the same basic cognitive capacities are to be found in all cultures; but they are differently developed and used. That is the view taken here. Scribner and Cole maintain: 'All culture groups thus far studied have demonstrated the capacity to remember, generalize, form concepts, operate with abstractions, and reason logically' (Scribner and Cole, 1973). Greenfield and Bruner similarly concluded from their work at the Harvard Center for Cognitive Studies that however diverse the cultures, cognitive

41

development is in the same direction. Some cultures push it earlier and further. 'What does not seem to happen is that different cultures produce completely divergent and unrelated modes of thought' (Greenfield and Bruner, 1966). But there are marked differences, say Scribner and Cole, in the way these capacities are brought to bear in various problem-solving situations.

Thought processes of different peoples are the same: it seems reasonable to assess them similarly. The same processes are used with dramatically different effects: there is, as Cole and Scribner say, 'massive evidence . . . [of] differences in mental functioning among cultural groups' (Cole and Scribner, 1974, p. 25).

Vernon's extensive cross-cultural studies produced precisely such evidence. In interpreting the manifest inequalities that his work revealed he recognized the influence of social circumstances but felt that 'the pendulum may well have swung too far towards environmentalistic explanations' (Vernon, 1959). Vernon conceded the possibility of genetic differences but emphasized overlap. The environment was important but: 'This does not mean that there are no innate differences in abilities, but they are probably small and we have no means of proving them' (Vernon, 1969, p. 215).

## 1. UNIFORMITIES AND INEQUALITIES: ANTHROPOLOGICAL AND PSYCHOLOGICAL EMPHASES

Anthropologists since Frazer have generally emphasized the cognitive uniformities of mankind; psychologists have highlighted inequalities. Psychologists' tests are undoubtedly 'contaminated' to some degree by different settings; their relevance and appropriateness may also be questioned. The Yale psychologist Leonard Doob said Western yardsticks are relevant everywhere because all men must become Western or perish. Vernon says the same. I agree with them. But even a Western yardstick will not do its job unless it is used with intelligent awareness of its meaning for subjects in non-Western circumstances. Tests may originate elsewhere, but they should have an analogue in the cultures in which they are used.

James Frazer was the first of a long line of anthropologists to put magic on a par with science. It is true that he talked of higher and lower mental operations: the higher were modern and scientific, the lower ancient and magical. But lower still, although nearer in time, was religious thinking, which assumed a capricious and arbitrary universe. The mind which conceived magic was essentially like the mind that conceived science: both recognized and in a measure controlled an orderly and rule-regulated world. Frazer upgraded magic, claiming that 'its fundamental conception is identical to that of modern science' (Frazer, 1957, p. 64).

The anthropologists have been saying for a century: primitive man is no more stupid than we are and he may be cleverer. His thinking seems bizarre only because we have not appreciated its context. Twenty years before Frazer roughly equated science and magic in *The Golden Bough* Tylor had done his own special form of 'cultural' upgrading. He gave a brief picture of the life and thought of a modern European peasant and claimed that there was 'scarce a hand's breadth difference between an English ploughman and a negro of Central Africa' (Tylor, 1871, p. 7). The pages of his book would be 'crowded with evidence of such correspondence' generally among mankind.

Durkheim attacked the problem of primitive logic (as it was misconceived, so he claimed, by both Frazer and Levy-Bruhl). For Durkheim men's thinking was derived from the form of their society: he rebuked Frazer for supposing the opposite (Durkheim and Mauss, 1963, p. 82). Society, whether primitive or modern, was itself the model for logical thought: 'So it is far from true that this [primitive] mentality has no connection with ours. Our logic was born of this logic. The explanations of contemporary science . . . do not differ in nature from those which satisfy primitive thought' (Durkheim, 1915, p. 238).

Today Lévi-Strauss analyses primitive myths and reveals a complex primitive mind. Primitive man living by myths is not a story-telling simpleton but a skilled dialectician solving complex problems based—like the digital computer—on binary opposition. The way minds work (in imposing form on content) seems to be fundamentally the same whether the minds are ancient or modern, primitive or civilized.

Mythologic is as good as scientific logic: 'the kind of logic in mythical thought is as rigorous as that of modern science . . . the differeence lies, not in the quality of the intellectual process, but in the nature of the things to which it is applied'. There is no notion of progression from lower to higher mental states or capabilities:

> The same logical processes operate in myth as in science . . . man has always been thinking equally well, the improvement lies, not in an alleged process of man's mind, but in the discovery of new areas to which it may apply its unchanged and unchanging powers. (Lévi-Strauss, 1972, p. 230)

Psychologists have been impressed by inequalities. Men everywhere are not thinking equally well. Psychologists do not necessarily deny underlying uniformities, and many concede that primitive people may have intellectual abilities of a kind we undervalue or have not yet identified. But in terms of actual behaviour, including memorizing and perceiving as well as 'problem solving', there are great observed differences among human societies.

Psychologists may be too simple-minded in their cross-cultural inquiries, but one Oxford-trained anthropologist, Hallpike, is very impressed by their work and charges his fellow-anthropologists with naiveté (Hallpike, 1976). He also makes the charge of obscurantism. Of Lévi-Strauss he observes: 'his basic contribution to the study of primitive thought has been to take an extremely difficult subject and make it impossible' (Hallpike, 1979, p. vii).

Psychologists are now enormously cautious about 'deficiency theories'. They are alert to the dangers of treating psychological processes as entities which a person 'has' or 'has not' (Cole and Scribner, 1974, pp. 173–174). But the fact, however interpreted, is this: that there is a 'vast difference' between the Temne of Sierra Leone and Eskimos of Baffin Island in the ability to pick out visual detail and to grasp spatial relationships. Technically highly competent and theoretically sophisticated psychological research leads to the unequivocal conclusion that 'a great gulf exists between Temne and Eskimo spatial ability' (Berry, 1966). The Temne are poor, but the Eskimos are almost as good as the Scots.

The Eskimos are far-ranging hunters over a featureless landscape who are reared to be self-reliant, independent, and resourceful; the Temne are sedentary cultivators in tropical West Africa who are reared to be cautious, conforming, and docile. They seem to illustrate exactly Rousseu's contrast between the sharp savage and the dull peasant. On tests with Kohs Blocks and Ravens Matrices the gap between them is enormous. Rousseau was wrong only in the detrimental effects he ascribed to literacy. The sharp savage is even sharper when schooled.

School equals hunting—in fact it is slightly better. When 'traditional' (mainly unschooled) Eskimos were compared with 'transitional' (schooled), the latter, although with less time for hunting, showed superior powers of visual discrimination:

> Transitional groups typically perform slightly better in the test [of visual discrimination] than traditional peoples [even though hunting activity usually is diminished], and this may be attributed to the effects of Western education, especially literacy. (Berry, 1971)

Just as literacy improves rather than impairs memory (see chapter 2), so it sharpens rather than dulls visual perception and grasp of spatial relationships. It did so for the Temne no less than for the Eskimos.

Eskimos generally do well on psychologists' tests of ability. Their utterly different ecology, culture, and society do not seem to be a handicap in their response to our psychological tests: they often perform at an average level comparable to middle-class Europeans and Americans. Vernon compared schooled Eskimos, North American Indians, Jamaicans, the Baganda of East Africa, and white Canadians on a variety of measures. The Indians generally did worse than the Eskimos, the Jamaicans roughly the same as the Indians, but the Baganda—one of the most progressive of East African tribes—performed badly.

The sample of Baganda children was superior to the population in general— it was urban, English-speaking, and middle class. They did especially badly on the vocabulary (word definition) test—'practically off the scale'—and Vernon concluded that they were unable to see words out of context: 'the notion that words can be isolated and defined in the abstract was unfamiliar, except to the most intelligent' (Vernon, 1969, p. 183).

The inequality among culture groups—not simply between 'Western' and 'primitive'—was Vernon's overriding impression. Abilities reached or surpassed Western standards in some cases, but in others fell below 'what we should regard as the borderline for mental deficiency' (Vernon, 1969, p. 213).

The environments of Vernon's groups were markedly different. Even the all-African samples of Doob, in a comparable study—Zulus, Baganda, and Luo—lived in widely different circumstances (Doob, 1960). But even when culture groups have grown up in the same city (Aden) and had similar schooling, differences in test scores are great. Hyde concluded that marked differences between Europeans, Arabs, Indians, and Somalis in Aden must be ascribed to 'their distinctive home background' (Hyde, 1970, p. 202). Genetic differences night, conceivably, play a part.

After reviewing their own work in West Africa and that of other specialists, Cole and his colleagues concluded:

> The almost universal outcome of the psychological study of culture and cognition has been the demonstration of large differences among culture groups on a large variety of psychological tests and experiments. (Cole *et al.*, 1971, p. 215)

They went on to ask: 'In the face of the experimental evidence of cultural differences, how can the anthropologist maintain his belief in the psychic unity of mankind?' He does so by denying the validity of the tests or saying that what they measure is 'irrelevant'. And it is true that in the traditional life high-level intellectual skills may not be 'needed': as Vernon says, backward people may develop lower-order cognitive skills 'which are highly effective for survival, [while] their reasoning capacities remain similar in many ways to those of younger children, or even regress through lack of appropriate stimulation' (Vernon, 1969, p. 215).

Cryns is a psychologist who thinks that psychological tests in primitive societies may have missed the point. He concedes that extensive tests of abilities over half a century show that Africans have about '85 per cent of White intelligence'. But the evidence is consistent and overwhelming that Western-type schooling goes far towards closing the gap. And it may be that Africans are 'intelligent' in some specifically appropriate African way: perhaps the African culture is essentially musico-choreographical in character, favouring the development of concrete perceptual and artistic abilities, whereas Western culture is computational-geometric, favouring predominantly mathematical ways of thinking (Cryns, 1962). Others have suggested qualitative differences between African and European thought along similar lines (for example, Beattie, 1966b). But the world into which traditional Africa is rapidly moving will not call heavily on such poetical and choreographical abilities.

## 2. PIAGET AND CROSS-CULTURAL RESEARCH

Extensive cross-cultural research using Piagetian tests seems firmly to establish three things: that cognitive development in childhood proceeds everywhere in the same way, in the same order, through the same 'stages'; that in primitive cultures it is considerably delayed; and that schooling is enormously potent in speeding it up. A fourth conclusion is more tentative: that in many non-Western cultures most people would never, without benefit of schooling, reach cognitive maturity at all.

Inequalities among the different culture groups of the world in the skills of thinking have been abundantly demonstrated in the past 20 years. All this cross-cultural research into Piagetian stages of cognitive growth is the most powerful argument for schools and literacy that we have. To deny a culture group formal, 'Western' education—or to play down the curriculum's numerical and and literate content—is to render them a grievous disservice.

This conclusion regarding the potency of schools may seem a little surprising in view of the emphasis that Piaget seems to place on the natural unfolding of cognitive abilities. Although he later moderated his views a little, in the early 1960s he was still asserting that 'development follows its own laws, as all contemporary biology leads us to believe'. New learning depended on the stage of development that had been reached and on the intellectual structures that the individual had at his disposal. People do not develop because they learn, they learn because they develop (Piaget, 1966a).

Learning theorists at this time certainly saw Piaget as holding a quasi-biological view of cognitive development. Patricia Greenfield, who made notable studies of the Wolof tribe in Senegal, was highly critical of Piaget's position: 'In his view, cognitive maturation is made to appear like a biologically determined and universal sequence.' While some reference was made by Piaget to the influence of the environment, there was no systematic attempt to relate development to class, urban location, or social cohesion. It was related only to age (Greenfield, 1966).

In 1966 Piaget published an important paper which took into account the very limited amount of cross-cultural research based on his theory of cognitive development that had then been accomplished. There were only five studies, and only three of these—carried out in Aden, Nigeria, and Hong Kong—had actually been published. He knew of a fourth (carried out in Martinique) from a personal communication, and the fifth, on which he drew heavily, was a Paris doctoral thesis reporting work done in Iran (Piaget, 1966b).

Piaget had over many years indicated three global stages of cognitive development: 'Sensori-motor (0 to 2 years); 'Preoperational' or egocentric (2 to 7 years); and 'Operational' (7 to 12). It is in the third stage, from 7 onwards, that logical thinking develops, first in relation to concrete, specific materials to hand (7 to 11), and finally, after the age of 11 or 12, in a more formal and abstract mode 'out of context', 'in the head'. A great deal of importance is attached to the first substage, 'Concrete Operations', from 7 to 11. This is the foundation for all logical and scientific thought. It depends on grasping the principle of 'conservation'—that when, for instance, a heap of sand changes shape, is flattened, the volume and weight are unchanged. Piaget had established three major substages in the acquisition of conservation: the conservation of mass or substance (age 7 to 8), of weight (age 9 to 10), and of volume (age 11 to 12). Extensive research throughout the world has now been conducted employing the methods and criteria used by Piaget for establishing the three global stages and the various substages, especially the substages of conservation.

The five studies carried out in other cultures to which Piaget referred in 1966 seemed to confirm the nature and invariant sequence of the stages he had discovered in white middle-class children in Geneva. Piaget took this as support for biological factors underlying intellectual maturation. But there was powerful evidence of lag. In Iran, rural illiterates were two or three years behind schooled children in Tehran on the operational tests, but these city children were not behind European children. In Nigeria, Price-Williams's evidence on stage sequence with illiterate Tiv children is convincing, but lag was more difficult to establish since age was judged by height and teeth (Price-Williams, 1961).

Piaget accepted the evidence on lag and conceded: 'This delay proves the intervention of factors distinct from those of simple biological maturation.' He was inclined to see passivity and docility in early childhood as the main retarding influence: in Iran there was 'astounding lack of activity of the young country children who do not go to school and who have no toys, except stones or sticks, and who show a constant passivity and apathy'.

The main weakness of these cross-cultural studies (then as now) was lack of work with children over the age of 9 or 10. Certainly at the age of 7 or 8 European boys at school in Aden were markedly ahead of Arab, Indian, and Somali boys at school in Aden; the Arab boys, in turn, were comfortably ahead of the Indian and Somali boys (Hyde, 1970). Both 'school-effect' and 'city-effect' are the same for these four culture groups, but differences in thinking skills as measured by Piagetian tests are pronounced. But we do not know whether the Arabs eventually catch up with the Europeans, and the Somalis with the Arabs.

Piaget recognized this weakness and urged more research in other cultures with older children, adolescents, and adults; but he felt able to suggest that in many primitive societies most adults never reach cognitive maturity:

> In particular it is quite possible (and it is the impression given by the known ethnographic literature) that in numerous cultures adult thinking does not proceed beyond the level of concrete operations, and does not reach that of propositional operations, elaborated between 12 and 15 years of age in our culture. (Piaget, 1966b)

A few years later Dasen cautiously endorsed this view. By now there had been a veritable explosion of Piagetian research in New Guinea, Hong Kong, and East, West, and Southern Africa, the West Indies, among the Eskimos, North American Indians, and the Australian Aborigines. Although extensive the research was still very inconclusive; but Dasen felt able to conclude: 'It seems that Piaget's "prediction" that the reasoning of many individuals in so-called "primitive" societies would not develop beyond the stage of concrete operations, may one day be verified' (Dasen, 1972).

Nevertheless, cross-cultural Piagetian research brings hope. It adds considerable weight to those studies carried out in England and America which show that education and training can accelerate and improve thinking skills. Churchill's work at Leeds in the 1950s was one of the first experiments to show that young children, given suitable experiences, could have a better understanding of number than they 'ought' to have for their age (Churchill, 1958); American work on conservation has produced similar results and shown how 'progress toward comprehensive logical thought can be developed' (Sigel *et al.*, 1966). Work by Lovell has shown the importance of the 'sheer experience of the physical world' in acquiring conservation (Lovell and Ogilvie, 1961). Lunzer has castigated teachers who, in the light of Piaget's theories, 'abdicate' in favour of discovery methods and wait for learning readiness (Lunzer, 1980). Cross-cultural studies powerfully reinforce this picture: that experience is very important and 'external' intervention in the maturational process is not only possible but within limits very effective. But whereas most of the experimental work in England and America has been with highly specific and directly geared training programmes, the cross-cultural work is coarser grained, pointing to wider cultural, environmental, and ecological influences.

## 3. BRUNER AND THE PREPOTENT SCHOOL

Cross-cultural psychologists have brought hope. Bruner has brought most of all. Piaget reproved him for thinking that 'one can teach anything at any age, if one goes about it adequately'. Quite the contrary, said Piaget: in Martinique, where there was a lag among schoolchildren of three or four years behind cognitive development in Europe, education could not close the gap: 'schooling . . . is not sufficient to ensure a normal development of operational structures' (Piaget, 1966b).

For Piaget development was largely from the inside, for Bruner from the outside. Bruner de-emphasized semi-automatic 'stages' of cognitive development although he saw a progression through three major emphases or modes of representing and interpreting experience—'enactive' (through action), 'iconic' (through imagery), and 'symbolic' (through language). But cognitive development depended on being equipped with an appropriate intellectual technology. The right tools were crucial: 'the development of human intellectual functioning from infancy to such perfection as it may reach is shaped by a series of technological advances in the use of the mind. Growth depends on the mastery of techniques' (Bruner, 1964).

The 'tools' were provided by a given culture and were 'internalized': development was not a question of 'capacity' but of unlocking capacity by techniques. The most important of these techniques was language and its overriding value was that it released the mind from its immediate context:

> Once language becomes a medium for the translation of experience, there is a progressive release from immediacy. For language . . . has the new and powerful features of remoteness and arbitrariness: It permits productive, combinatorial operations in the absence of what is represented. (Bruner, 1964)

The 'tools' approach led Bruner to place enormous emphasis on education and to assert: 'Cognitive growth, then, is in a major way from the outside.'

Bruner's Harvard Center for Cognitive Studies promoted cross-cultural inquiries which 'explored the role of culturally transmitted technologies in intellectual growth' (Greenfield and Bruner, 1966). Greenfield did work in Senegal, Maccoby in Mexico, Lee Reich in Alaska. The Center stood in conscious and growing opposition to the approach of Piaget: 'Cambridge has steadily disagreed with Geneva on the fundamental "how" of intellectual growth. Our own work has emphasized the role of internalized, culturally transmitted technologies' (Greenfield, 1966).

Without schooling, concluded Greenfield, intellectual development among the Wolof of Senegal ceases effectively at the age of 9. But if they were schooled, they were, intellectually speaking, more like white middle-class children in Boston than they were like their unschooled Wolof friends. Greenfield's work has been criticized on the grounds of method and inadequate statistical analysis (Furby, 1971) and sheer common sense: how could people so uncomprehending of weights and measures without schooling have survived? (Cole and Scribner, 1974, pp. 151–152). The study has weaknesses and the case has been overstated, but the Wolof experiments remain a powerful argument for the potency of the school.

By the age of 8 most European and American children understand that if you change the shape of a lump of clay the actual amount is unchanged; and that if you pour water from a short, squat container into a tall thin one, the volume of water is the same. Fewer than half of the 8-year-old Wolof children in Senegal who have not been to school grasp this 'invariance' of amount and volume in spite of change of shape. By the age of 12 all schooled Wolofs have grasped this, but the proportion of unschooled Wolofs who have done so is unchanged at about 50 per cent. Moreover, there was good though indirect evidence that unschooled adults never caught up: 'without school, intellectual development, defined as any qualitative change, ceases shortly after age nine' (Greenfield, 1966).

No inconsistency is seen with the rather different results of Price-Williams (1961). He claimed that all unschooled Tiv children in Nigeria achieved conservation probably by the age of 8. This is taken by both Greenfield (1966) and Bruner (1974, pp. 45–46) as further evidence of the decisive influence of culture. Although the Tiv were unschooled, a more adventurous, active, and manipulative childhood provided experiences unavailable to passive and inactive Wolofs. Certainly the independence training of young Tiv children, who are sent early from home to widen their horizons, is well documented in the ethnographic literature (Bohannan, 1954).

Experiments in New Guinea, though differently constructed, have produced results which are strikingly like Greenfield's in Senegal. Prince did not investigate unschooled groups but compared conservation results at different levels of various educational establishments. This inquiry points to the importance of the quality of schooling and the 'training-effect' of well-designed science curricula. Conservation results were more closely related to school grade and curriculum content than to chronological age. The vernacular teacher training college results were poor. Prince sees his results as confirming Greenfield's. 'These parallel findings certainly cast strong doubts on any simple maturational notion of development' (Prince, 1968).

Bruner and Greenfield are convinced of the tremendous effect of schooling on cognitive development. So is Vernon. 'It is clear', says the latter, 'that sheer amount of schooling, even—in backward countries—of low-quality education, helps to promote both school achievement and the kind of reasoning measured by non-verbal tests' (Vernon, 1969, p. 219). But native teachers using traditional rote methods are relatively ineffective, and in Africa it is particularly important for children to have opportunities for concrete, manipulative activities 'to compensate for the inadequacies of psychomotor stimulation at home'.

For Greenfield and Bruner the power of the school has two principal sources: it gives primitive children consciousness of self and use of language which facilitates out-of-context learning. Children in poor, collective, subsistence economies may not have a strong consciousness of self: they are not sufficiently important and indulged. Any Western-style school in such a culture is inevitably child-centred: it picks (some) children out and makes them the centre of attention. An unschooled Wolof cannot understand the question: 'What do you think . . . ?' He has never thought of himself as having thoughts. School invents children as a separate category for special treatment: they don't just tag along with (but behind) everyone else, picking up know-how as best they can.

But it is 'school language' that is the real key to advanced conceptual development. It helps that it is written: 'We may hypothesize that it is the fact of being a written language that makes French such a powerful factor in the cognitive growth of the chldren we have studied.' But language used in school, whether written or spoken, takes communication out of the context of immediate reference:

> But school itself provides the same opportunity to use language out of context, even spoken language, for to a very high degree, what one talks about are things that are not immediately present.

Some environments 'push' cognitive growth better, earlier, and longer than others; Western-type schooling is a very important aspect of a primitive environment: 'it makes a huge difference to the intellectual life of a child simply that he was in school' (Greenfield and Bruner, 1966).

This is all too simple. School-effect will vary with the extent of other Western influences, notably urbanization. And there is the nagging suspicion that innate endowment play a larger part than most psychologists nowadays concede.

Schooling does not always get children in a primitive society, even after considerable delay, to the same eventual 'stage' as European children. Some primitive people, like the Tiv, seem to achieve 'conservation' (roughly the second of Piaget's three global stages) without benefit of schooling; some, like the Wolof, do so after a highly sophisticated Western-type education; but some, like a significant proportion of schooled Australian Aboriginals, never get there at all.

Marion De Lemos investigated Australian Aboriginal children between the ages of 8 and 15. They were attending a mission school. Her inquiries once again provided confirmation for Piaget's developmental sequence, but showed not only massive retardation but failure in many instances ever to arrive at all: 'The results of the study clearly indicate that conservation is developed much later in Aboriginal children than in European, and in some cases appears not to develop at all' (De Lemos, 1969). A comparison was made between a group of part-Aboriginals of mixed race, and the rest. There were no environmental or cultural differences between Aboriginals and part-Aboriginals: they were all members of the same community. But the part-Aboriginals did much better on the tests and showed a faster rate of development. De Lemos concluded that genetic differences must be part of the explanation.

## 4. CITY-EFFECT

Cities may achieve much of what schools achieve in 'pushing' cognitive development, but city-effect cannot entirely take the place of schools. City and school together make a prepotent contribution to cognitive growth.

School-effect in other cultures has been studied in relation not only to the acquisition of 'conservation' but to the change-over from colour to form as the preferred basis for classifying objects and figures. In America the change-over from colour to form occurs at 4 years 2 months (Suchman and Trabasso, 1966). In Africa it is very much later and may not occur at all with people who have neither been to school nor lived in cities. The changeover seems to be related to overall cognitive development (Cole and Scribner, 1974, p. 92). If primitive children have had experience of both cities and schools they may move not simply from colour to form but to function.

This is broadly the picture that emerges from the Harvard investigations in Senegal. When unschooled bush Wolofs were asked to group objects and figures which were alike, they did so at all ages on the basis of colour; bush children who attended school relied less on colour and more on form as they got older; city children at school (in Dakar) made the change-over between the third and sixth grades not only to form but to more functional and nominal concepts: 'In terms of content, bush children who do not go to school end up with nothing but colour-oriented concepts; all school children move away from an initial reliance on colour, but bush children mainly towards form, the city chldren toward form and function' (Greenfield *et al.*, 1966).

The Harvard team interpreted these findings in terms of the influence of both cities and schools in promoting powers of abstraction and more complex perceptual analysis:

> We believe that the difference between the city child and the rural child derives from a differential exposure to problem solving and communication in situations that are not supported by context—as is the case with, for example, most reading and writing, the use of monetary exchange, and schooling. Rural life, it appears, is somewhat less conducive to the development of abstraction.

Schooling is not enough. Change-over from colour to form in primitive societies perhaps depends on the quality of schooling (not based on rote learning) and more certainly on city location. But in the few studies that we have got, good quality schooling and city location tend to go together. City-effect may be the dominant one.

No change-over occurred among schoolchildren attending a Koranic school in Northern Nigeria: 'The results were unequivocal. There is no developmental transition from colour to form preference at any age level' (Suchman, 1966). But the children read the Koran without understanding it. Mere sensitivity to the shape of words does not in itself lead to a preference for form in equivalence grouping as some have (tentatively) suggested (Cole and Scribner, 1974, p. 94). In a racially mixed private school in Lusaka, Zambian children, like Indian and English children, changed from colour to form; but in remote bush schools there was little sign of change-over: 'The effect [of schooling], however, is less pronounced among Zambian children [in the city school] and may be entirely absent in remote rural populations' (Serpell, 1969).

The progression: bush unschooled, bush schooled, city schooled has been a familiar one for more than 50 years in the psychological and educational literature on primitive peoples. Biesheuvel reported psychological testing with Zulus in the 1930s in which mean scores with Kohs Blocks rose steeply from bush school to city school: but unschooled (9), bush schooled (12.5), city schooled (20.6) (Biesheuvel, 1949). This is now a familiar gradient.

Cities, perhaps, attract 'superior', more able people. But marked urban–rural differences have been found in some aspects of mental functioning which have little or no relationship to levels of 'intelligence' (or school attainment). Equivalence grouping by children in Mexico City was based far more on abstract qualities than was the case with children attending village schools. By the age of 9 city children in Mexico were almost like city children in America: 'We are struck by how much closer Mexico City is to Boston than to a *mestizo* village' (Maccoby and Modliano, 1966). There was no relationship between performance on equivalence tasks and either scores on a non-verbal intelligence test or levels of academic attainment.

In their interpretation the investigators placed emphasis on the city environment which calls for abstraction in exchanging, cataloguing, and coding diverse and complex pieces of information. In the rural situation interest centres on particular and specific people, objects, and events. City-effect, it was claimed, is 'transcendental', overriding national, regional, and cultural differences:

> The similarity of results in Mexico City and Boston, Massachusetts, and the dissimilarity of both from a small Mexican village give us reason to suspect that modern urban development everywhere may produce a certain style of equivalence judgments, and that this influence may transcend national and other differences in cultural content. (Maccoby and Modliano, 1966)

This is a massive oversimplification. It fails to discriminate between different forms of city life, development, and ecology—the perhaps crucial distinction that is made, for instance, by Robert Redfield between primary and secondary urbanization. Urban–rural differences are not invariable—even in Dakar, children lagged behind rural children on conservation tasks until the age of 12 (Greenfield, 1966); and Doob did not find Baganda children in Kampala significantly more Westernized in outlook and thinking than their country cousins— with whom they were in close contact (Doob, 1960, p. 49). The Zulus in Durban, by contrast, were far superior to rural Zulus on a variety of tests and 'acculturation' measures (Doob, 1957).

It is arguable that Kampala in the 1950s was at an early stage of growth, still largely systematizing and extending an old culture and in close contact with it, whereas Durban lived by mainly new and discontinuous modes of thought and authority. The distinction is that made by Redfield and Singer between primary and secondary urbanization. And for them the crucial distinction is between the abstract and generalizing culture of the 'secondary' city and the particularistic folk culture of the primary city (Redfield and Singer, 1954–1955).

Certainly city-effect, though powerful, was not sufficient to equalize the performance of schoolchildren in a Northern Nigerian city and of lower-class children of average intelligence in an English city on a range of conservation and reasoning tasks (Poole, 1968). Hausa children attending schools in a Nigerian city were markedly superior to Hausa children in remote village schools, but the city children were in turn markedly inferior to the English city children.

In a test of conservation of weight only 24 per cent of the rural Hausa were successful, 57 per cent of the city Hausa, but 77 per cent of the city English; in estimating time intervals only 2 per cent of the rural Hausa were successful, 10 per cent of the city Hausa, 40 per cent of the city English; in estimating lengths only 8 per cent of the rural Hausa were correct, 26 per cent of the city Hausa, 38 per cent of the city English; in a test of mechanical principles (where weights should be put on a see-saw) 16 per cent of the rural Hausa were right, 30 per cent of the city Hausa, but 62 per cent of the city English. The potency of the urban environment in cognitive development is clear from these results, but equally clearly it falls short of the transcultural omnipotence claimed by the Harvard Center for Cognitive Studies.

When children grow up in urban-industrial countries or in modern cities (at a stage of secondary urbanization) elsewhere, they are likely to make considerable intellectual progress even though unschooled; in these circumstances we must expect school-effect to show up only as an additional increment of development at the upper end of the developmental range. If schooling is poor, no school-effect may show at all—and this probably explains the developmental equality of some unschooled and schooled Negroes in America (Mermelstein and Schulman, 1967). Research in Italy (Genoa), in Hong Kong, and in Ibadan seem to support this 'marginal' view of school-effect in modern cities.

In the Italian study 11-year-old children born and schooled in Genoa were superior to children in the rural south of Italy on the most difficult of the conservation subtests, the conservation of volume; rural immigrants to the city caught up with the city-born within 3 years. The same picture emerged on the advanced Piagetian test of combinational thinking (Peluffo, 1967). It was these difficult tests that effectively discriminated between schooled and poorly or little schooled in a modern European society.

A roughly comparable situation was shown by research in Hong Kong. Chinese boys who had grown up there but had little or no schooling did as well as English boys attending school in Hong Kong on conservation tests, but 'In contrast, the unschooled Chinese were markedly poorer than the schooled European on another Piaget test, one of combinatorial reasoning' (Goodnow and Bethon, 1966). And in Ibadan children who had grown up there with inferior or little schooling were distinguished from better-off Yoruba children with superior schooling only on advanced number conservation tasks (Lloyd, 1971). The additional increment of development that city-schooled have over city-unschooled (or over non-urban residents in urban-industrial societies) is at the top end of the range of cognitive development and probably arises because at this level it is necessary 'to work things out "in the head" rather than by hand or by eye'—and it is this kind of experience that schools provide and city life *per se* does not (Goodnow and Bethon, 1966).

These explanations of city-effect are inevitably speculative. But clearly the experience of life in modern cities can take young children a considerable distance along the path of cognitive development without benefit of schooling. It has been argued that one advantage of cities is their 'carpentered' environment which fosters visual discrimination and analysis, but research in deserts, forests, and cities gives little support to this view (Jahoda, 1966).

Hallpike thinks that a mechanical city environment helps children to grasp the principle of 'reversibility' which underlies scientific causal analysis. The world of nature which the child knows in the bush, on the other hand, does not go into reverse and cannot be taken apart and reassembled in quite the same way (Hallpike, 1979, pp. 96–97, 437–439). Other intepretations focus on 'mapping' as an abstract activity developed by living in and moving around cities.

There is probably substance in this view. Even those who have claimed that modern cities are really collections of villages nevertheless tend to talk about their city world in abstract, formal, geometric terms—as Robert Roberts described his Salford 'village' in terms of intersections, networks, and grids: 'some thirty streets and alleys locked along the north and south by two railway systems a furlong apart' (Roberts, 1971, p. 3).

Primitive children have difficulty with intellectual tasks which involve 'shifting and shuffling things around in your head'. Schooling helps this process; a city's construction and the life lived within it give it an added boost to this facility (Goodnow, 1969). In mastering the layout of a city, in converting and transforming topographical detail into mental diagrams, maps, and charts, the city child develops skills of abstract reasoning on which the school can build.

It would be utter folly to conclude from all this either that we do not really need schools or that we should put all our children into great cities to ensure their full cognitive growth. Our Western urban-industrial countries are pervasively suburbanized and a discrete 'big-city' effect is probably minimal. But in primitive countries this is by no means the case: the difference between bush and city is vast and a period of city life would almost certainly help cognitive development.

In Britain and similar advanced industrial countries pervasive urbanization and suburbanization are likely to get all children a long way, cognitively speaking, even without benefit of schooling. The conclusion is not that we should put all our children in cities or close our schools, but that all our schools must be elite schools. They must all be very good indeed in a straightforward intellectual sense, with everyone in them at intellectual full-stretch. Their job is to 'top up', at the difficult end, on what urban culture has already achieved. In an urban culture even passably average schools are redundant.

## 5. NAVIGATION AND ABSTRACTION

Navigation in general and the triangle of velocities in particular have come to symbolize or represent abstract thought. They are the touchstone of modernity. Primitive people who can navigate or think as if in terms of a triangle of forces are claimed to have minds equivalent to our own.

Gilbert Ryle referred to mapping and contours when he wished to illustrate abstract or theoretical thinking (Ryle, 1949, pp. 290–291); Robin Horton presented African thought at its most theoretical and abstract as a triangle of forces (Horton, 1962, 1967); and Gladwin's study of Polynesian canoe navigation has been seized upon by all those educationists who wish to proclaim the abstract character of primitive thought—or to argue that primitives have a different and special logic which is in no way inferior to our own.

Ryle was concerned to play down the difference between mind and matter, abstract and concrete thought. He argued that learning an abstraction was simply acquiring a knack. It will be argued below that in fact primitive navigation is all knack and no abstraction. Even Ryle conceded that a contour line was at a higher level of abstraction than the map of a river—there was nothing to be seen on a hillside answering to a 300-foot contour. It is not easy to see what knack corresponds to grasping the distinction between a rhumb-line and a great circle, although Western navigators make important practical decisions in the light of it.

Horton maintained that African thinking, although effectively pragmatic in practical spheres, was also highly theoretical: religious thought was abstract because it parsimoniously selected the common factor in diversity and found order in apparent disarray. Society was basically stable, orderly, and regular, rather than the physical world, and it was to this social order that African abstract 'science' addressed itself.

For the Kalabari, said Horton, the three-sided relationship between ancestors, heroes, and water-spirits constituted a triangle of forces. 'In this triangle we have a theoretical scheme in terms of which Kalabari can grasp and comprehend most of the vicissitudes of their daily lives' (Horton, 1967). This abstract, triangular scheme is 'responsible for almost everything that happens in the immediate world of the Kalabari villager' (Horton, 1962).

The triangle of forces (or velocities) is basic to modern navigation. It is, indeed, a parsimonious selection of relevant factors from the multitudinous buffetings that beset an aircraft in flight or a ship at sea. It is neither a knack nor a recipe. Details constantly change and can be reordered and interpreted only if underlying relationships (and the principle of 'reversibility') are understood. To impose the triangle of forces on African thinking about famine and flood is not only intellectually pretentious—it is to be guilty of the fallacy of misplaced abstractness.

The activities of Puluwat canoe navigators have likewise been credited with highly abstract qualities. Gladwin's first accounts emphasized heavy reliance on memory and concrete observation and quite explicitly contrasted this with the 'relational or abstract thinking' to which we attach great value. The Polynesian navigators relied instead 'on the cumulative product of the adding together of a great number of discrete bits of data, summed together in accordance with predetermined parameters, to arrive at a desired conclusion'. In a manner strongly reminiscent of the Cape Coast market women (described in chapter 2), the Trukese (Polynesian) canoe navigator draws on 'vast amounts of data stored in memory' rather than working deductively from an overall principle or plan. The navigator worked with an immense number of details but never arrived at any discernible principles: 'We might refer to this kind of ability as a "knack"' (Gladwin, 1973). But in subsequent writing Gladwin stridently insisted that 'Abstract thinking is . . . a pervasive characteristic of Puluwat navigation' (Gladwin, 1971). This is the interpretation that has been taken up no less stridently by English sociologists of education.

Gladwin first set out to make a study of the 'intelligence' of people living on the islands of Polynesia. They did remarkably badly on intelligence tests and showed no aptitude as motor mechanics. For Gladwin there was a problem: how could such stupid people routinely accomplish the remarkable feat of sailing—without maps, charts, or even compasses—over vast areas of the Pacific Ocean to arrive safely at remote and tiny islands?

The answer was this: that prospective navigators spent years memorizing all the signs that might indicate their position. Thus star positions were memorized, and they were learned for every pair of islands between which a navigator might conceivably find himself sailing. Since there were 26 islands, the number of possible islands pairs between which star courses must be learned 'grows to formidable size'. This body of knowledge was 'taught and memorized through endless reiteration and testing'.

This is a remarkable achievement by any standard, and some inference and abstraction are involved. But Gladwin emphasizes the prepackaged answer and claims that the navigator's job was essentially information processing. This was map reading without maps and all relevant information had to be carried in the head: in that sense it was assuredly an 'abstract' activity. But that is playing with words. This was a massively memory-based, semi-automatic intellectual task:

> Each observation a navigator makes of waves, stars, or birds is related directly without any logical recording or interpretation to a conclusion about position, direction, or weather. Each such conclusion in turn permits of only one or at most two or three clearly defined alternative responses . . . once the intial observation has been made the steps which follow upon it are unequivocal.

Astonishingly, our neo-contextualists—Nell Keddie and M. F. D. Young—imagine that this is a new kind of logic comparable to the logic used by English academics. The key words are 'situated' and 'contexted'. In *Worlds Apart* the editors (Young and Keddie are two of the four) refer to Gladwin's work as evidence that 'theorizing, abstraction and inference' are to be found in primitive cultures and 'are not inherently different from the cognitive processes of members of "academic" cultures in industrial societies' (Beck *et al.*, 1976, pp. 159–160). In *Tinker, Tailor* the editor (Keddie) takes a stronger position, arguing that Gladwin's work shows that logic itself is not absolute but 'socially situated' and cannot be treated by the learner as if it were 'context free' (Keddie, 1973, p. 17).

Young has advanced a similar view based on Horton's writings on African thought (Young, 1971, p. 14). Elsewhere he cites the massively memory-based arithmetic of the Kpelle and the even more massively memory-based navigation of the Polynesians as supreme examples of primitive abstract thought: 'The situated and contexted features of "abstraction", a process all too easily seen as limited to academic knowledge, are illustrated in such diverse examples as African traditional religion, Polynesian navigation and Kpelle mathematics' (Young, 1974). These scarcely credible views are being presented to schoolteachers and curriculum experts with the clear message that Western (especially 'middle-class') ways of thinking are not necessarily superior to primitive thinking and have no exclusive claim to be the basis of the school curriculum.

It would be preposterous to say that primitive peoples cannot 'abstract': they are able to classify and reclassify objects and events and, even though illiterate, do so using increasingly abstract criteria as they grow older (Price-Williams, 1962). They are able to do Western tests of abstract thinking, like the Goldstein-Scheerer Cube Test—although Ghanaian schoolboys obtain significantly poorer results than European children (Jahoda, 1956). This ability to abstract is not in question. It is precisely the universality of abstracting and logical behaviour that have led some anthropologists to seek an explanation not in 'context' but out of context—in transcultural problems like the selection of foods to eat. Rationality, abstraction, and logic are products of planning the menu (Wilson, 1977). People may be more or less logical (Jackson, 1965) and more or less prone to use abstract criteria for classification (Price-Williams, 1962) according to context and materials. But that is an utterly different proposition from saying that logic itself is 'different' according to the context in which it is used.

The fact is that Puluwat canoe navigation is not very abstract and relies very little on deduction and problem solving. When I graduated as a Royal Air Force navigator in the early 1940s and flew with Bomber Command I was routinely engaged, during flight, in obtaining data for the solution of triangles of velocities. (As the relevant details constantly changed, a new solution was needed every 10 or 20 minutes.) The three 'sides' of the triangle were: track and ground speed, course and air speed, wind speed and direction. If data were obtained for two of these 'sides', the third could be deduced and appropriate action (course recalculated, times for turning revised) taken. This was intellectually parsimonious, economical, and elegant. It was also highly abstract. Map reading, by contrast, was a very minor, subsidiary aid to navigation and very concrete and non-theoretical. Of course, if there had been no maps, charts, compasses, or air speed indicators, the only means of navigation would have been 'map reading', having memorized the 'map'. Puluwat canoe navigators have developed techniques entirely appropriate to their circumstances. But to claim that their navigation is 'abstract' or employs some special, perhaps 'superior', non-Western logic is simply absurd.

## 6. LANGUAGE, THINKING, AND TRUTH

Benjamin Lee Whorf said that 'there is no primitive language' and concluded from this that there is no primitive thought. It is not a remarkable idea that the language we use influences the way we think. This simple notion underlies the writings, for instance, of Basil Bernstein on 'orders of meaning' and the different linguistic 'codes' through which they are realized (Bernstein, 1958, 1970). It is a much stronger proposition (which lies further back in Bernstein's thought) that the form of language we use shapes the reality we see and experience. On this stronger view language has a double effect on cognition: it influences not only the way we think, but the reality that is presented to us to think about. This in essence is the famous 'Sapir-Whorf hypothesis'.

Rousseau had held a similar view of language; but whereas those who have been influenced by Sapir and Whorf place language at the centre of the educational process, Rousseau would have banished it to the outer perimeter. He regarded the study of languages as 'among the useless lumber of education'. But it was not simply useless, it was dangerous; language did not simply mirror reality but modified our conception of it. Different languages, said Rousseau, 'as they change the symbols, also modify the ideas which the symbols express. Minds are formed by language, thoughts take their colour from its ideas' (Rousseau, 1911, p. 73). It was for this reason that Rousseau advocated an education based not upon words but things: the child should experience reality directly and not through a linguistic intermediary.

Whorf, whose papers (mainly on Hopi grammar) were first written in the 1920s and 1930s and published, some of them posthumously, in the 1940s and 1950s, argued that the picture of the universe was different from language to language. The worlds in which different language groups lived were quite distinct worlds and not merely the same world with different labels attached. Whorf claimed a major disjunction between Standard Average European (SAE) languages and other language families, notably Hebrew, Aztec, and Maya. The former were civilized and inferior, the latter primitive and superior. Each language, said Whorf, artificially cuts up the continuous flow of existence in a different way: it analyses nature and picks out or ignores certain types of relationship and phenomena. 'We dissect nature along lines laid down by our native language. The categories and types that we isolate in the world of phenomena we do not find there because they stare every observer in the face . . .' (Whorf, 1956, p. 212).

Whorf said that some languages chopped up and organized experience with finer discrimination and more powerful logic than others. He claimed that American Indian and African languages abounded in 'finely wrought, beautifully logical discriminations about causation, action, result . . .'. These primitive languages did not lead their users into confusion, like European languages: they showed the quintessence of the rational and 'In this respect they far outdistance the European languages'. We have the unfortunate practice of stretching terms to cover quite dissimilar phenomena, as when we talk of 'seeing' the colour red and 'seeing' that something is new. By comparison with Hopi, English, French, and German were poor and jejune:

> Does the Hopi language show here a higher plane of thinking, a more rational analysis of situations, than our vaunted English? Of course it does. In this field and various others, English compared to Hopi is like a bludgeon compared to a rapier. (Whorf, 1956, p. 85)

Whorf, then, is claiming two things: that reality does not have an independent, autonomous existence, but is in large measure created by the particular language we use; and that many primitive languages are superior to modern languages. On both counts he is wrong.

There are serious methodological and empirical problems about the Whorfian view of language and reality. Whorf's method of relating the two, in which the evidence of a changed reality is taken from the change in language, is tautological. Linguistic and non-linguistic events must be separately observed before they can be correlated.

The empirical testing of the relationship has come principally from research on colour discrimination and colour vocabulary in different cultures. There seemed, at first, to be some support for Whorf: the Zunis have no separate words for orange and yellow and in practice they do confuse these colours. But Brown and Lenneberg, who conducted these Zuni studies, were very cautious in interpreting their results. There was no warrant for saying that language was the cause of a particular way of dividing up the colour spectrum (Brown and Lenneberg, 1954).

The Harvard psycholgists who investigated the Wolofs claimed that they had refuted Whorf. The Wolofs have a very restricted colour vocabulary but nevertheless rely heavily on colour (rather than, say, form or function) for purposes of classification. Although young, unschooled, monolingual Wolofs made mistakes in colour grouping (but not on any major scale), these mistakes declined with age and finally disappeared. 'We began to wonder whether the lexical features of language should be assigned as large a role in thought as has been claimed by Whorf . . .' (Greenfield et al., 1966). The Harvard team placed great emphasis on language in conceptual growth but concluded that with increasing age reality triumphs over language if the two conflict. They felt they were justified in their emphasis on language while 'at the same time rejecting almost completely Whorf's simple notions about the relation between language and reality'.

The team from Bruner's Harvard Center looked for the triumph of environment over inborn or quasi-inborn factors wherever they could. But other research supports their doubts about Whorf. Osgood's extensive cross-cultural work (across six language families) on concept evaluation provides indirect evidence, underscoring the universality of the way people in all language groups construct meanings. Osgood's subjects were all schooled and he was aware of the possible homogenizing effects of schooling, but he claimed that his work cast doubt on Whorf and observed: 'Indeed, if the Sapir-Whorf psycholinguistic relativity hypothesis were taken literally . . . such comparisons would be impossible' (Osgood, 1964).

The Yurok, Karok, and Hupa Indians of north-western California have a similar culture but strikingly different languages. The way they classify plants and animals is substantially the same in all three tribes. Their separate and distinctive languages do not, it seems, enclose them in distinct worlds, and Jane and William Bright, who made this study, concluded that the three tribes' biotaxonomies were as similar as their languages were different, 'contrary to predictions from the Sapir-Whorf hypothesis' (Bright and Bright, 1969).

The theory of linguistic relativity has now been seriously challenged even in the colour domain (Cole and Scribner, 1974, pp. 43–50). Heider has shown how eight or nine basic or 'focal' colours (red, yellow, green, blue, pink, orange, brown, and purple) are most easily named and remembered in different cultures. She is inclined to interpret the universal features of colour recognition in terms of the physiology of colour vision. Far from being well suited to the study of the effect of language on thought, 'the colour space would seem to be a prime example of underlying perceptual-cognitive factors on the formation and reference of linguistic categories' (Heider, 1972).

Whorf's claim that primitive languages are generally 'superior' to modern (SAE) languages is singularly perverse. The Eskimos have more words for 'snow' than Europeans, the Arabs have more words for 'horse'. This is supposed to indicate greater powers of discrimination. Durkheim had similarly argued, in his attack on Levy-Bruhl, that Australian Aborigines, who had one word for white cockatoo and a quite different one for black cockatoo, showed superior powers of both discrimination and rationality. Their language would save them from the errors and confusion to which we are prone (Durkheim, 1915, p. 238).

In fact it was likely to save them from the higher form of abstract, relational thinking that Piaget called 'combinativity'. If a red cow and a brown cow have quite different names, there is an inbuilt obstacle in the language to combining them into one class ('coloured cows') which embraces both. To have distinct names for members of the same class of thing does not promote logical thinking: it prevents it.

Our own language is adjectively rich and has relatively few nouns: a great range of classification and recombination is facilitated by the language itself. Our language is also rich in prepositions and auxiliaries—the support parts of language—which makes for great flexibility and subtlety of recategorization. The single words of primitive languages become numerous words in advanced languages: the one Latin word 'fuissem' is four words in English: 'I should have been'. The many different notions embedded in the one primitive word are available for redevelopment and recombinations in endless new contexts.

This was the essential argument of Logan Pearsall Smith: that 'simplification is the law of development in all language'. The development of English as a superior language had been through a series of losses: with the loss of gender we had also discarded agreement of adjectives, pronouns and the article with their nouns. This makes our language a very powerful and sophisticated analytical tool: relationships once expressed by verbal terminations are now expressed by separate words of an abstract character. This, said Logan Pearsall Smith, 'is one of the most remarkable triumphs of the human intellect' (Smith, 1912, p. 13).

He addressed himself to the aspect of primitive languages which Whorf (and Durkheim) had thought signalled their superiority—their use of single words where we would use many:

> In primitive forms of speech whole complexes of thought and feeling
> are expressed in single terms. 'I said to him' is one word, 'I said to her'

another; 'my head' is a single term, 'his head' a different one. My head is, of course, to me an enormously different thing from his head, and it is an immense advance in the clearness of thought when I analyze the thought of 'my head' into its different parts, one of which is peculiar to me and named 'mine', the other that of 'head' which I share with other human beings.

Basil Bernstein, in his first important paper (1958), referred approvingly to Sapir's claim that the forms of language 'predetermine for us certain modes of observation and interpretation'. Thirteen years later he told us how Whorf had alerted him to 'the selective effect of culture' and had, more than anyone, opened up for him 'the question of the deep structure of linguistically regulated communication' (Bernstein, 1971). In fact Bernstein's contribution, over the years, to the study of language and thought has been dedicated to the view which is the antithesis of Sapir and Whorf's: that the symbolic order (including language) is modelled on the social order, rather than the other way round. Neither proposition is in fact true. Language and 'reality' (whether social or physical) have independent existences. It is an echo of an older magic to say that language does not simply reflect or retrieve reality but creates it.

## 7. CONCLUSION: THE IMPORTANCE OF OUT-OF-CONTEXT LEARNING

School is preeminently a device for taking learning out of context. That is its point—compared, say, with family instruction, workshop training, or apprenticeship. The main conclusion of this chapter is that it is vital, in both primitive and modern countries, to keep it that way,

It is curious that Bruner, whose work (with that of his colleagues at the Harvard Center for Cognitive Studies) strongly supports this view, has a hankering for 'contexted' learning situations. He says that primitive societies are disrupted when schooling separates knowing from action and the value of knowledge from the authority of the person who transmits it. The culture cannot then operate as a 'support system' for the learner. He says that a study by Cole and Scribner shows this but gives no reference. The work by Cole and Scribner among the Kpelle of Liberia does not show this, but underscores even more than the research of Bruner's colleagues the vital importance of getting learning out of the context in which it has been traditionally embedded. It is doubtless true, as Bruner says, that the young learn better if they think their knowledge will be needed. But that is no reason for embedding the learner in his culture in the way that Bruner now seems to commend (Bruner, 1980).

What the work of Cole and Scribner does show preeminently is not only the limitation of in-context learning but the critical weakness of in-context teaching. It suppresses both curiosity and intelligent understanding. The learning tends to be 'rote' and not very intelligent because questions are not encouraged (Gay and Cole, 1967, p. 20); and the teaching is inadequate because 'in-context

teachers' have difficulty abstracting themselves from the situation and understanding the learner's difficulties. The schoolteacher, who does not practise the
arts he teaches but stands outside them, understands more readily their difficulty for someone else. Kpelle adults do not give adequate instructions. Their
thinking appears to too 'egocentric'. In a communication experiment involving
the identification of differently shaped twigs, they simply did not give the
'learner' enough information to pick a particular twig out (Cole and Scribner,
1974, pp. 177–179). He who normally teaches by doing and showing rather than
by talking and explaining may, when he attempts the latter, fail to put himself in
the other person's place and give all the information needed for understanding
the message. Much of what is taught by doing and showing is not necessarily understood by the learner: it is simply performed.

If the new contextualists are Keddie and Young, the old contextualists were
Margaret Mead and Meyer Fortes. They gave accounts of in-context learning in
primitive societies not only for our admiration but emulation. Margaret Mead
strongly approved of the upbringing of Samoan children: 'From the time they
are four or five years old they perform definite tasks, graded to their strength
and intelligence, but still tasks which have meaning in the structure of the whole
society' (Mead, 1943, p. 181). American education was reproved because 'children spend hours in school learning tasks whose visible relation to their
mothers' and fathers' activities it is quite impossible to recognize'.

The Tallensi of Ghana have a similar 'integrated' or 'holistic' mode of education and Meyer Fortes gave a very sympathetic account of it. He contrasted our
out-of-context drill techniques unfavourably with Tale educational methods
which worked 'through the situation, which is a bit of the social reality shared
by adult and child alike' (Fortes, 1938, p. 27).

In Taleland, said Fortes, the social sphere of adult and child is unitary and
undivided; from the very beginning the child is oriented to the same social
reality as his parents: 'Nothing in the universe of adult behaviour is hidden from
children or barred from them. They are actively and responsibly part of the
social structure, of the economic system, the ritual and ideological system.' The
Tallensi did not, like us, use 'atomic' and 'factitious' training situations which
involved being drilled in skills taken out of their context: 'The Tallensi do not
make systematic use of training situations. They teach through real situations
which children are drawn to participate in because it is expected that they are
capable and desirous of mastering the necessary skills.'

Fortes called this situation organic and holistic; we used to call it child labour.
Modern industrial societies invent three closely related institutions: childhood,
school, and children's play. All three mark off the child from the adult world
and afford him a protracted period of exploration and relatively autonomous
development. Play is no longer at best frivolous but more probably sinful: it is
the condition of mental health and is actively encouraged, particularly by middle-class parents.

Margaret Mead said with approval that Samoan children did not play, and
equal disapproval that American children did. Samoan children joined in the

festivals, ceremonials, and games of adults, but they did not have a special child's version of play. Meyer Fortes gave a careful account of children's play in Taleland and emphasized its 'training' character in promoting competence, for instance, in using a bow and arrow. 'When adults are asked about children's mimetic play they reply: "That is how they learn"' (Fortes, 1938, p. 13).

Such strictly utilitarian, non-fantasy play, directly related to real-life tasks, was precisely what I found when I investigated play in the preliterate tribes of Uganda. Young children 'played games which were mostly anticipatory of the traditional life of their people. Their games were marked by a strong utilitarian aspect, of which the boys themselves are fully conscious. They may even describe the play of their early years as "training"' (Musgrove, 1953).

Those who approve of this strongly 'integrated' mode of informal education, in contrast to the alleged unreality of both our schools and our children's less 'contexted' play, have paid little heed to its cognitive costs. Fortes conceded that children in Taleland accepted unquestioningly what adults told them: by 9 years of age they had memorized a vast amount of information about trees, grasses, herbs, and the anatomy of small field animals, but 'listening to children's talk for "why" questions I was surprised to note how rarely they occurred' (Fortes, 1938, p. 30). Gay and Cole (1967) make exactly the same point about Kpelle children. Unlike Fortes they fully recognize its disastrous cognitive consequences.

In summary: the evidence of cross-cultural research points strongly to the importance of schools and cities in getting children to look beyond their own back yards and move from concrete to more abstract thought. It also points, though less conclusively, to the importance of free-ranging play in early childhood, especially manipulative play with physical objects. The attributes of schools which seem particularly relevant are alphabetic literacy, 'school language', both spoken and written, and probably the use of European languages. The attributes of cities that are significant are probably the need for complex information processing, for 'mapping', and for handling more 'distanced' social relationships. Schools and cities are important in advanced no less than in primitive societies, but in extensively suburbanized countries 'city-effect' is likely to be widely diffused and all-pervasive. It is not necessary to live within the boundaries of a city to experience it.

The evidence from cross-cultural research on the significance of play is less conclusive. Indeed, the evidence of intra-cultural research on the cognitive effects of play (compared, for instance, with more structured training or drill) is fragmentary and relatively weak. Fantasy play is common among English and American children between the ages of 3 and 7 and seems to help them to cope well with innovative as compared with routine and standard tasks (Smith, 1980).

Restricted and directly 'relevant' or focused play is more generally the picture in Africa—even restricted physical movement. Vernon pointed to the way infants are carried for many hours on the backs of their mothers while they work in the fields and are limited in their opportunities to grasp and manipulate

(Vernon, 1969, p. 44); another study maintained that 'the typical African is somewhat arrested in mental development' and attributed this to dependency arising at least in part from the fact that the mother carried the young child 'on her back all day, in a cloth or a buck-skin, and he sleeps in her arms or by her side at night' (Ritchie, 1944). The 'performance' aspects rather than the verbal aspects of African culture have been seen as limiting intellectual growth (McFie, 1961).

The psychologist Leonard Doob, in striking contrast to the anthropologist, Meyer Fortes, regretted that less civilized people had 'a tendency to unify experience' (Doob, 1960, p. 187). In consequence, he said, 'they are less likely to view objects, other people and themselves out of context'. But if they went to Western-style schools this was to some extent rectified, and this was reflected in their improved performance in cognitive tests. Doob is not prepared to deride 'school skills' as irrelevant and unrepresentative of life; indeed, school skills, to all intents and purposes, equals 'civilization'. The tests revealed children's improved ability to cope with novel situations and at least 'In this restricted sense they are better prepared for a more civilized world'.

## REFERENCES

Beattie, John (1966a), *Other Cultures*, Routledge & Kegan Paul, London.
Beattie, John (1966b), 'Ritual and social change', *Man*, **1** (n.s.).
Beck, J., Jenks, C., Keddie, N., and Young, M. F. D. (1976), *Worlds Apart*, Collier-Macmillan, London.
Bernstein, B. (1958), 'Social class and linguistic development: A theory of social learning', *British Journal of Sociology*, **9**.
Bernstein, B. (1970), 'Education cannot compensate for society', *New Society*, 26 February.
Bernstein, B. (1971), 'Social class, language and socialization', in B. Bernstein, *Class, Codes and Control*, vol. I, Routledge & Kegan Paul.
Berry, J. W. (1966), 'Temne and Eskimo perceptual skills', *International Journal of Psychology*, **1**.
Berry, J. W. (1971), 'Ecological and cultural factors in spatial perceptual development', *Canadian Journal of Behavioral Sciences*, **3**.
Biesheuvel, S. (1949), 'Psychological tests and their application to non-European peoples', in *Year Book of Education*, Evans Bros, London.
Bohannan, Paul (1954), 'The migration and expansion of the Tiv', *Africa*, **24**.
Bright, Jane O., and Bright, William (1969), 'Semantic structure in north western California and the Sapir-Whorf hypothesis', in Stephen A. Tyler, *Cognitive Anthropology*, Holt, Rinehart & Winston, new York.
Brown, R. W., and Lenneberg, E. H. (1954), 'A study of language and cognition', *Journal of Abnormal and Social Psychology*, **49**.
Bruner, J. S. (1964), 'The course of cognitive development', *American Psychologist*, **19**.
Bruner, J. S. (1974), *The Relevance of Education*, Penguin, Harmondsworth, Middx.
Bruner, J. S. (1980), 'Patterns of growth', in Peter Gordon (ed.), *The Study of Education*, vol. 2, Woburn Press, London.
Churchill, E. M. )1958), 'The number concepts of young children', *Researches and Studies*, **17** and **18**.

Cole, M., Gay, John, Glick, J. A., and Sharp, D. W. (1971), *The Cultural Context of Learning and Thinking*, Methuen, London.

Cole, M., and Scribner, S. (1974), *Culture and Thought*, Wiley, New York.

Cryns, A. G. J. (1962), 'African intelligence: A critical survey of cross-cultural intelligence research in Africa south of the Sahara', *Journal of Social Psychology*, **57**.

Dasen, P. R. (1972), 'Cross-cultural Piagetian research: A summary', *Journal of Cross-Cultural Psychology*, **3**.

De Lemos, Marion (1969), 'The development of conservation in Aboriginal children', *International Journal of Psychology*, **4**.

Doob, L. W. (1957), 'An introduction to the psychology of acculturation', *Journal of Social Psychology*, **45**.

Doob, L. W. (1960), *Becoming More Civilized. A Psychological Exploration*, Yale University Press, New Haven, Conn.

Durkheim, É. (1915), *The Elementary Forms of the Religious Life*, translated by Rodney Needham, Allen & Unwin, London.

Durkheim, É., and Mauss, M. (1963), *Primitive Classification*, Cohen & West, London.

Fortes, Meyer (1938), *Social and Psychological Aspects of Education in Taleland*, Oxford University Press, London.

Frazer, G. J. (1957), *The Golden Bough*, vol. I, Macmillan, London.

Furby, L. (1971), 'A theoretical analysis of cross-cultural research in cognitive development: Piaget's conservation task', *Journal of Cross-Cultural Psychology*, **2**.

Gay, J., and Cole, M. (1967), *The New Mathematics and an Old Culture*, Holt, Rinehart & Winston, New York.

Gladwin, T. (1971), *East is a Big Bird. Navigation and Logic on Puluwat Atoll*, Harvard University Press, Cambridge, Mass.

Gladwin, T. (1973), 'Culture and logical process', in N. Keddie (ed.), *Tinker, Tailor . . . The Myth of Cultural Deprivation*, Penguin, Harmondsworth, Middx.

Goodnow, J. J. (1969), 'Cultural variations in cognitive skills', in D. R. Price-Williams (ed.), *Cross-Cultural Studies*, Penguin, Harmondsworth, Middx.

Goodnow, J. J., and Bethon, G. (1966), 'Piaget's tasks: The effects of schooling and intelligence', *Child Development*, **37**.

Greenfield, P. M. (1966), 'On culture and conservation', in J. S. Bruner, R. Olver, and P. M. Greenfield, *Studies in Cognitive Growth*, Wiley, New York.

Greenfield, P. M., and Bruner, J. S. (1966), 'Culture and cognitive growth', *International Journal of Psychology*, **1**.

Greenfield, P. M., Reich, Lee C., Olver, R. (1966), 'On culture and equivalence: II', in J. S. Bruner *et al.*, *Studies in Cognitive Growth*, Wiley, New York.

Hallpike, C. R. (1979), *The Foundations of Primitive Thought*, Clarendon Press, Oxford.

Hallpike, C. R. (1976), 'Is there a primitive mentality?', *Man*, **11**.

Heider, Eleanor Rosch (1972), 'Universals in color naming and memory', *Journal of Experimental Psychology*, **93**.

Horton, R. (1962), 'The Kalabari world-view: An outline and interpretation', *Africa*, **32**.

Horton, R. (1967), 'African traditional thought and Western science', *Africa*, **37**.

Hyde, D. M. G. (1970), *Piaget and Conceptual Development*, Holt, Rinehart & Winston, New York.

Jackson, S. (1965), 'The growth of logical thinking in normal and subnormal children', *British Journal of Educational Psychology*, **35**.

Jahoda, G. (1956), 'Assessment of abstract behaviour in a non-Western culture', *Journal of Abnormal and Social Psychology*, **53**.

Jahoda, G. (1966), 'Geometric illusions and environment: A study in Ghana', *British Journal of Psychology*, **57**.

Keddie, N. (1973), *Tinker, Tailor . . . The Myth of Cultural Deprivation*, Penguin, Harmondsworth, Middx.

Lévi-Strauss, C. (1972), *Structural Anthropology*, Penguin, Harmondsworth, Middx.

Lloyd, Barbara (1971), 'Studies of conservation with Yoruba children of differing ages and experience', *Child Development*, **42**.

Lovell, K., and Ogilvie, E. (1961), 'A study of the conservation of weight in the junior school child', *British Journal of Educational Psychology*, **31**.

Lunzer, E. A. (1980), 'On children's thinking', in Peter Gordon (ed.), *The Study of Education*, vol. 2, Woburn Press, London.

Maccoby, M., and Modliano, N. (1966), 'On culture and equivalence: I', in J. S. Bruner *et al.*, *Studies in Cognitive Growth*, Wiley, New York.

McFie, J. (1961), 'The effect of education on African performance in a group of intellectual tests', *British Journal of Educational Psychology*, **31**.

Mead, Margaret (1943), *Coming of Age in Samoa*, Penguin, Harmondsworth, Middx.

Mermelstein, E., and Schulman, L. S. (1967), 'Lack of formal schooling and the acquisition of conservation', *Child Development*, **38**.

Musgrove, F. (1953), 'Education and the culture concept', *Africa*, **23**.

Osgood, C. E. (1964), 'Semantic differential technique in the comparative study of culture', *American Anthropologist*, **66**.

Peluffo, N. (1967), 'Culture and cognitive problems', *International Journal of Psychology*, **2**.

Piaget, J. (1966a), 'Foreword', in M. Almy, E. Chittenden, and P. Miller, *Young Children's Thinking*, Teachers' College Press, Columbia University, New York.

Piaget, J. (1966b), 'Necessité et signification des recherches comparatives en psychologie génétique', *International Journal of Psychology*, **1**; reprinted in J. W. Berry and P. R. Dasen, *Culture and Cognition: Readings in Cross-Cultural Psychology*, Methuen, London.

Poole, H. E. (1968), 'The effect of urbanization upon scientific concept attainment among Hausa children in northern Nigeria', *British Journal of Educational Psychology*, **38**.

Price-Williams, D. R. (1961), 'A study concerning concepts of conservation of quantities among primitive children', *Acta Psychologica*, **18**.

Price-Williams, D. R. (1962), 'Abstract and concrete modes of classification in a primitive society', *British Journal of Educational Psychology*, **32**.

Prince, J. R. (1968), 'The effect of Western education on science conceptualization in New Guinea', *British Journal of Educational Psychology*, **38**.

Redfield, R., and Singer, Milton, B. (1954–1955), 'The cultural role of cities', *Economic Development and Cultural Change*, **13**.

Ritchie, J. F. (1944), 'The African as grown-up nursling', *Rhodes-Livingston Institute Journal*, no. 1.

Roberts, Robert (1971), *The Classic Slum*, Manchester University Press, Manchester.

Rousseau, J.-J. (1911), *Émile*, Dent, London.

Ryle, Gilbert (1949), *The Concept of Mind*, Hutchinson, London.

Scribner, S., and Cole, M. (1973), 'Cognitive consequences of formal and informal education', *Science*, **182**.

Serpell, R. (1969), 'Cultural differences in attentional preference for color over form', *International Journal of Psychology*, **4**.

Sigel, I. E., Roeper, A., and Hooper, F. H. (1966), 'A training procedure for acquisition of Piaget's conservation of quantity: A pilot study and its replication', *British Journal of Educational Psychology*, **36**.

Smith, Logan Pearsall (1912), *The English Language*, Thornton Butterworth, London.

Smith, Peter K. (1980), 'Play and its role in education', *Educational Analysis*, **2**.

Suchman, R. G. (1966), 'Cultural differences in children's color and form preferences', *Journal of Social Psychology*, **70**.

68

Suchman, R. G., and Trabasso, T. (1966), 'Color and form preference in young children', *Journal of Experimental Child Psychology*, 3.

Tylor, E. B. (1871), *Primitive Culture*, vol. I, John Murray, London.

Vernon, P. E. (1959), 'Race and intelligence', *New Scientist*, 29 January.

Vernon, P. E. (1969), *Intelligence and Cultural Environment*, Methuen, London.

Whorf, Benjamin Lee (1956), *Language, Thought and Reality*, MIT Press, Cambridge, Mass.

Wilson, P. J. (1977), 'La pensée alimentaire: The evolutionary context of rational objective thought', *Man*, 12.

Young, M. F. D. (1971), *Knowledge and Control*, Collier-Macmillan, London.

Young, M. F. D. (1974), 'Notes for a sociology of science education', *Studies in Science Education*, 1.

# CHAPTER 4

# *The Social Basis of Rationality*

Anthropologists are agreed that a primitive society's belief in witchcraft and magic reflects no discredit on the minds of its members. A primitive people may impress European travellers, missionaries, anthropologists, and traders as highly intelligent and their practical arts in the spheres of farming, fishing, and building may be, and usually are, perfectly 'scientific'; and yet they may be steeped in witchcraft beliefs and practices. These beliefs may be highly coherent and well defended with logic. Nevertheless, in this chapter I shall take witchcraft as the supreme manifestation and symbol of irrationality.

Large claims have been made in recent years for primitive magic; but I agree with Tom Settle's argument that 'by the standards of rationality customarily used in the West, magic is irrational' and 'declaring magic to be irrational seems to be required if proper attention is to be paid to science (including technology) as a paradigm of rationality' (Settle, 1971). In addressing the question, 'under what circumstances are people most likely to hold rational beliefs?', witchcraft, sorcery, and magic will remain near the centre of attention.

The subject abounds in paradox. It has been claimed that witchcraft beliefs and practices among primitive people are increased by the introduction of Western education—or at least that Western schooling does nothing to eradicate them. The connection between witchcraft and schooling is the focus of this chapter. There has often been a close connection between higher education and witchcraft both in Europe in the past and in Africa today; and an education based on the Bible and the Christian religion is more likely to support than to challenge magical beliefs. The broad influence of a secular Western education is undoubtedly towards a greater scientific rationality, but this will take firm root only when society itself shifts in emphasis from 'Gemeinschaft' to 'Gesellschaft', from community to association.

In this chapter an attempt will be made to examine the social circumstances in which irrational beliefs arise and persist. Reference will be made to witchcraft, sorcery, and magic in primitive societies and in medieval and Renaissance Europe; to millennial cargo cults in the Pacific; and to witch-finding movements and extreme separatist Christian sects under conditions of 'culture contact'. There are problems about grouping these diverse phenomena together: but they all afford evidence of behaviour and belief unsupported by adequate evidence and held even when they clearly do not 'work'. Societies do not abandon these beliefs when the errors are explained; nor when the anxieties which they seem to reflect are removed; but when community yields to association. The basic condition for rationality is a weak sense of community and abundant opportunities to get out.

No attempt will be made to explain irrational systems of belief in terms of individuals' thought processes. Seventy years ago Franz Boas argued correctly (in *The Mind of Primitive Man*) that the traditional and customary beliefs of a society provide no evidence about the way individuals think. Beliefs that an outsider considers bizarre are not evidence of bizarre thinking. They tell us something about social tradition, little about individual thought. Boas thought he was attacking Levy-Bruhl's view of 'primitive mentality'. In fact, Levy-Bruhl had said exactly the same. He had argued that beliefs tell us about a people's 'collective representations': about patterns of thought, which are a social product. They do not tell us about the working of individual minds.

## 1. WITCHCRAFT REVALUED

In the past 50 years anthropologists have done two things with regard to witchcraft: they have shifted the blame from primitive minds to primitive societies; and they have shown that witchcraft beliefs are logical. They have also claimed a third thing: that witchcraft beliefs uphold society. They are the mainstay of morality. All this amounts to a massive upgrading of witchcraft. But logical beliefs are not necessarily rational beliefs. Good logic can defend utterly stupid beliefs which find no support in experience and observed reality. Logic is effectively used by primitives to show that the failure of witchcraft is its proof of success: the incompetence of magicians does not invalidate magic. It would be a profound error, when considering witchcraft, to confuse logic and rationality.

Lucien Levy-Bruhl (1857–1939) has been severely censured for claiming that primitive mentality was prelogical and mystical. Evans-Pritchard's classic study of witchcraft and oracles among the Zande of the Sudan showed how apparently weird beliefs were not only eminently practical and sensible but even more eminently logical. Yet Evans-Pritchard's interpretation was greatly influenced by the writings of Levy-Bruhl whose general theory he was supporting.

When Max Gluckman wrote an extended review of Evans-Pritchard's work he called his article 'The logic of African science and witchcraft' (Gluckman, 1944). Logic was at the very centre of Evans-Pritchard's account of Zande sorcery. As an account of causation in personal affairs witchcraft offered a superior explanation because it was more complete—it did not leave gaps, as our explanations do, which we fill in with the notion of 'chance'. 'Anyone', said Gluckman, 'who follows Evans-Pritchard's exposition of the intellectual aspect of Zande magic and witchcraft will be fascinated by their logical skill.'

When a raised granary falls on men who are sheltering under it from the heat of the sun they know that it collapsed because termites had eaten away the supports: but why did it collapse at that particular moment on these particular men? Witchcraft explains why two unconnected chains of events intersect at a particular time and place (Evans-Pritchard, 1976, pp. 22–23). Our own explanation in terms of chance or coincidence appears to an African an intellectual evasion. As Monica Wilson observed: 'The decline in belief in witchcraft and sorcery is not purely a matter of extending scientific knowledge—our answer must cover the astute Pondo teacher who said to me: "It may be quite true that typhus is carried by lice, but who sent the infected louse? Why did it bite one man and not another?" ' (Wilson, 1951b). I have reported similar conversations with highly intelligent African schoolboys who were explaining to me why some boys (but not others) had gone down with malaria. They differed from their pre-Christian fathers only in attributing the witchcraft to God (Musgrove, 1953).

But people who believe in witchcraft and magic have not worked out a system of beliefs for themselves; they do not believe in magic because they have reasoned incorrectly from evidence: they believe in magic because they were born into a community which has magical beliefs. This is Levy-Bruhl's essential and not especially remarkable point. It is also Evans-Pritchard's. The beliefs are already 'there', external to the individual and imposed upon him. They are 'collective representations'. Different types of society, said Levy-Bruhl, had their own mentality, 'but let us abandon the attempt to refer their mental activity to an inferior variety of our own' (Levy-Bruhl, 1926, p. 26).

Boas had argued similarly in *The Mind of Primitive Man*, pointing out that if common American beliefs about nature and society were used as evidence of logical thought, the result would be very unflattering to the American mind (Boas, 1911, p. 128). Evans-Pritchard wrote in a similar vein in a very sympathetic analysis of Levy-Bruhl's views which he published in the bulletin of the Faculty of Arts of the Egyptian University at Cairo in 1934:

> The fact that we attribute rain to meteorological causes alone while savages belief that Gods or ghosts or magic can influence the rainfall is no evidence that our brains function differently from their brains. . . . It is no sign of superior intelligence on my part that I attribute rain to physical causes. I did not come to this conclusion myself by observation and inference and have, in fact, little knowledge of the meteorological processes that lead to rain. I merely accept what everybody in my society accepts, namely that rain is due to natural causes. . . . He (the savage) and I are both thinking in patterns of thought provided for us by the societies in which we live. (Evans-Pritchard, 1934)

And so the witchcraft beliefs which characterize most primitive societies are rescued from explanations in terms of defective primitive minds; and if we ask why these beliefs are never seriously challenged or overthrown, the answer again is commonly in terms of society rather than individual abilities. Horton says that primitive societies experience a 'closed predicament' wherein there is no developed awareness of alternatives (Horton, 1967); Settle says they have no custom of criticism and this is 'a matter of corporate tradition rather than individual intelligence' (Settle, 1971). Other anthropologists (and philosophers) have in recent years said exactly the same, shifting the responsibility from individual intelligence to social institutions. Magical beliefs will persist, they say, when a society has no habit of taking up critical attitudes to beliefs and values: 'This is a question of sociological fact: the presence or absence of a tradition. It reflects in no way upon the intelligence, stupidity, human dignity, or mental capabilities of the peoples of the societies in question' (Jarvie and Agassi, 1967).

Levy-Bruhl himself was a principal exponent of the social interpretation of primitive thought. He did not say that men's thinking was everywhere the same: he said it varied with the type of society. Primitive thinking, he said, was indifferent to contradiction and relied heavily on memory rather than reason. He did not say that this was because primitive men had weaker or inferior minds: he said it was because they had a different kind of society. This was a 'structuralist' argument based on alleged concordance, correspondences, and homologies between form of society and form of thought. Evans-Pritchard's only serious criticism of Levy-Bruhl was that he failed to follow through this structuralist argument by making systematic, comparative analyses and showing how modes of thinking and forms of society varied together. But his work was of such exceptional brilliance, said Evans-Pritchard, that it could survive even major deficiencies of this kind (Evans-Pritchard, 1934).

Anthropologists have tried to rescue 'cargo cults' as well as witchcraft from the charge of irrationality. These millennial movements developed in Melanesia towards the end of the nineteenth century and continued until recent times. Prophets arose, like Buka in the Solomon Islands in the early 1930s, who promised that ships would come over the horizon carrying unending cargoes of calico and tinned salmon, axes, tobacco and firearms; natives would become the equals of whites; and all work would cease. The religious secrets which were hidden by the white man would be revealed to all, and the first cargo would arrive in April 1935. It failed to arrive—as it had failed to arrive when expected in Fiji in 1885, in New Guinea in 1893, in Papua in 1919. The Melanesians did not learn from their 'mistakes', yet failure to learn was a serious matter: the prophets' adherents ceased to cultivate their gardens and ate all their pigs. But, argued Worsley (1957), their beliefs were eminently sensible in view of what was known of nonproductive white men and the way they received their supplies. No explanation was needed in terms of primitive psychology.

Lucy Mair was very sharply and properly critical of Worsley's attempt to play down the irrationality of cargo cults. She castigated him especially for his shift in meaning from the rationality of individual action to the rationality of social systems, when he claimed that the cults were far less irrational than the capitalist system. The cults, insisted Mair, were irrational—or at least non-rational—'in the sense in which the word is applied to means which cannot possibly achieve their ostensible ends' (Mair, 1958).

The cults on the face of it deserve the charge of fantasy and unrealistic escapism; but Jarvie contends that they are rational because they constitute, in effect, a religion:

> In arguing that the cults are rational, I am saying that religion is rational too. . . . In the sense that religious beliefs are theoretical explanations of things and events in the world, then they are as rational, I would say, as any other (say scientific) explanation. (Jarvie, 1963–1964)

And so the criteria of rationality are changed by anthropologists to accommodate the varieties of primitive belief and clear them of any charge of 'inferiority'. But in fact these beliefs are inadequate for an effective handling of reality, however consoling they may be to those who embrace them. That is not to say that 'primitive psychology' is to blame: the fault may well lie in social circumstances. (That is not necessarily a 'structuralist' argument: the structuralist case is scarcely more advanced today than at the point where Levy-Bruhl left it.) It is the social circumstances which seem to breed and nurture irrational beliefs which will now be my concern. Education itself, in certain circumstances, does not entirely escape suspicion, and this possible linkage will be dealt with next.

## 2. EDUCATION AND IRRATIONALITY

The touchstone of rationality in England since the late seventeenth century has been the use of evidence provided by the mathematical and experimental sciences rather than reasoning based on analogy and syllogism. And yet the man who is held to embody the new rationality—'the gigantic figure who summed up the new reason for the next two centuries' (Hill, 1969)—Sir Isaac Newton, was deeply involved in the study of alchemy and biblical prophecy. The man who wrote *Principia Mathematica* also wrote *Observations upon the Prophecies of Holy Writ*. The close association of advanced learning and belief and behaviour which by our standards are wholly irrational extended from the late fifteenth to the early seventeenth century. Over this period the association intensified rather than diminished. The age of Shakespeare, the high Renaissance, saw a crescendo of witchcraft accusations and trials. As the Elizabethan grammar schools were founded and what Lawrence Stone calls England's 'educational revolution' took off, the witch-craze reached its height. Throughout Western Europe witchcraft grew with a learned literate elite.

The Protestant Reformation made neither the syllogism nor experimental science, but a sacred book, the test of truth. Max Weber emphasized the rationality of Protestantism and highlighted the Quaker contribution to taking magic out of the liturgy (Weber, 1930, pp. 148–149); but the new literacy-based and Bible-centred version of Christianity accompanied the upsurge of witchcraft activity and undoubtedly made some contribution to it. The persecution of witches reached its height at the centres of Puritan sentiment: 'the history of the persecution of witches in England (also the history of the practice of witchcraft) directly parallels the career of the Puritans' (Walzer, 1968). But more generally Protestant irrationalism, as Christopher Hill (1969) maintains, was underpinned by biblical fundamentalism.

Two distinguished historians have examined witchcraft and associated phenomena in Europe between the fourteenth and the seventeenth centuries: Richard Kieckhefer made a notable study of the fourteenth and fifteenth centuries (Kieckhefer, 1976), Hugh Trevor-Roper of the sixteenth and seventeenth centuries (Trevor-Roper, 1967a). There are serious problems attached to defining and categorizing the beliefs and behaviour they studied. There is not only the familiar problem of distinguishing witchcraft from sorcery, but that of distinguishing both from demonology and heresy. But what seems to have happened from the fourteenth century onwards was that a subterranean tradition of pagan folk witchcraft was reinterpreted by men of great learning. Their essential contribution was to bring the Devil into it.

In fifteenth-century Europe there was a sharp increase in witchcraft accusations accompanied by more frequent charges of diabolism. The introduction of diabolism was the work of the literate elite. It was the subject of elaborate and learned theological and judicial treatises. The first well-authenticated trials for diabolism occurred in Italy, for 'it was there that legal scholarship was most developed, and it was in the Italian courts that one might expect to find ideas of the literate elite reflected in judicial practice' (Kieckhefer, 1976, p. 23). The infusion of diabolism into witchcraft was the supreme achievement of late-medieval European scholarship.

Trevor-Roper ties sophisticated scholarship and demonology even more tightly together in the sixteenth and seventeenth centuries. The self-confessed activities of witches who had made pacts with the Devil reached a crescendo in the time of Bacon, Montaigne, and Descartes. Trevor-Roper points to the astonishing paradox of Bodin, 'the undisputed intellectual master of the later sixteenth century', a pioneer of comparative history and of the philosophy of law, who in 1580 wrote a book, *De la demonomaine des sorciers*, which 'more than any other, re-animated the witch-fires throughout Europe'. But Bodin was merely the most eminent of a host of erudite men whose monstrous treatises justified ferocious witch-hunts and executions. 'Indeed, the more learned a man was in the traditional scholarship of the time, the more likely he was to support the witch-doctors.'

No one has suggested that high learning actually caused witchcraft beliefs or even demonology; but it undoubtedly, for a time, encouraged both. Mary Douglas sees the irrationality of sixteenth-century academics as rooted in the social insecurities of the time, especially their personal dependence on the caprice of Renaissance princes and their courts (Douglas, 1970a). It is in the tight but brittle social relationships of courtly life that the answer may in large measure lie and to which I shall return.

In modern Africa there is a similar paradox of an apparently intimate connection between witchcraft and Western education. Of course, witchcraft was there first, but Western education often seems to be associated with its extension.

Malinowski did not say that Western schooling produced more widespread witchcraft practices in Africa but he never tired of saying that it was powerless to eradicate them (Malinowski, 1943). Evans-Pritchard took a similar despairing view: not only did witchcraft beliefs underpin morality and the social order (witchcraft accusations were against social undesirables), but, 'To reason against African belief in witchcraft is useless because intellectually it is perfectly coherent' (Evans-Pritchard, 1935). But some anthropologists have gone further than this, strongly suggesting (what is in fact superbly untestable) that Western education has actually extended witchcraft accusations and beliefs.

This was the contention of Audrey Richards when she reported in 1935 on witch-finding movements among the Bemba. Certainly the Bamucapi, the witch finders who were sweeping through Bemba country, were Westernized, well dressed in European clothes, usin. Western implements such as mirrors, and proceeding with the brisk bureaucratic efficiency of white officials conducting a census. Audrey Richards claimed that 'the result of white contact is in many cases an actual increase in the dread of witchcraft'. As the old order broke down and uncertainties increased witchcraft became more rather than less relevant: 'Nowhere did I feel this more strongly than in the most civilized part of Northern Rhodesia, the copper belt' (Richards, 1935).

Similar interpretations have come more recently out of Ghana. Barbara Ward claimed that the Ashanti Social Survey of 1948 showed that 'the spread of Christianity and school education had been accompanied not simply by the persistence of witchcraft beliefs but by their very considerable increase . . .'. On the basis of her own experience as a teacher in Ghana she linked education closely with witchcraft and witch finding although she was cautious about claiming an actual increase in witchcraft beliefs (Ward, 1956).

This thesis has been most systematically developed by Marwick. In a series of publications in the 1950s and 1960s (Marwick, 1952, 1956, 1965), he argued that the Westernization of Africa, including the spread of Western schooling, actually meant more witchcraft and not less:

> Many people assume that the African's beliefs in witchcraft are being reduced by his contact with Western culture. Their optimism is based on the fact that the civilization into which the African is being drawn is founded on a scientific technology. . . . I am going to suggest that exactly the opposite is true. (Marwick, 1956)

At least in the short term witchcraft beliefs were encouraged:

> It seems to me that the immediate effect of contact with Western influence is not a decrease but an increase in the African's preoccupation with beliefs in magic, witchcraft and sorcery.

The effect was often indirect: in a partially Westernized Africa infringements of old rules were inevitable—thus an educated, Christian African who already had one wife could not inherit the widow of his deceased maternal uncle. The affronted widow would be suspected of witchcraft whenever trouble afflicted the nephew and his family.

Marwick's case studies with the Cewa tribe do not in fact suggest a flood of witchcraft accusations arising from modernity: only 19 out of 101 instances of personal misfortune which led to witchcraft accusations arose out of circumstances brought about by modern influences (Marwick, 1965, pp. 254–255). There is powerful testimony from other anthropologists, notably Mitchell and Goody, that suggests that Marwick's thesis is the opposite of the truth.

Yao tribesmen who moved from their rural villages to work in European enterprises on the Copperbelt were less given to witchcraft practices and accusations, says Clyde Mitchell, than those who were left behind. They were less inclined to blame their misfortunes on the witchcraft of kinsmen, and witchcraft was seen as 'weaker', less likely to kill. Mitchell does not ascribe these 'improvements' to greater Westernization and intellectual enlightenment but to the looser and more transient social relationships of urban life (Mitchell, 1965).

The change-and-witchcraft thesis has been seriously questioned for England: witchcraft died out precisely as rapid industrialization set in (Douglas, 1970a; Gillies, 1976). Goody has questioned the argument that change brings anxiety and more witchcraft, making special reference to Ghana. In any event, he says, formerly there was slavery, warfare, and wholesale executions; Westernization meant a steep decline in personal insecurity. It is true that ancient ways of detecting witches were now forbidden, and new ways, not surprisingly, evolved. But the 'anomie' thesis of (increased) witchcraft, says Goody, is based wholly on inadequate evidence (Goody, 1957).

Westernization in general and schooling in particular almost certainly undermine the more powerful forms of witchcraft belief. But their influence is probably indirect, changing the social relationship out of which witchcraft has grown.

### 3. SCHOOLING AND THE MILLENNIUM

Education is not the cause of witchcraft: it is probably not the cause of *more* witchcraft; but it may peacefully coexist with 'weaker' forms of irrationality, like sorcery. And Western education and religion are clearly implicated in millennial movements. These are a social phenomenon quite distinct from witchcraft. Witchcraft underpins tradition and order, it is part of the social cement (Nadel, 1952); millennial movements are a symptom of change. They do not occur in 'precontact' primitive tribes: they arise out of rapid social transformations in which education usually has a crucial role.

The distinction between witchcraft and sorcery is controversial. Marwick (1965, p. 81) sees the former as deeper and more intellectually baffling, the operation of internal, psychic powers; the latter as relatively trivial, the use of external techniques, potions, and 'medicines'. Mary Douglas (1967) is unhappy with this contrast, but other anthropologists have distinguished between them in these terms, and it squares with my own experience in Uganda. The precautionary use of 'medicines' to ensure a safe journey is not of the same order as the Nyakyusa tribesman, for instance, accusing a neighbour of witchcraft because his son has died, and believing that the neighbour has a python in his belly which he rides around on at night, and that he eats his victim with his own (the victim's) teeth (Wilson, 1951a).

Sophisticated, educated Africans, said Monica Wilson, do not see 'medicines' and charms as seriously at odds with a Westernized outlook: 'Sorcery is felt by them to be compatible with Western science in a way in which witchcraft is not' (Wilson, 1951b). Jahoda has described the coexistence of 'instrumental magic' and a higher education in Ghana: he sees it simply as 'a continuing part of the culture ethos' and does not attach great significance to it. 'Instrumental magic' is 'external'—the use of 'medicines' and charms—mainly for protective purposes: it would be used to help, for example, in passing examinations or obtaining promotion (Jahoda, 1966). What Jahoda is referring to is sorcery and compared with the complex theoretical assumptions and far-reaching social implications of witchcraft it is relatively trivial.

I have documented beliefs similar to those described by Jahoda among Uganda college boys (Musgrove, 1952a). At high levels of seniority (age 17, 18, or 19) they still talked freely about 'charms' and 'medicines' and perhaps had some lingering belief in their efficacy. But junior boys (around the age of 12 or 13), new to this residential college from remote tribal homes, believed in human metamorphosis. They also knew of trees that could talk and stones that might bleed; and storms, famines, and earthquakes (earth tremors occurred frequently) as well as more personal misfortunes might be attributed to the demon Bachwezi, light-skinned spirits with one arm, one leg, and one eye, who lived in the lakes.

The aspect of Westernization that might support such beliefs, I argued, was not change arising from science, technology, or a market economy, but Bible-based Christianity:

> The Hebrew cosmology which has been presented to them as Christianity has not upset their traditional mental picture of the universe. The Batoro, for example, imagine a flat-earth and a heaven (*iguru*), fitting like a bowl over the earth, peopled by creatures with long hair and tails (the *abaana bahaiguru*). *Iguru* is ruled by Ngarwa. Under the earth is a subterranean region with a lake, and here are the Bachwezi. Although these are not the spirits of the dead, they are the ancestors of the Batoro, the historical light-skinned invaders of Toro now living as spirits. The Christian geography of Heaven and Hell can be accommodated easily within this pattern with a slight change in terminology. (Musgrove, 1952b)

Millennial movements do not simply coexist with Western education, they develop along with it. They are closely related features of culture contact, conflict, and change. In Oceania they have taken the form of 'cargo cults'; in Africa usually separatist Christian sects like the Balokole. They have 'educated' Western attributes but they oppose Western power. They are puritanical and also by

78

implication deeply political—the 'Mau Mau' revolt among the Kikuyu of Kenya in the 1950s was a spectacular illustration of such a millennial cult (Mair, 1959). Less spectacular but of the same utopian genre are the West Indian Rastafarians in Jamaaica and in the immigrant communities of contemporary Britain. They are strikingly like the Balokole in many respects: a separatist, puritanical, millenarian and spiritually elitist Christian sect with its roots in colonial oppression and its imagination in biblical mythology. It promises a Second Coming. There will be salvation and deliverance.

Leaders of cargo cults in the Pacific were mission-school educated and usually called themselves 'scribes'. Senior officials were 'destroying angels'. They believed that pages of the Bible had been withheld from them and that these pages contained the white man's 'secret'. In Africa the Balokole are a separatist Christian sect of the 'saved'. Even among the highly conservative cattle-keeping people of Ankole they are notable for their Westernization: 'They are more ready purchasers of Western goods, such as European dress, bicycles, domestic utensils, light furniture and medicine' (Stenning, 1965).

The Balokole are key men in the process of modernization and culture-change. Under the conditions of colonial administration in the 1950s they emerged as teachers, chief clerks, store-keepers and bookkeepers: reliable and methodical men with the Weberian virtues of thrift, sobriety, and application. A majority of the college boys I taught were Balokole and so were most of their fathers. Some students saw the Christian religion as the ideology of imperialism, but the salvationist and spiritually elitist Balokole had embraced an ideology very similar to Calvinism which provided a spearhead into independence and modernity. In the study that I made of them I said:

Some boys reject the Christian teaching of meekness and allege that this is taught by Europeans in order to emasculate the African. . . . Others, and particularly those under the influence of the Balokole, accept the Christian virtue of meekness as a central tenet; it provides them with a strong defence mechanism in the culture conflict. . . . The influence of the Balokole movement is itself an expression of culture tension; the sect is essentially separatist; it is also salvationist, and its members can relegate all Europeans who are not within its ranks to an inferior standing on earth and eternal torment in Hell. (Musgrove, 1952a)

The sect was salvationist and millenarian but firmly reality-based. Balokole were an effective mutual aid society for entrepreneurial economic activity. But many of them took a correspondence course from Cape Town called 'The Voice of Prophecy'. I reported as follows:

Coaching in the evidence for the Second Coming is one of the main purposes of the correspondence course, the 'Voice of Prophecy'. (This course is taken not only by boys but by two of the four African members of staff.) Instruction is given in the signs which foretell the Day of Judgement—earthquakes, stellar indications, social degeneration etc. It is demonstrated on the basis of such evidence that the Judgement began in 1884; and Armageddon is now being forecast for the close of the century in the Middle East. (Musgrove, 1953)

The cure for this kind of irrationality is a more settled life and freedom from colonial rule. (In the case of the Rastafarians in contemporary Britain it is equal employment opportunities for black youth.) The cure for witchcraft lies in a deeper social surgery which weakens rather than strengthens social bonds.

## 4. DANGERS OF COMMUNITY

We have had more than half a century of very competent comparative studies of witchcraft. Evans-Pritchard's doctoral study at the London School of Economics in the 1920s compared magic among the Trobriand Islanders as described by Malinowski and among the Zande as investigated by himself (Evans-Pritchard, 1929); Monica Wilson compared witch beliefs among the Nyakyusa and the Pondo (Wilson, 1951b); Nadel compared the Nupe and Gwari of Northern Nigeria with the Korongo and Mesakin of the central Sudan (Nadel, 1952); Mary Douglas has compared the Lele, Cewa, Yao, and Ndembu of Central Africa (Douglas, 1967). In recent years historical studies of witchcraft in England and Europe have been made and brought within this comparative framework. All this comparative work throws light on the role of witchcraft in social control and in social change. There are unresolved theoretical issues and the comparison between primitive witchcraft and European Renaissance witchcraft raises particular difficulties (Gillies, 1976). One thing is clear: witchcraft thrives on community. It flourishes when you are packed in with folk and cannot get away from them.

Witchcraft is both a theory of personal misfortune and a method of coping with it. Both Evans-Pritchard and Malinowski said you cannot get rid of witchcraft until you have largely eliminated misfortune, and it might be disastrous to get rid of it anyway. 'To abolish the belief in sorcery', said Malinowski, 'seems a very simple and invariably desirable achievement.' It was certainly not simple and not necessarily desirable. He warned: 'To tamper with any part or aspect of culture' might have disastrous consequences. Moreover:

The real cure for the belief in witchcraft and sorcery must go to the root of the evil. . . . Give the Africans better nourishment, better housing, systems of preventative medicine, and adequate medical care, and then, but then only, will they stop bothering about sorcerers, flying witches, and ancestral spirits. (Malinowski, 1943)

Malinowski did not include education in his list of improvements.

Evans-Pritchard also thought that eradicating witchcraft would be regrettable: it was 'an essential concomitant to social organization' and it played a vital part 'in the preservation of morality, kinship, and political authority' (Evans-Pritchard, 1935). To educate the Zande out of their witchcraft beliefs—if that were possible—would destroy society. When witchcraft collapsed in England, said Lucy Mair, we were saved by insurance (Mair, 1972).

Very similar 'functionalist' views were held by Nadel, but he recognized the deep conflicts that existed in societies which witchcraft sustained, and was prepared to regard them as 'pathological' and to question whether they were worth sustaining. Witchcraft provided a kind of 'solution', explaining misfortune in terms of personal malevolence; but this merely distracted attention from the institutional deficiencies which gave rise to chronic conflict, hatred, and suspicion in the first place (Nadel, 1952).

The socially destructive and personally damaging consequences of witchcraft beliefs and practices are beyond question, in spite of older functionalist views. What is difficult to explain in functionalist terms is why such destructive ideas and practices survive. (They are not even convincing as an ideology of the ruling class in highly egalitarian societies—like the Dinka—which have no ruling class.) The enemy is within. Societies may find strength and cohesion from enemies outside; they are unlikely to prosper when the enemy is inside the gates, and will survive only by accommodating great personal anguish and grief.

Winter makes this abundantly clear in his account of witchcraft among the Ba'amba. I taught Ba'amba boys at the time Winter was doing his witchcraft research and was always impressed by their appearance of being perpetually afraid. They came from their remote and isolated villages in the Semliki swamps; they were small, near-pygmy in stature; they were despised by the lordly Batoro and Banyankole as unclean, eaters of snakes.

The villages of the Ba'amba are small, isolated, self-contained, and almost politically autonomous. Each village is organized around a lineage and consists of a group of patrilineally related men plus their wives and children. Within these tight-knit family groups living a close-packed village life, witchcraft is rife. Your child's death, your leprosy, were deliberately caused by your nearest and dearest.

The result is horror: and it is horror for the Ba'amba no less than for an anthropological observer. The outcome, says Winter, 'can only be described as tremendously disruptive'. The villager lives with constant hatred and fear for the people closest to him and from whom he has no escape. Witchcraft is devastating in its effects:

> It gives rise to feelings of suspicion, fear and hatred among those living in the same village. It is tragic for people who are bound together by the strongest ties, for those who must depend upon one another in the crises of their lives, to feel that there are some among their number who gather together secretly to bring about the destruction of

their kinsmen and neighbours. By the time a man has reached the age of thirty or so it is almost inevitable that at least one of those closest to him, his mother or his father, a wife or one of his children, will had died, having been killed, he will believe, by the witches. The hatred which he must feel towards those fellow-villagers whom he thinks responsible can well be imagined. (Winter, 1963)

Witchcraft accusations are by no means invariably 'within the family', but they are seldom 'long distance' in either a social or geographical sense. They may be restricted to blood relations, to in-laws, or (less common) to neighbours who are not members of the family. In-laws (affinal kin) are, of course, 'outsiders' compared with blood relations. But generally speaking as we move nearer to the 'inside' witchcraft seems to increase. Leach points out that 'in matrilineal Ashanti, the witch is habitually a lineage kinsman and the same is true of the patrilineal Tiv. Furthermore throughout patrilineal Polynesia it is the father's sister who must be particularly respected lest she invoke supernatural sanctions' (Leach, 1961, p. 22).

But among the Nyakyusa, who live in 'age-villages' and not with their kin, it is neighbours and not kinsmen who are accused. By contrast the Pondo (also a patrilineal tribe) mainly accuse their kinsmen. Kinsfolk live in the same tight-knit village: residential patterns reinforce kinship ties:

The local group, the homestead, is a kinship group, comprising agnatic lineages, together with wives and unmarried daughters. The men of a homestead form a single close-knit group, commonly eating in company and formerly being jointly responsible for each others' torts and fighting as a unit in the army of the district. (Wilson, 1951b)

It is among these close and highly interdependent relatives that witchcraft is rife.

When the family is weaker witchcraft accusations within it decline. When divorce is easy, as among the Cewa, even polygynous marriages—a powerful breeding ground for witchcraft—are not highly productive of witchcraft accusations. 'If tension develops between spouses, they can easily part, before it grows into the intense hatred that is characteristically expressed in terms of sorcery' (Marwick, 1965, p. 179). Unreason finds a secure foundation in strong and stable family life.

The social relationships of the people involved in witchcraft accusations and trials in late sixteenth- and seventeenth-century Essex have been closely examined by historians. There were virtually no accusations of blood relations, although some convicted witches confessed that they had bewitched their in-laws. 'On the other hand, almost all bewitchings occurred within a village and within groups of neighbours' (Macfarlane, 1970a). Two other features emerge: the accused were mainly women—the proportion had risen from earlier times—and there was usually an ambiguous or uncertain social relationship between the accuser and the accused (Macfarlane, 1970b). The accusation of women has been ascribed to their low social status (Anderson and Gordon, 1978); in Africa where women are mainly the accused—for instance among the Nupe—it is because their status is high and their power in economic life great (Nadel, 1952). This was probably the case also in England: as the education and status of women improved in the sixteenth century they were cast more often as witches. But the overriding and central conclusion from the studies of English witchcraft is that accusations were almost wholly among neighbours in tight village communities (Thomas, 1970).

All primitive societies are not equally witchcraft-ridden. What is it that distinguishes those that are from those that are not (and our own witch-crazed epoch from the centuries that followed)? It is perhaps unfortunate that Evans-Pritchard's famous study was made of a society relatively free from witchcraft, in which it was perfectly 'normal' but not in fact really extensive—it was 'thought to operate only in the cracks and crevices of their social system' (Douglas, 1967). There were large witchcraft-free zones.

In both Europe and Africa it is clear that the involved interdependence of people in small and isolated communities provides a fertile ground for witchcraft. (The situation is probably made worse if social roles and obligations are not too clearly understood.) But smallness, remoteness, dependence, and lack of role definition would not be decisive if people could easily get out. It was in isolated villages high in the Alps and the Pyrenees that the witch-craze of the sixteenth century was most intense and prolonged: 'As a continuing social phenomenon, involving not merely individuals but whole societies, the witch-craze would always be associated particularly with the highlands. The great European witch-hunts would centre upon the Alps and their foothills, the Jura and the Vosges, and upon the Pyrenees and their extensions in France and Spain' (Trevor-Roper, 1967b, p. 105).

The Zande as described by Evans-Pritchard (1929) are a scattered people with no village life: they live in isolated homesteads and have few communal undertakings. There is a lack of cohesion in social life and 'the Azande move their homesteads over the countryside'. The incidence of witchcraft accusations falls within a very narrow range of social relations and the highly formal political superstructure is witchcraft-free. It is the very formality, thinness and impersonality of these relationships that guarantees their immunity.

This in essence is the argument that Mary Douglas advances, based on a comparison with witch-ridden societies of Central Africa like the Cewa, Yao, Lele, and Ndembu. Virtually all their social relationships give rise to witchcraft accusations, and the distinctive character of these societies is their highly concentrated social life: 'The whole society barely rises above the small, face-to-face level of the neighbourhood. There are practically no social relations which are clearly structured, nor which are free from witch-beliefs' (Douglas, 1967). Geoffrey Lienhardt drew a precisely similar picture when he compared the scattered, pastoral Dinka and the sedentary, agricultural Anuak of the southern Sudan. Witchcraft is not at all prominent among the Dinka, 'In fact one could understand much of their social structure without reference to it'

(Lienhardt, 1951); but it is rife among the Anuak who live in 'many distinct largely self-sufficient and often very crowded village communities, where they are in constant and intense individual contact' (Lienhardt, 1970).

Elsewhere Mary Douglas has distinguished between 'small group' and 'strong grid'. Small-group societies impose insistent personal pressures and people have a sense of 'having no option but to consent to the overwhelming demands of other people'. Virtually everyone is a 'potential reject', open to the charge of witchcraft. But 'strong-grid' societies are formal, with relatively low levels of communal involvement. Life is lived within grids of impersonal forces and rules. Social contacts are infrequent and irregular. But only small and well-defined categories are 'rejects', exposed to the suspicion of being a witch (Douglas, 1973, p. 88). In impersonal, strong-grid societies, rationality has a chance.

## 5. CONCLUSION: WITCHCRAFT OR SUICIDE

The distinction that Mary Douglas made between 'small group' and 'strong grid' is roughly the distinction that Tonnies made about a century ago between 'Gemeinschaft' and 'Gesellschaft'. Tonnies was greatly influenced by the writing of Henry Maine on the historical shift from status to contract; but he saw the first spokesman and representative of the new Gesellschaft society as Thomas Hobbes. The *Leviathan*, which stated the rationalist-contractual principles of the new form of society, was published in 1651. And it was almost precisely from that time that witchcraft in England declined.

Gemeinschaft societies are based on blood ties and sentiment, Gesellschaft societies on contract and calculation. Gemeinschaft societies are tribes and villages, Gesellschaft societies are cities and states. Gemeinschaft, said Tonnies, is peasants, people with family ties, natives, people in mountains; Gesellschaft is urbanites, people with weak family ties, strangers, people in valleys. The shift from the tribe based on blood to the state based on 'local contiguity', said Henry Maine, was one of 'those subversions of feeling which we call emphatically revolutions' (Maine, 1959, p. 76). Tonnies wrote similarly of the shift that occurs from Gemeinschaft to Gesellschaft: a complete reversal of intellectual life takes place (Tonnies, 1955, p. 264). The basis of the new life is reason and not sentiment, 'rational will' and not 'natural will'. Its fullest support and expression are in cities.

And it was the temporary eclipse of the city by the court in Renaissance Europe, says Mary Douglas, that goes far to explain the recrudescence of witch beliefs. Princely (and ecclesiastical) courts are 'small group', cities are 'strong grid'. The princely courts of witch-crazed Europe were strikingly like the witch-infested villages of the Anuak. There was great zeal for burning witches, for example, at the court of the scientist and mathematician Heinrich Julius, Duke of Brunswick, and at that of the learned Catholic Prince-Bishop of Wurzburg, Julius Echter von Mespelbrunn (Trevor-Roper, 1967a, p. 154). In such courts intrigue was rife, great fortunes were made and spent and great names met disaster: 'Their cosmos was dominated . . . by other dangerous humans competing against them with demonic powers. We recognize an Anuak style of cosmology filling the minds of people in an Anuak style of social situation' (Douglas, 1970b).

This is the opposite of 'anomie'. Anomie produces suicide, its opposite produces witchcraft. Anomie is thin social relationships; witchcraft thrives on thick. The following go together: on the one hand small, self-contained communities, weakly defined, diffuse social roles, strong local and family ties, irrationality, and, in certain historical circumstances, witchcraft; on the other hand cities, impersonal, infrequent, and 'segmented' social relationships, ease of divorce, working wives, anomie, rationality, and suicide. The broad trend of history is from the former to the latter. It is the process of 'modernization'.

It is not wholly automatic and it does not always develop at a uniform rate and equally on all fronts. Schools in particular have stubbornly and quite explicitly refused to fall into line: they are Gemeinschaft in spirit rather than Gesellschaft: they emphasize their community character, loyalty, intense personal involvement, and *esprit de corps*. Today they may even wish to embed themselves *in* local communities and to discredit and discourage movement out. We now applaud the 'community school'.

I have elsewhere commented critically on this trend which I regard as wholly retrograde (Musgrove, 1979, pp. 183–185). Of course, it would be preposterous to suggest that schools which emphasize their community, as distinct from their associational, aspects will today breed witchcraft. But rationality will be harder to come by, and prejudice with regard to colour, class, and creed more difficult to eradicate. It is not a question of the intelligence or logical abilities of the pupils. The clear conclusion from the studies of other cultures referred to in this chapter is that with regard to rationality logic and intelligence are largely irrelevant.

The associational (Gesellschaft) model is now to be found in colleges of further education—and that is some indication of the low regard in which it is held in the educational world. But this must be the future model for all our schools. The future must see tertiary colleges (developed on Further Education lines) and not sixth form colleges which hark back to Arnold's Rugby. Ronald King has discussed the ideology of the tertiary college interestingly and illuminatingly in these terms (King, 1976). I have argued previously that the school-as-a-community must be superseded by a quite different kind of organisation:

> Voluntary in character, sensitive to the needs of clients and consumers, tolerant of diversity, unceremonious and indifferent to tradition, careful of the contractual rights of its members, consultative and participatory in its style of management. It probably will not have a football team; there may be neither school crest nor colours. It will be an asociation and not a community. (Musgrove, 1979, p. 185)

It will be low on loyalty; but reason will be enthroned.

# REFERENCES

Anderson, A., and Gordon, R. (1978), 'Witchcraft and the status of women—the case of England', *British Journal of Sociology*, **29**.

Boas, Franz (1911), *The Mind of Primitive Man*, Free Press, New York.

Douglas, Mary (1967), 'Witch beliefs in central Africa', *Africa*, **37**.

Douglas, Mary (1970a), 'Thirty years after *Witchcraft, Oracles and Magic*', in M. Douglas, *Witchcraft Confessions and Accusations*, Tavistock, London.

Douglas, Mary (1970b), 'Introduction', in M. Douglas, *Witchcraft Confessions and Accusations*, Tavistock, London.

Douglas, Mary (1973), *Natural Symbols*, Penguin, Harmondsworth, Middx.

Evans-Pritchard, E. E. (1929), 'The morphology and function of magic: A comparative study of Trobriand and Zande ritual and spells', *American Anthropologist*, **31**.

Evans-Pritchard, E. E. (1934), 'Levy-Bruhl's theory of primitive mentality', *Bulletin of the Faculty of Arts*, **II**, Egyptian University, Cairo.

Evans-Pritchard, E. E. (1935), 'Witchcraft', *Africa*, **8**.

Evans-Pritchard, E. E. (1976), *Witchcraft, Oracles and Magic Among the Azande*, Clarendon Press, Oxford.

Gilles, Eva (1976), 'Introduction', in E. E. Evans-Pritchard, *Witchcraft, Oracles and Magic Among the Azande*, Clarendon Press, Oxford.

Gluckman, M. (1944), 'The logic of African science and witchcraft: An appreciation of Evans-Pritchard's "Witchcraft, Oracles and Magic Among the Azande" of the Sudan', *Rhodes-Livingstone Institute Journal*, no. 1.

Goody, J. (1957), 'Anomie in Ashanti', *Africa*, **27**.

Hill, Christopher (1969), ' "Reason" and "reasonableness" in seventeenth-century England', *British Journal of Sociology*, **20**.

Horton, R. (1967), 'African traditional thought and Western science', *Africa*, **37**.

Jahoda, Gustav (1966), 'Social aspirations, magic and witchcraft in Ghana: A social psychological interpretation', in P. C. Lloyd, *The New Elites of Tropical Africa*, Oxford University Press, London.

Jarvie, I. C. (1963–1964), 'Theories of cargo cults: A critical analysis', *Oceania*, **34**,

Jarvie, I. C. and Agassi, J. (1967), 'The problem of the rationality of magic', *British Journal of Sociology*, **28**.

Kieckhefer, Richard (1976), *European Witch Trials*, Routledge & Kegan Paul, London.

King, Ronald (1976), *School and College*, Routledge & Kegan Paul, London.

Leach, E. R. (1961), *Rethinking Anthropology*, Athlone Press, London.

Levy-Bruhl, Lucien (1926), *How Natives Think*, Allen & Unwin, London.

Lienhardt, G. (1951), 'Some notions of witchcraft among the Dinka', *Africa*, **21**.

Lienhardt, G. (1970), 'The structure of death: An aspect of Anuak philosophy', in Mary Douglas, *Witchcraft Confessions and Accusations*, Tavistock, London.

Macfarlane, Alan (1970a), 'Witchcraft in Tudor and Stuart Essex', in Mary Douglas, *Witchcraft Confessions and Accusations*, Tavistock, London.

Macfarlane, Alan (1970b), *Witchcraft in Tudor and Student England*, Routledge & Kegan Paul, London.

Maine, Henry (1959), *Ancient Law*, Everyman, London.

Mair, L. P. (1958), 'The pursuit of the millennium in Melanesia', *British Journal of Sociology*, **9**.

Mair, L. P. (1959), 'Independent religious movements in three continents', *Comparative Studies in Society and History*, **1**.

Mair, L. P. (1972), 'Witchcraft', *British Journal of Sociology*, **23**.

Malinowski, B. (1943), 'The pan-African problem of culture contact', *American Journal of Sociology*, **48**.

Marwick, M. G. (1952), 'The social context of Cewa witch beliefs', *Africa*, **22**.
Marwick, M. G. (1956), 'The continuance of witchcraft beliefs', *Listener*, 26 April.
Marwick, M. G. (1965), *Sorcery in its Social Setting*, Manchester University Press, Manchester.
Mitchell, J. Clyde (1965), 'The meaning of misfortune for urban Africans', in M. Fortes and G. Dieterlen, *African Systems of Thought*, Oxford University Press, London.
Musgrove, F. (1952a), 'A Uganda secondary school as a field of culture change', *Africa*, **22**.
Musgrove, F. (1952b), 'Teaching geography to the peoples of western Uganda', *African Studies*, **11**.
Musgrove, F. (1953), 'Education and the culture concept', *Africa*, **23**.
Musgrove, F. (1979), *School and the Social Order*, Wiley, Chichester.
Nadel, S. F. (12952, 'Witchcraft in four African societies', *American Anthropologist*, **54**.
Richards, Audrey (1935), 'A modern movement of witch-finders', *Africa*, **2**.
Settle, T. (1971), 'The rationality of science versus the rationality of magic', *Philosophy of the Social Sciences*, **1**.
Stenning, D. J. (1965), 'Salvation in Ankole', in M. Fortes and G. Dieterlen, *African Systems of Thought*, Oxford University Press, London.
Thomas, Keith (1970), 'The relevance of social anthropology to the study of English witchcraft', in Mary Douglas, *Witchcraft Confessions and Accusations*, Tavistock, London.
Tonnies, F. (1955), *Community and Association*, Routledge & Kegan Paul, London.
Trevor-Roper, H. R. (1967a). 'The European witch-craze of the sixteenth and seventeenth centuries', in H. R. Trevor-Roper, *Religion: The Reformation and Social Change*, Macmillan, London.
Trevor-Roper, H. R. (1967b), *Religion, The Reformation and Social Change*, Macmillan, London
Walzer, M. (1968), 'Puritanism as a revolutionary ideology', in S. N. Eisenstadt, *The Protestant Ethic and Modernization*, Basic, New York.
Ward, Barbara (1956), 'Some observations on religious cults in Ashanti', *Africa*, **26**.
Weber, Max (1930), *The Protestant Ethic and the Spirit of Capitalism*, Allen & Unwin, London.
Wilson, Monica (1951a), *Good Company*, Oxford University Press, London.
Wilson, Monica (1951b), 'Witch beliefs and social structure', *American Journal of Sociology*, **56**.
Winter, E. H. (1963), 'The enemy within: Amba witchcraft and sociological theory', in John Middleton and E. H. Winter, *Witchcraft and Sorcery in East Africa*, Routledge & Kegan Paul, London.
Worsley, P. (1957), *The Trumpet Shall Sound. A Study of 'Cargo' Cults in Melanesia*, MacGibbon & Kee, London.

# CHAPTER 5

# *Learning to be Modern*

## 1. RESPONSES TO MODERNITY

'Modernity' for social scientists, as for tribal elders, is often a pejorative term. It is rather disreputable; it suggests the abandonment of old standards; it is 'fast'. Those who turn from the traditional life to embrace it are defectors, unreliable, morally weak. Moreover, it is darkly said, under stress they always 'revert to type'.

In fact they are usually both happy and stable. They are certainly much happier than the country cousins they have left behind. Park, in a seminal essay, discussed 'human migration and the marginal man' (Park, 1928). I have elsewhere examined the unsatisfactory studies that followed (Musgrove, 1977, pp. 5–11, 230). It is a highly conservative ideology that equates modernity with moral collapse.

But there are strains; and those who are happy with modernity have embraced it of their own free will. There may have been background pressures: taxes imposed by a colonial government may have prompted them to turn from subsistence farming to wage labour for at least part of the year; new laws may have 'modernized' land tenure and dispossessed customary tenants. But the choice to move from a traditional life has essentially been theirs. By contrast there have been notable, even notorious examples of forced change: the 'collectivization' of peasant farmers and the enforced enrolment of North American Indians in Federal boarding schools dedicated to turning them into Americans. This chapter is not about forced modernity in this sense of imposed, wholesale change.

It is by no means all primitive people who turn to modernity when the chance occurs. Those who do so seem generally to be cultivators who live in permanent villages. Those who show no interest in modernity and actively resist it are generally pastoralists who move freely with their herds over open country. This chapter will examine the significance of this difference.

Becoming civilized or modern has often been seen as deeply disturbing for individuals and destructive for their societies. There are certainly examples of calculated change backed by force which seem to have had these effects. But the cataclysmic view of change is not generally supported by the evidence. The 'functionalist' anthropologist of the interwar years saw change on any but minor scale as demoralizing and destructive; today Peter Berger's popular writings on modernization give us an unappetizing picture of 'homeless minds'. Freud, too, said that the principal consequence of civilization was unhappiness and frustration. All the evidence we have points to an opposite conclusion: it is frustration that predisposes primitive people to become more civilized.

Thirty years ago when I taught in Africa anthropology had a simple message: the new must fit in with the old. This was known as functionalism. The idea was similar to that of spare-part surgery some years later: if new customs and knowledge did not 'fit', tissue-rejection occurred and the transplant failed. My own experience of teaching and research in Africa led me to the opposite conclusion: new knowledge and customs were sought and accepted precisely because they were at odds with the old.

Thirty years ago we talked about 'culture contact and change'; today we talk about 'modernization'. The former was about customs and values; the latter is more about economic growth. But both are about the way primitive people come to resemble ourselves.

This chapter will examine how and why some people become 'modern'. The subject is complex but the final conclusion is simple: modernity is where, at least for the moment, they feel 'at home'.

It may be, as Leonard Doob says, that primitive peoples are doomed to modernity or extinction; but 'modernization' does not proceed evenly, uniformly, or automatically. And it can seldom be total. Poor, low-income countries in the Third World can support only a relatively small segment of their people in genuine modernity—perhaps no more than 10 or 15 per cent (Belal, 1979).

Modernization means a dual economy and a dualistic society: cash crops, capitalism, and international commerce cheek by jowl with a traditional subsistence economy, ancient hoe cultivation alongside the runways of international airports, grass huts beyond the line of a new city's skyscraper blocks. Modern technology—especially 'supercultural communications systems' like motorways, air traffic, and telecommunications—can peacefully coexist with a Stone Age way of life and scarcely disturb it (Leach, 1973).

The sharp contrast between primitive pastoralists and cultivators in their inclination to be 'modernized' has often been observed. The pastoralists are contemptuous of Western civilization and effete white men; they are proud of themselves and their traditional life; they reject with disdain the European, his life-style and consumer goods. The settled, sedentary cultivators, on the other hand, are generally open to new ideas and more receptive to modernity: they send their children to Western-style schools (and may pay a disproportionate amount of their annual income to meet the fees).

It is not a matter of intelligence. The pastoralists are clever in living a demanding life which often calls for quick decisions and ingenious improvization. They acquire difficult traditional skills and learn awesome quantities of knowledge relating to climate, terrain, plants and herbs, and especially to cattle and their welfare. But they refuse to learn Western ways.

When I worked in Uganda I was constantly struck by the difference in response to Western education among the pastoral Banyankole and the agricultural Batoro. It seemed to me that in this contrast was an important key to understanding differences in educability: why some people would learn more than their fathers could tell them and others would not. Across the length and breadth of Africa we find, for example, the Tiv, Baganda, Cewa, Tonga, and Babemba all essentially agricultural tribes and all prone to modernity; and in contrast the Nuer, Nandi, Masai, Kipsigis, and Ngoni: pastoralists whose way of life is strongly resistant to change. This chapter is about 'modernization' and why some primitive peoples opt for it and others do not. At the heart of the difference lies a clue to educability which may not be entirely flattering to those with open minds and a thirst for new knowledge who flock into our schools.

The symbols of modernity, says Peter Berger, are the city, the wristwatch, and the ballpoint pen. The pen signifies literacy and new knowledge, the watch a restructuring of time which 'lies at the very roots of modern technological production and modern bureaucracy, and thus of modern society as such' (Berger and Kellner, 1974, p. 130).

The city, the wristwatch, and the ballpoint pen are the outward signs of a transformation of consciousness. For modernization, according to Berger, is the growth of institutions rooted in the transformation of traditional economies by modern technology. And the principal consequence is the 'pluralization of life worlds'. Simple and homogeneous societies are internally diversified and the consequences are secularization, rationality, future-planning, and the openness of personal identity. There is a split between public and private spheres (in a tribal context, between family and kin). And the upshot according to Berger is the 'homeless mind'.

There are discontents, says Berger, which are specifically derived from the pluralization of life-worlds: more people are migratory, ever-changing, mobile. 'Generally, these discontents can be subsumed under the heading of "homelessness".' This is a catastrophic view of modernization scarcely different from the pessimism of an earlier generation of 'functionalists'. Both are wrong. The response to modernization varies systematically across cultures in a way which will be indicated in this chapter. It is not all gloom, marginality, angst, anomie, and despair. Quite often there is joy. 'Home', where the mind formerly was, is commonly deeply restrictive and destructive. 'Homelessness' is a delerium of liberation from witchcraft and formerly inescapable frustration and oppression by neighbours and kin.

## 2. FUNCTION, NEEDS, AND CHANGE

My interest in modernization and culture contact and change goes back 30 years. The prevailing theories and methods of inquiry then were those of the late Bronislaw Malinowski. I attempted to interpret the 'function' of schools in Uganda as I observed and experienced them in his terms. I was unable to do so.

Functionalism was deeply discouraging. Preferably one should leave well alone; but if changes were made they should be limited and cautious and carefully in line with tradition. All action on other cultures was unpredictable in its consequences and probably catastrophic. Thus one of our most gifted social anthropologists, Lucy Mair, who did distinguished fieldwork in Buganda in the

1930s, saw 'culture contact' as inevitably pathological. The primitive society in question might be already pathological at the zero point of contact and change, but further penetration could only dislocate a going system which satisfied needs at least 'with a reasonable degree of general satisfaction' (Mair, 1934).

Lucy Mair was not prepared to concede that any healthy consequences came from 'culture contact' in Buganda. She instanced two examples which were on the face of it benign but in practice either null or catastrophic. The colonial government had abolished forced labour by peasants for chiefs in 1923, but this seemed to have had no effect on the wider society at all ('there is no feature of modern Ganda society which I could identify as its product'); the government had also ruled that a man whose wife left him could not demand a refund of the bride-price through the native courts. The results of this enlightened decree were calamitous. There was more witchcraft as deserted husbands turned to it to 'further their just claims' when they could no longer turn to the courts.

It was not only in British colonies that functionalism prevailed: this alleged ideology of Empire—which was undeniably highly conservative in its implications—was also adopted by Unesco. The handbook of 1953, which gave guidance to officials working in 'developing' countries, well illustrates functionalism's daunting and dispiriting message. The handbook was prepared for such 'agents of change' as teachers and agricultural experts. They were told of the dire consequences of introducing even the most apparently beneficent change:

> Where a change may seem to the expert to be merely a better way of feeding cattle, or of disposing of waste, to the people it may seem to be a rejection of the commands of the gods, or a way of giving their welfare and safety into the hands of sorcerers. . . . Substitution of a more or less destructible cooking pot may be seen as lowering the value of a bride because of a change in the cost of her dowry. (Mead, 1953)

The agent of change was further warned: 'There is no available body of knowledge which makes it possible to predict in advance the way in which individuals will respond.' Only one thing was sure: change meant more tension and not less.

Functionalism, it is now said, provided a theoretical underpinning of Empire. Gouldner argues that Malinowski and Radcliffe-Brown produced an anthropology which justified the preservation of primitive life: there was nothing in it that was really non-rational or, on close scrutiny, useless (Gouldner, 1971, pp. 125–134). Maquet concedes that anthropologists in the interwar years may not have done it deliberately, but 'anthropology was oriented as though it wanted to preserve the existing situation' (Maquet, 1964).

Anthropologists did not provide the ideology of Empire, because district commissioners took little notice of them (Kuper, 1975, pp. 139–140). Colonial governments introduced fundamental changes with regard to marriage and family life and traditional authority with scant regard for anthropological theory. As Meyer Fortes pointed out in 1936, colonial governments were 'deliberately and energetically active in transforming native society' and their front-line agents, the district commissioners, were men of great power backed in the final analysis by military might. The problem was not to explain how native society was being preserved, but how 'any of its traditional forms of social life survive the process of civilization' (Fortes, 1936).

For Malinowski change was difficult and infinitely complicated. The key to change was the 'institution' and this was 'an indefinitely ramified, dovetailing and intertwined reality . . . [which] cannot be easily, in a piecemeal fashion, dropped out of Native culture' (Malinowski, 1945, p. 53). But Malinowski's basic proposition was this: 'One kind of institution can be replaced by another which fulfills a similar function.' Political, religious, and economic institutions were 'commensurable across the dividing line of culture', they satisfied needs, and the new Western institution might satisfy them more effectively than the old. Indeed, it must do so to survive.

It was within this simple framework of ideas that I examined a 'Western' school in Uganda and corresponding indigenous educational institutions as competitors in the satisfaction of 'needs'. The 'Western' school ignored the ancient 'needs' of the traditional society. It did not fail for that reason: it succeeded.

Thus training in sexual competence was central to most traditional forms of African education. It was wholly unthinkable that it could ever find a place in the curriculum of a mission or even a government school. Sexual competence was a matter not only of personal gratification but of tribal fertility and survival. Hoernlé (1931) gave a good account of the way initiation schools met this need. Songs and dances were used to arouse sexual passions and break down the barriers of modesty and reserve. Restraint was also taught, but so was achievement:

> Among many of the tribes the sexual life is regarded as vitally important, not only to the individuals themselves, but to the social whole of which they form a part. Every individual wishes to have his or her sexual powers developed to the maximum, and people feel that they are helping to this end in the initiation rites.

This was a need not only disregarded but even explicitly denied by the new educational institutions. And the consequent disabilities were clear to everyone. Girls who went to mission schools and not to the traditional girls' initiation rites were sexually incompetent and Luvale women warned their socially aspiring sons against them: 'You are going to marry one of these mission girls who has not been to the puberty rites; she will give you no sexual satisfaction and will not know how to do her work properly' (White, 1953).

As with sexual training, so with Christianity: it was not accepted because it did a better job than traditional religious beliefs. In a root-and-branch attack on Malinowski's functionalism Gluckman made exactly the same point:

> Conversion [to Christianity] cannot be studied only as the supplanting of one set of religious beliefs by another. . . . Not all Zulus are converted because they feel that Christianity is a better religion than the ancestor-cult. (Gluckman, 1949)

The functionalists said, in essence, that the new would be accepted only if it fitted in with and supported the old. It seemed to me that it was accepted principally because it subverted it. Meyer Fortes very properly rebuked Monica Hunter for her 'spare-part' interpretation of social change and her argument that 'Elements which fit in with the existing culture and which do not raise any direct opposition to it, are quickly taken over' (Hunter, 1934).

Fortes described this 'theory' as a lame tautology. He pointed out that anthropologists must be able to explain why new ways of life deeply at odds with the traditional culture were adopted: why 'Christian teaching gains converts despite bitter opposition in many parts of Africa, or why labour migration rapidly becomes a habit among a sedentary agricultural people unaccustomed to wage labour, as has happened in the hinterland of the Gold Coast' (Fortes, 1936). New Patterns of life emerged in the culture-contact situation and, said Fortes, change could not be understood as 'a mechanical pitchforking of elements of culture, like bundles of hay, from one culture to another'.

Schooling gave no support to the most cherished institution of all: polygyny. It undermined it. A Western school—especially if it were a mission school—might explicitly condemn polygyny; but it was the indirect consequence of Western schooling, followed by a Western career in Kampala, that made it virtually impossible. My students at Government College—all fee-paying volunteers for modernity—knew this quite well and resented it deeply. It was a grievous price to pay for education, far in excess of school fees (which they would be repaying to their maternal uncles for the rest of their lives). But five wives on a country 'shamba' were an economic asset; in Kampala a crippling liability. The new institution which was so eagerly embraced was at odds with the central values and institutions of the traditional life.

I was forced to conclude that this explained its success. It was utterly irrelevant to old needs and was successful precisely because it ignored them. As I wrote at the time:

> The school, far from flourishing in response to 'indigenous' needs, appears to flourish in despite of them. Thus before the English contact family instruction placed great emphasis on correct speech, clear articulation and respectful address. The modern secondary school . . . starves this need. . . . And yet the school enjoys widespread popularity. . . . My pupils seem to feel little need for the new knowledge to be related to the concrete situations of their home lives and regard such treatment with suspicion, as a frivolous evasion of the real work of the school. (Musgrove, 1952)

Modernity was embraced although it hurt. Modern consciousness as represented by timetables and the long shadow of bureaucratic employment was particularly repellent to my pupils. But this was undoubtedly the 'hidden curriculum' of modernity. A tidily reconstructed time was certainly quite pointless for the traditional life; but it was looked forward to with foreboding in the new.

It has been persuasively argued that the rational ordering and sequencing of school life is more potent than the explicit school curriculum in modernizing the traditional mind: 'principles directly embedded in the daily routine of the school teach the virtue of planning ahead and the importance of maintaining a regular schedule' (Inkeles and Smith, 1974, pp. 141–142). It was precisely over this centrepiece of modernity that my African pupils were most in conflict with their school.

I examined this conflict in my study of the school as a 'need-satisfying' institution in Malinowski's sense: 'In particular', I reported, 'they lament the regular routine and comprehensiveness of the school time-table' (Musgrove, 1952) and 'The school time-table itself is a great burden—perhaps the greatest frustration which these boys feel in a school run on European lines' (Musgrove, 1953). Moreover, they knew that modernity meant careers in similar time-regulated institutions and they were dismayed at the thought of becoming modern on these terms:

> 'European-type' employment in offices and Government departments has no allurement for them—it is bondage, slavery to a routine and to a hierarchy, distasteful even though it involves European dress and other desirable features of European life. (Musgrove, 1952)

Malinowski would have saved them from themselves. He advocated segregation. The schoolteacher should encourage children to respect tribal elders and 'even to be aware of the value of ancestor-worship'. The 'European' school for Africans should sustain the tribe (Malinowski, 1943).

Malinowski was uneasily aware (in 1943) that his argument for separate development was close to the policy of South Africa, but he insisted that 'an equitable system of segregation' was possible. The European-style school should be no more than a skills centre which would equip blacks to compete on equal terms with whites. But tribal culture should be strengthened and transmitted through the family, initiation ceremonies, and age-grade institutions. 'The schooling we give him [the African] should never be subversive of his respect for his own tribal dignity or racial characteristics.' Although Malinowski had argued convincingly that culture contact produced a third cultural reality with its own determinism that was neither black nor white (Malinowski, 1945, pp. 20–26), he failed to follow up the educational implications of this analysis. In the end he parcelled up the parent cultures separately and would use education to maintain their integrity—in other words, to keep them apart.

### 3. PASTORALISM AND ANTI-MODERNITY

Many primitive people take to modernity at least in the form of Malinowski's 'third cultural reality': they are mostly agricultural tribes. Some primitive people still reject modernity outright. They are mainly small-scale pastoral societies. In examining these contrasted types of society we find a clue to 're-educability' and the dynamics of change.

The pastoralists have no problem of sustaining their sense of identity and pride in themselves. They have never for a moment doubted it. Conversely, the people most avid for modernity and the schooling that leads to it often have a rather poor 'self-concept'. They have sometimes been slaves of powerful cattle folk. As they seek Western education and the cattle men reject it, it is they who become the new overlords in a modernized world.

My contacts with a dozen tribes in East Africa led me to pinpoint a marked degree of 'specialization to environment' as the root of conservatism. Some agricultural tribes like the Bakonjo, who farmed the difficult lower slopes of the Ruwenzori Mountains, and the Ba'amba, who farmed the low-lying swamps of the Semliki River, were notable for their resistance to change. Thirty years ago I discussed these differences in inclination for new (Western) learning in terms of 'mimesis' and interpreted them in terms of specialized adaptation to especially difficult environments. This analysis cut to some degree across the simple distinction between pastoralists and farmers:

> The Masai of Kenya and the Bakonjo of Uganda . . . have retained to a considerable extent their traditional habits, dress, and pursuits; they are relatively specialized to their environments, wandering pastoralists on the one hand and mountain cultivators on the other. Cattle-keeping peoples generally, whose lives tend to be far more specialized than agriculturalists', show comparatively little interest in education. The cattle-owning Bahima of Ankole, the aristocrats and former conquerors, appear to be losing ground politically and economically to the peasant cultivators of the same district, the Bairu, who are more willing to turn from traditional pursuits in imitation of imported customs and to take advantage of educational opportunities. (Musgrove, 1953)

But the pastoral–agricultural distinction remains a basic and important one. Many social scientists have pointed to the way tribes vary in their interest in schooling and Westernization and have regretted that there is no satisfactory explanation. Goldthorpe says tribes differ in these respects 'in ways that are not always easy to explain, whether in terms of the indigenous social structure or the history of missionary penetration and government activity' (Goldthorpe, 1975, p. 201). Josef Gugler has discussed the same problem with special reference to labour migration and the lure of commodity consumption. He points to the distinction between pastoralists' conservatism and agriculturalists' greater inclination to change, but concedes that there is an important puzzle here that has yet to be solved:

> The theoretical challenge this presents to social scientists has not yet been met, presumably because of the difficulties inherent in a comparative study of societies that would have to deal with numerous variables. (Gugler, 1969)

His own 'explanation' is in terms of the remoteness and inaccessibility of pastoralists, but he knows that this simple explanation is weak.

It was often claimed in the past that pastoralists were 'innately' conservative. This view was attacked by Kalervo Oberg in the 1930s in the light of the studies he made in Ankole of Bairu agriculturalists and the Bahima pastoralists who were their erstwhile conquerors and overlords. He also rejected explanations in terms of social and political structure which in any event is very varied among pastoral people: to the west of Lake Victoria they established great centrally organized kingdoms but to the east they did not. Economic organization varied, too: 'cattle-keeping in Ankole works in a different setting from that in Masai-land' (Oberg, 1938).

'It is a well-known fact', said Oberg, 'that such exclusively pastoral tribes as the Bahima and the Masai offer a much greater resistance to European influences than the surrounding agricultural people.' The pastoralists were even able to sidestep the pressures of the poll tax: the Bairu cultivators could pay it only by going away to work for wages for 2 to 6 months every year; a Muhima simply sold a cow. But the key to his conservatism, said Oberg, was in 'the restricted and highly specialized situation established by cattle-keeping'. Cattle were his only means of support: he must remain constantly with them and move with them from place to place. The Bairu were no more 'naturally' adaptable than the Bahima were 'naturally' conservative, said Oberg: 'Their respective responses to external stimuli are different because of the different ways in which they are bound to nature.'

A few Bahima, it is true, attended mission schools and went away to become clerks and schoolteachers: but they spent their salaries not on shoes and bicycles but on cows. One Muhima teacher bought two or three female cows every year and sent them home to his herdsman: 'He told me that he was able to visit his kraal only twice a year but looks forward with interest to seeing his herd' (Oberg, 1938).

In a number of important studies Margaret Read gave a strikingly similar picture of the Ngoni of Central Africa (Read, 1936, 1938a, 1959). The pastoral Ngoni had also conquered a population of indigenous agriculturalists and established a centralized state; they in turn were conquered by the British in 1898 and almost half a century later, when Margaret Read worked among them, they showed 'a pronounced antipathy to European contact' (Read, 1938a, p. 14). Unlike the neighbouring agricultural Cewa tribe they appeared not to covet the white man's material possessions: 'Their houses, both in the villages and on the copper mines, were noticeably bare of "store goods", and their expenditure on clothes and "trash" is low in comparison with the wages earned' (Read, 1936). They are infinitely more civilized than the white men: 'Their standards of hospitality, of courtesy, and of mutual assistance they believe to be much superior to the Europeans' ' (Read, 1936).

Only the children of non-Ngoni cultivators attended mission schools and were held in contempt by young Ngoni herdsmen for doing so: 'School was regarded as an easy option where you sat still all day and repeated things after the teacher' (Read, 1959, p. 100). When Ngoni tribesmen, whether pastoralists or (more commonly) cultivators went away to work for wages, on their return they converted cash into cows (Read, 1938a, p. 32). Migrant labour and involvement in the cash economy did not 'modernize' traditional society but preserved it.

The cattle-keeping Tallensi of northern Ghana similarly absorbed and incorporated the potentially disruptive effects of migrant labour. There was no poll tax in the northern provinces of the Gold Coast to drive the Tallensi to work in the towns, but family quarrels might cause some of them for a time to do so. Meyer Fortes plays down the consequences of their 'modern' experiences: 'The foreign ideas and exotic information brought back by the young men arouse curiosity but have no appreciable impression on the native scheme of values and beliefs . . .' (Fortes, 1945, p. 11). Men who had been abroad as labour migrants, soldiers, or policemen were among the most loyal members of the community. Meyer Fortes's garden boy, who had worked as a gardener in Kumasi for some years and had actually learned to use a spade, 'reverted absolutely to the native hoe' on his return (Fortes, 1936).

Unlike the Ngoni and the Bahima many pastoral tribes—for instance the Nuer, the Kipsigis, the Nandi and the Pokot—did not establish centralized, highly hierarchical states. But these egalitarian people had a similar pride in themselves and their culture and contempt for the white man's civilization. Margaret Read suggested that Ngoni rejection of European life was 'perhaps the struggle of a disappearing aristocracy' (Read, 1959, p. 99). But many pastoral people have no aristocracy: on the contrary, status among them is often achieved 'in the field' rather than ascribed through birth and inheritance—as Peristiany (1954) describes the situation among the Nilo-Hamitic Pokot of north-western Kenya. The proud and intensely conservative Nandi (Huntingford, 1950, p. 108), like the Nuer of the Sudan, are not reactionary aristocracies defending threatened privileges. They had neither social hierarchies nor tribal chiefs. Evans-Pritchard, who 'found Nuer pride an increasing source of amazement', thought it was their initiation rites that, more than anything else, gave the Nuer their arrogance and 'that sense of superiority which is so conspicuous a trait of their character' (Evans-Pritchard, 1940, p. 182).

There are few studies of the fate of European-style schools in such societies, but some account has been published of a government school and a mission school among the Pokot (or Suk) (Bascom and Herskovits, 1959). These people have no centralized, hierarchical political system; they are strikingly different from their agricultural neighbours in their powerful resistance to Euroamerican life.

In 1928 a government school was established at Kapenguria and shortly afterwards a mission school was set up by the Bible Churchmen's Mission Society. Twenty years later the poor attendance at these schools was a cause for concern; and yet the government school had enjoyed the leadership of a pioneering headmaster, G. H. Chaundy (from 1930 to 1943). The curriculum of his school was carefully adapted to local circumstances and apparent needs. It was 'heavily biased toward "good" farming techniques in the hope that the pupils would disseminate the knowledge they gained'.

Chaundy failed. He had attempted a dual task—not only to modernize the Pokot but to convert them to the life of settled agriculturalists. 'Aside from the limited acceptance of maize, his work met with strong resistance, despite his sincerity, good intentions, and zealous efforts.' The Pokot were as contemptuous of African cultivators as they were of white officials. Schooling was a serious distraction from the important things in life like herding cattle. In the 1950s the Pokot way of life was virtually unchanged. The women wore goatskin skirts and capes, the men wore hardly anything at all. They carried their eight-foot spears, wore elaborate head-dress, tended their flocks and drank great quantities of their millet or honey beer:

> They continue to . . . remain unconvinced of the alleged benefits of government, schooling and Christianity. Their herding life provides all they need and all they want, and they have found almost nothing in Euroamerican culture that will entice them to abandon their old ways. (Bascom and Herskovits, 1959)

The Tonga of central Africa (Malawi) stand in striking contrast. They are an agricultural tribe who have often been depicted as a disorganized rabble without any obvious or effective means of social control (Colson, 1953). And they are education-mad. The Scottish Presbyterian Mission has a long history of successful educational effort among them, 'but this itself is the result of Tonga enthusiasm rather than its cause' (Lloyd, 1966, p. 21). In the past they were a source of slaves for neighbouring pastoral tribes; they are not a tribe of high prestige and their social organization does not offer individuals much opportunity for obtaining positions of standing. They are not a proud people: 'The Tonga are a people lacking in marked self-identification and great traditions, formed by refugees from Ngoni slave raids' (Lloyd, 1966, p. 21). But in the modern states of Zambia and Malawi it is the mission-educated Tonga who have made a disproportionate contribution to the new elites.

## 4. PSYCHOLOGICAL EXPLANATIONS

Teams of American psychologists have now investigated the process of 'acculturation' (or becoming more civilized) in East Africa. One team (from the

Johns Hopkins University) investigated the connection between change and happiness (Ainsworth and Ainsworth, 1962); another team (on the 'Culture and Ecology in East Africa Project' based on UCLA) investigated personality differences between pastoralists and agriculturalists (Edgerton, 1971). It is now clear that tight interpersonal relationships from which it is difficult to escape provide a powerful impulse to labour migration, witchcraft, and a Western education.

In *Civilization and its Discontents* Freud dwelt on the unhappiness of being civilized. Like Thomas Hobbes before him he said civilization was possible only when we curbed our aggression. Hobbes gave the job of curbing it to an all-powerful state; Freud internalized it and gave it to a no less punitive 'superego'. And so it is odd that the best evidence we have shows that becoming more civilized is by and large a joyous affair.

It is true that forcibly civilized people have not usually been joyous—like such North American Indian tribes as the Sioux who were ruthlessly put to school by the Federal Indian Affairs Department (MacGregor, 1946). If the Nuer were forcibly enrolled in Western-type schools it is probable that they would not be joyous either. But when becoming civilized has been in large measure a voluntary and selective response to new opportunities, people generally seem pleased with the change.

When Daniel Lerner made a study of the process of becoming modern in six countries in the Middle East he found that the urbanized and modernized man was far more likely to rate himself 'happy' than his country cousin. It was those who were loyal to traditional ways and values who were dissatisfied: 'those who embody tradition are most unhappy while those seeking to forsake it become increasingly happy in the measure that they succeed' (Lerner, 1958, p. 101). The contrast that is often made between urban anomie and rural stability was not supported by Lerner's inquiry:

> In every country the rural villagers declare themselves the most unhappy fellows. In every country, the modernizing individuals are considerably less unhappy—and the more rapidly the society around them is modernized the happier they are. . . . Traditional society is passing away from the Middle East because relatively few Middle Easterners want to live by its rules. (Lerner, 1958, p. 399)

The key to this puzzle lies not only in the nature of 'modernity' but in the nature and organization of rural village life.

The 'Culture–Ecology Project', which was carried out in the 1960s, involved a study of four Kenyan tribes: the Hehe, Kamba, Pokot, and Sebei. All four had a predominantly pastoral group as well as a sector devoted to agriculture. Thus the Pokot of the plains lived a semi-nomadic existence as herdsmen, constantly on the move, but the Pokot of the hills depended on the produce of their fields and maintained a complex irrigation system which required the constant vigilance of those who exploited it. Pastoralists were defined as unmounted herdsmen who maintained cattle and perhaps some sheep and goats; farmers were defined as cultivators engaged in hoe agriculture, without ploughs or draft animals. The pastoralists were distinguished by their high degree of mobility, the farmers by their ties to local communities which they could leave only by abandoning their capital. A herdsman moved on and took his capital with him.

This comparative study of pastoralists and farmers was based on survey data obtained from interviews and from the use of a range of appropriately adapted psychological tests. The use of such tests was made cautiously, expertly (and apologetically). A systematically modified form of the thematic apperception test (TAT) was used, the Rorschach (inkblots) test, and 85 interview questions designed to explore values. Highly sophisticated methods of scoring, coding, and analysing the data were employed. The project team were very sensitive to methodological criticism and conceded that by making a study of 'verbal behaviour' they could be charged with opting for 'neatness and precision of measurement, and thus for convenience, not for behavioral reality in all its contradictory complexity' (Edgerton, 1971, p. 27). Nevertheless, within the conventions of this kind of research the results are impressive. And they are generally consistent with conclusions reached by less tidy methods of living with people and observing what they do.

The farmers were more Westernized than the pastoralists. An 'index of acculturation' was based on such characteristics as the amount of school education the subject and his sons and daughters had had, whether he wore shoes, and the type of roofing he used for his dwelling. 'In each tribe, the farmers in our sample were more acculturated than their pastoral counterparts.' In a factor-analytical study of personal characteristics, acculturation variables were most closely associated with farming variables—and both with a tendency to go to law and to be sensitive to insults (Edgerton, 1971, p. 241).

The evidence from interviews, the Rorschach test, and the TAT was unequivocal: the cultivators differed psychologically from the pastoralists in important ways. They were more anxious, subservient, and prone to witchcraft accusations; they were also more concerned to avoid conflict, and they attached more importance to neighbours in times of trouble and crisis than to kin. (The importance of kinsmen to pastoralists and immediate family to farmers is a major point made by Oberg in his Ankole studies.) Even in the way they responded to the test situation differences were striking. Farmers' perceptual and verbal skills seemed to be more facile and fluent, and 'the farmers were also more eager to please, less prideful, and less arrogant than the pastoralists, who retained their independence even in the Rorschach performance' (Edgerton, 1971, p. 205).

Peristiany (1954) found that the agricultural Pokot were riven by feuds which resulted in bitter and enduring enmity, but 'as the lineages of the western pastoral Pokot are not localized and their villages lack corporateness and continuity, feuds do not occur in this pastoral section'. The report of the 'Culture–Ecology Project' confirms this picture: references to vengeance and insults were far more common among farmers than pastoralists. The very importance of their neighbours made them a source of tension and spite. 'Given this response pattern, we would expect witchcraft to be higher among farmers than pastoralists. And so it is.'

The farmers are anxious people, avoiding direct conflict, dealing with threats real and imagined circuitously, through litigation or witchcraft. The pastoralists are directly and openly aggressive, they are prepared to take risks, they are brave and self-controlled. They are independent but respect authority, especially the authority of the elders. They have a capacity for rapid action and decision making. It is the ability and confidence to take independent decisions which more than anything else distinguishes the pastoral personality.

There is normally neither time nor opportunity for the herdsman to refer back to higher authority when he makes crucial decisions for himself and his herd. And his decisions must take a range of often complex factors into account:

> The care of livestock involves the husbandman in a constant pattern of decision making. His seasonal round of activities is not routinized; he must decide each day where to take his animals, and he may have to include many diverse factors in his computation—the potential quality of the grass, the availability of water, the probability of predators, the competitive action of other herders, and so on. (Edgerton, 1971, p. 297)

But the evidence of the Rorschach test was also that pastoralists are greater 'perseverators' and have greater 'cognitive rigidity'. When they have made up their mind they tend to stick to it even when new and contrary evidence is produced. They are not only independent: they are obstinate.

There has been only one psychological study of any consequence that has not sharply contrasted personality in pastoral and in agricultural societies: Barry *et al.* (1959) said they were virtually the same. Their correlational study was based on ratings of socialization practices and form of economic life as described in more than a hundred ethnographic reports of nonliterate societies throughout the world. Astonishingly, they concluded that pastoralists no less than cultivators were reared to be obedient, highly responsible, and cautious because both had to accumulate food and protect it over long periods of time. The only difference was that cultivators stored the harvest while pastoralists cared for food on the hoof. Pastoral peoples were prudential and lived carefully by the rules: 'In this type of society future food supply seems to be best assured by faithful adherence to routines designed to maintain the good health of the herd.' It was hunters, who lived from day to day without storing food, who were self-reliant and independent and notable for their initiative.

An intensive psychological study in two communities in the highlands of southern Peru showed the familiar differences between cultivators and pastoralists. Children in cultivators' and pastoralists' families were closely observed and given tasks which revealed different aspects of personality. It is true that pastoralists' children, like farmers' children, were extremely obedient and had a highly developed sense of responsibility; but the former were significantly more independent and self-reliant. Pastoralists appeared to have much in common with hunters, little with farmers. The study was seen as supporting the Culture–Ecology Project in East Africa and refuting the correlational study of Barry and Child:

> The pastoralist–agricultural personality differences have appeared despite the shift in setting and in herd type, they have emerged in early childhood, and they have evidently arisen as a function of pastoral versus agricultural activities. (Bolton *et al.*, 1976)

But the personality characteristics do not in themselves account for the unwillingness of pastoralists to learn more than their fathers can teach them. Indeed, their independence and initiative might suggest a more innovative and experimental approach to life. The answer lies in their free-ranging movements and their ability to put values into practice. In striking contrast, the way that cultivators behave is not in line with the values they hold: they do not think that they ought to be vengeful, anxious, servile, and sly. 'Conversely', says the Culture–Ecology Project, 'many of the characteristic pastoral variables are regularly expressed as values.' The pastoralists are open and aggressive, self-controlled, brave, industrious, and appreciative of kinsmen, and the evidence of the Culture–Ecology Project is that this is exactly what they think they ought to be. The cultivators' psychological orientations are not supported by their cultural values, but the pastoralists' behaviour finds support and reinforcement in their culture at every turn.

Interpersonal tension in his close-packed village, where he is heavily dependent on his immediate family and neighbours, as well as the discrepancy between what he is and what he thinks he ought to be, makes the cultivator open to opportunities to enter new worlds. Even the remote and very primitive Ba'amba may now escape from the intolerable stress of village community life to wider and looser social networks in Kampala, Nairobi, even Mombasa. They leave to escape the constraints of their restricted world. 'Serious friction within the family and trouble with neighbours who are suspected of practising witchcraft have long been features of Amba society. In the past, when such situations become unbearable, the individual moved to another village' (Winter, 1955, p. 38). Today he moves to another country, a distant town.

## 5. OBEDIENCE TRAINING AND SOCIAL CHANGE

Are primitive peoples so trained in obedience that they have great difficulty in questioning authority and tradition and changing their ways? And does this apply particularly to pastoralists? It has often been said that Africans in general have strict obedience training in infancy and youth and consequently accept even the most exacting authority without protest. In the past colonial officials took this view and justified forced labour and heavy obligations of service to chiefs on the grounds that they were customary and accepted as 'natural'. The Uganda Development Commission said in 1920: 'We submit that there is no injustice in compulsion as such. In the Uganda Protectorate compulsory labour for the Kabaka or chief is too ancient and accepted a fact to be challenged.' More than 50 years later an American psychologist who had worked in Africa advanced the same argument, asserting that schoolchildren in Africa were exploited by their teachers and used as servants and garden boys and that no one complained 'except where the practice extends to using the female students sexually'. For Africans, it was argued, there was nothing demeaning in being used as a lackey to a leader: 'Africans do not see it that way' (Le Vine, 1973). Both ancient social custom and traditional child-rearing practices ensured a remarkable docility.

All this is extremely doubtful, as I have argued from my own observation and experience. Forced labour for chiefs was bitterly resented in Uganda in the 1950s: the Uganda Agreements of 1900 had confirmed and perpetuated the ancient *kasanvu* and *luwalo*, although they were commuted into taxes in the 1920s; but customary services (*burungi bwensi*) in building roads, hunting, digging wells, and the like were still expected, and they were seen as an affront to personal dignity even by the uneducated peasant (*mukopi*), and especially by the educated. These services were avoided if at all possible (Musgrove, 1955). By the 1950s Africans berated the Europeans of 1900 not for subverting their culture but for preserving it.

The picture presented by the American psychologist (Le Vine) of African docility is altogether extraordinary. He relates it elsewhere to 'traditional child-rearing formulas evolved to protect the child from risk of economic disaster' (Le Vine, 1974). Parents are anticipating the occupational demands their children will eventually have to face: they are concerned that they will have the capacity to survive in a world of scarce and unstable resources. And in fact it is now a widely accepted view among behavioural scientists that obedience training will be severe where life is hard.

It is true that most African peoples attach considerable importance to obedience in their children. What is far less certain is the connection between this and adult values and behaviour. Obedient children may be very useful as children; adult life later on may require, promote, and reward quite different attributes.

It is not surprising that warrior tribes like the Zulus have emphasized discipline, obedience, and respect for the elders in their puberty ceremonies (Mahlobo and Krige, 1934). The Ngoni likewise taught endurance and obedience as the prime virtues, and as young boys listened to the instruction of their fathers at the kraal gate, they did so passively, silently, asking no questions (Read, 1938b). Among the Chaga, initiation schools subjected adolescent boys to the 'tiring repetition of their ethical teaching' and in the longer rites the boys would sit quiet and inactive, 'haggard, drowsy, often insensible to what is going on around them' (Raum, 1938).

These are pastoral tribes, but a similar picture emerges from recent studies of agricultural people like the Kikuyu of Kenya. In an intensive study of 5-to-9-year-old Kikuyu children obedience to mothers and other women was measured: the children obeyed their mothers completely. (In comparable American studies children of the same age tended to 'take advantage' of their mothers.) The Kikuyu children showed extremely high levels of obedience, but the investigators do not relate this to future work requirements but more plausibly to current heavy involvement in household tasks (Munroe and Monroe, 1972).

The situation among the Tallensi of Ghana is exactly the same: a strong emphasis on obedience coupled with early responsibilities and duties. From the age of 4 or 5 boys help in pegging out goats and scaring birds from newly sown fields; by 6 or 7 they help with house building, sowing, and harvesting; by the time they are 12 they may own property and have heavy responsibilities as leaders of herdboys. This is the context of obedience:

> A parent's authority may not be flouted, though he or she is expected to be affectionate and indulgent. . . . Children are, as a rule, very obedient. If they refuse to carry out an order there is usually some very valid reason—acknowledged as such by both parents and children. (Fortes, 1938, p. 17)

Educated African elites (and elites in the making) show no tendency to reduce the traditional emphasis on obedience in child rearing. This is so among elite Yoruba parents in Nigeria (Lloyd, 1966); and secondary school pupils in Tanzania take a similar view when they look forward to their responsibilities as parents.

The inquiry in Tanzania was carried out with more than 3 000 students attending secondary (high) schools. They were asked what they would try to teach their children if and when they became parents. 'Obedience and manners' was the overwhelming response. Academic attainment and skills were also given great emphasis; honesty and religious values were mentioned; but by far the greatest weight was given to manners, obedience, respect. 'Secondary school students in Tanzania express the determination to stress obedience training in the upbringing of their own children with the resolve holding equally across sex and ethnic [Asian and African] lines' (Klingelhofer, 1971).

This, it is suggested, is regrettable. Modernizing individuals should be reared not to be obedient but 'autonomous'. Modernization in Africa is put in jeopardy by this continuing emphasis, even among the educated, on good manners and docility:

> Aside from the affirmation of the importance of education and the need to assist in the academic training of children there seems to be no indication in these data of a strong identification with training of children in the independent, individualistic, autonomous attributes which are considered to be so important in modern technological societies. (Klingelhofer, 1971)

Middle-class parents in industrial countries are reported to attach less importance than working-class parents to children's obedience and more to their independence and curiosity. The middle class is seen as the spearhead of modernity and its child-rearing methods peculiarly appropriate to modern (and modernizing) societies. Kohn's (1969) social-class comparisons in Washington and Turin are commonly cited in this connection. It is true that middle-class parents picked out 'obedience' less often than working-class parents as an important characteristic of children; but only about a third (37 per cent) of working-class parents thought it important even so. Nevertheless Kohn feels justified in claiming that the work experience of lower-class people leads them to see obedience and conformity as essential to survival. This conclusion has been extrapolated to primitive societies (Le Vine, 1974).

This is dangerous. In Kohn's study, working-class mothers saw no conflict between obedience and curiosity (although middle-class mothers did). Certainly the observed behaviour of pastoral tribes suggests that there is no necessary conflict between obedience training and independent decision making. And under modernizing conditions early childhood socialization seems to be far less secure, according to the extensive evidence assembled by Inkeles and Smith (1974, p. 303), than psychologists commonly suppose.

I found Uganda schoolboys who had been reared under traditional tribal conditions quite extraordinarily and exhilaratingly curious and questioning by English standards (Musgrove, 1955). My experience was exactly like that of a Cambridge scientist, Patrick M. Synge, who taught for a time at Makerere College (then a secondary school) when he was in East Africa in 1934–1935 as a member of the British Museum Expedition. He was astonished and delighted by the searching questions that were put to him:

> The Baganda have shown a most unusual adaptability to modern European civilization and a real seeking after knowledge, as I discovered at their Makerere College when I found it difficult to answer their straight questions on elementary biology, questions which hardly any undergraduate in England would be likely to ask, but which were perfectly logical.

The teacher, said Synge, needed 'an almost endless patience in answering questions'. The boys had developed an inquisitive faculty; by contrast 'The majority of English public schoolboys will accept any fact they are told, even if they do not understand how it is arrived at' (Synge, 1938, p. xxiii).

This exactly parallels my own experience some 20 years later. And when I subsequently taught boys in an English grammar school, I found the work by contrast boring and dispiriting: they asked no questions unless prodded hard, and they believed everything they were told.

This, then, is the paradox: pastoral people, who emphasize obedience in rearing the young, show a remarkable capacity for independent decision taking in their traditional lives as herdsmen, but they do not take readily to the white man's schools and new knowledge; the cultivators place similar emphasis on obedience, show less independence and resourcefulness in their daily lives as farmers, but are avid for European education and ask searching and highly pertinent questions when they get it. Obedience training in childhood seems to explain very little in subsequent behaviour. We must look elsewhere for explanations of intellectual curiosity and the willingness and ability to challenge what 'authorities' say.

## 6. CITIES AND ELITES

Cities and elites provide the key to modernity. They are usually found together. Both turn outwards from the home-base community to a wider network of connections and involvements. In some respects they still turn inwards, too. It is this that gives them a pivotal position in the modernizing process.

The new city in a developing country, with its Westernized elites and shanty towns, is Malinowski's 'third cultural reality' *par excellence*: a 'tertium quid' to be understood in its own terms. It is this and not the parent cultures to which education refers and in terms of which the new school systems make sense.

The mystique of modernity finds its most powerful manifestation in the city. It is true, as Peter Berger says, that the fastest-growing urban agglomeration in the Third World is the slum and that the city nevertheless is enormously attractive and has great drawing power: 'Whatever its frustrations and degradations, the city continues to be the place where things are happening, where there is movement and a sense of the future.' Throughout the Third World the culture of modernity is closely linked with city life (Berger *et al.*, 1974, pp. 128–129).

Cities in the Third World do not have quite the same role and significance as cities in the West: Goldthorpe says they are more important agents of modernity, Norton Ginsburg says they are less. For Goldthorpe 'development' and 'urbanization' are virtually interchangeable terms: 'Urbanism, indeed, may be regarded as part of the definition of development' (Goldthorpe, 1975, p. 120). Daniel Lerner similarly tied urbanism, literacy, and media participation together to mark the passing of traditional society. Ten per cent urbanization was necessary before literacy began to rise, 25 per cent before literacy 'took off' independently (Lerner, 1958, pp. 59–60).

But Ginsburg says that cities in Third World countries are swamped by rural immigrants who are often unemployed, under-employed, or employed in 'non-modern' service work. Urbanism as a way of life does not develop and the rural immigrants are unable to take advantage of urban living. Consequently, says Ginsburg, cities 'cannot play the same modernizing role that has characterized the cities in the West' (Ginsburg, 1966).

This is almost certainly wrong. There is a very powerful relationship between modernity of outlook and city life in developing countries. Inkeles and Smith constructed an 'Overall Modernity' scale which they administered in six such countries—Argentina, Chile, Pakistan, India, Israel, and Nigeria. The scale measured sense of personal efficacy and of living in a manageable and calculable world, orientation to the future rather than the past, inclination to long-term planning, openness to new experience, and readiness to change. City dwellers everywhere had higher modernity scores than their country cousins and modernity scores rose steadily with years of urban residence: 'For example, in Nigeria . . . only six per cent of those just arrived in the city [from rural areas] scored as modern, whereas among those who had spent 14 years or more in town, the proportion scored as modern was 42 per cent' (Inkeles and Smith, 1974, p. 219).

Nevertheless Inkeles was inclined to discount any special effect of the city over and above the effect of institutions commonly though not necessarily found in cities—schools, factories, the communications media. But in Nigeria there was a distinct 'city-effect' over and above these separate influences (Inkeles and Smith, 1974, p. 221). Inkeles reports this but then ignores it and makes no attempt to explain it. In fact, it is precisely what we might expect: the other five countries in this study were far less primitive. Nigeria is still a country of tribal societies in which everyone can think of himself related to everybody else.

The contrast between city and bush in tropical Africa is still dramatic and stark. The city is a highly distinctive physical configuration and way of life: its characteristics are not extensively diffused through suburbs and suburbanized villages. In the primitive countries which are the main concern of this book we should expect that the highly distinctive physical and social complex that makes a city would have a uniquely modernizing effect.

An older generation or urban sociologists—Park, Burgess, Redfield, and Louis Wirth—had doubtless overstated the modernizing consequences of urban life. Park and Burgess maintained that modern men were more rational than their forebears because they lived in cities (Park and Burgess, 1925, p. 130); Louis Wirth painted a gloomy picture of congestion, irritation, loneliness, and 'anomie' but argued that the juxtaposition of diverse groups bred a relativistic outlook, tolerance, and rationality (Wirth, 1938). Cities may, in fact, be congeries of villages which support ancient and irrational beliefs; and tolerance and community size do not appear to be closely linked (Fischer, 1971). But the sheer distinctiveness of cities in tribal worlds promotes not only cognitive development and rationality—as has been argued in earlier chapters of this book—but a more generalized openness to new experience and awareness of alternatives.

The modern city in a tribal world turns outwards. It is essentially a centre of foreign influence. This, says Goldthorpe, 'is an important difference between those towns and the towns of the already industrialized nations' (Goldthorpe, 1975, p. 119). The Westernized elites turn outwards, too, and Nettl and Robertson (1966) relate modernization very closely to this outward-turning posture of the new elites.

Nettl and Robertson break away from economic definitions of modernization in terms of per capita income and growth of the GNP; their emphasis is on the involvement of modernizing countries with other 'well-placed' nations in a worldwide system. This involvement is mainly through new national elites. Modernization is the process whereby elites reduce their international isolation. Nettl and Robertson question the value of the concept of industrialization in interpreting modernity; they say that industrialization does not have the homogenizing effect on developing nations that is often claimed; and that in so far as modern nations are in fact alike, this arises largely from their dealings with one another on an international stage. For Nettl and Robertson the study of modernization focuses on the international system and the 'prismatic role of elites'.

But modernity is not all of a piece and the new outward-turning elites look inwards, too. They are not interchangeable, international civil servants who happen to be black. As I have indicated above, the boys I taught in Uganda—elites in the making—reacted strongly against key aspects of a modernized life. Their heart was in farming and their strongest identification was with a new class of educated men.

This is also the picture that comes out of Goldthorpe's (1955) study of an East African elite and Philip Foster's (1977) study of Ghanaian secondary school boys. Here are new social worlds which Malinowski said had their own determinism and whose constituent parts could not be invoiced back to their place of origin. These new cultural realities, said Malinowski, 'are without precedent in either of the cultures. They are not to be understood by direct reference to any parent culture but must be studied as processes running on their own specific lines' (Malinowski, 1945, p. 80).

Even Gluckman (1949, pp. 11–14) thought that Malinowski was broadly correct in this view, although he thought he overstated the separateness of the 'third cultural reality'; Beattie (1964, p. 243) endorsed this particular aspect of Malinowski's theory without any serious reservation. The concept of a third cultural reality made sense to me in interpreting my observations and experiences in Uganda when Malinowski's institutional-substitution theory did not (Musgrove, 1952).

Goldthorpe's account of an East African elite seems to me to illustrate this concept well. The study is based on Africans who attended Makerere College (then a secondary school) in the 1930s and in the 1950s were, in the main, government clerks. They were not well-to-do: their salaries did not even support their families—'that must be done off the land'; they were not men of great power in a British protectorate. But they had a strong sense of belonging to a new category of educated men. They all wanted their children to have as much education as possible but had little notion of specific careers to follow. Their salaried jobs were important to them for providing cash for school fees.

They had a strong sense of identity as educated men; they worked in city offices; and their abiding passion was for a stake in the land. As one government servant said when interviewed: 'You know how it is with us Africans; we must be cultivators first and foremost.' Goldthorpe saw a pattern of life emerging rather like an eighteenth-century English gentleman's, with a house in the town and one in the country. A typical remark, said Goldthorpe, was the following:

'It is very important to me to develop my land, now that I have bought it, while I am still in the service. Later the money will not be available.' But for many their land must for the time being lie idle until they retire.

An academic and non-applied education is as passionately desired as a landed estate. This is also what Foster found in the late 1950s among secondary schoolboys in Accra. Roughly two-thirds ideally wished to be farmers; all wanted a highly academic, non-applied education; only 5 per cent wanted white-collar work, but virtually all of them thought they would get it (Foster, 1977).

Within the new social reality of Westernized elites and modern cities it is traditional kinship ties that 'give'. It is true that uneducated wives are often preferred who will live in a village, maintain old ties, and dig the banana garden. But the nuclear family of husband, wife, and children generally turns in upon itself. The Nyakyusa once talked in shocked whispers about government clerks who bought luxuries like butcher's meat and sugar and regularly ate alone with their families. 'It was terrible! The sharing between neighbours had gone' (Wilson, 1956). So, too, had the sharing with kin. Modernization meant more saving and less hospitality: the tribesman in Central Africa 'must therefore reject the claims of his kinsmen and turn them hungry from his door' (Mitchell, 1956). In Accra in the 1950s a clerk with only £10 a month might allocate £3 to support kinsfolk outside his own household, but increasingly these city men had to learn how to protect themselves: 'Faced with insistent, even predatory claims, they may begin to restrict the range of relatives to whom they recognize an obligation' (Marris, 1959).

The new world is lighter in its social constraints and obligations; it is part of an international network of relationships; but it is not homogenized in any but a superficial, technical sense. Modernization is not conformity but a constellation of new social realities; and the new man, as Malinowski said, has abilities and energies, advantages and handicaps, to which 'neither his European neighbour nor his "blanket" brother are heirs' (Malinowski, 1945, p. 25).

## 7. CONCLUSION: MODERNITY AND FULFILMENT

Learning to be modern, or 'more civilized' as Leonard Doob would say, seems generally to have brought satisfaction, pleasure, and fulfilment. But those who have moved away from a traditional life have in the main been volunteers. There are still highly resistant enclaves that have refused to move. Doob recognizes that these exist but says they must eventually follow suit. The result will not be total uniformity, says Doob (native languages, for instance, are remarkably resilient); but 'all will share to a certain extent some core attributes of civilization' (Doob, 1960, p. 253).

Marxists now say that primitive peoples have been held back from modernity in the interests of capitalism: they have been systematically 'underdeveloped'. Somewhat inconsistently they also complain that Africans have been Westernized and robbed of their pride and sense of identity (Rodney, 1972). It is a highly reified capitalism that is held to impinge on primitive societies and have this retarding effect. Schools play a key role in underdevelopment. Both mission schools and government schools have alienated and subjugated Africans for the benefit of capitalism: 'Colonial schooling was education for subordination, exploitation, the creation of mental confusion and the development of underdevelopment' (Rodney, 1972, p. 264). It is nowhere explained why Africans so readily paid for it.

The Christian missions, in fact, have been and still are powerful agents of modernity. Although in the West modernization nowadays goes hand in hand with secularization, in primitive societies the opposite is still the case. (African parsons often emerge as key men in modernizing power structures.) Christianity provides a modernizing ethic (Wilson, 1956) just as Calvinism did, according to Max Weber, in seventeenth-century Europe; but the missions have promoted economic change more directly, if only because cash crops were needed if converts were to buy Bibles and pay school fees. Thus the Church Missionary Society established a great commercial enterprise, the Uganda Company, and was largely responsible for introducing cotton as a cash crop into Uganda (Goldthorpe, 1975, p. 53).

The Marxist charge against colonial governments is also very weak. Even Rostow gave them a positive role in his theory of semi-automatic stages of development. Colonial governments often operated with very limited budgets. Rostow says they did not always optimize the development of the preconditions for 'take-off'; nevertheless, they could hardly avoid moving colonial society along the transitional path 'and they often included modernization of a sort as an explicit object of colonial policy' (Rostow, 1960, p. 27).

But the Marxists are quite right to bring power to the centre of social analysis. The cultural anthropologists almost completely ignored it (although Gluckman emphasized conflict as well as cooperation in culture contact and change). They were, in the main, politically naive. Hoogvelt's strictures on Talcot Parsons apply equally to Malinowski and his followers:

> In Parsons' approach one gets the impression that the history of mankind has been one happy, relaxed exchange of ideas. . . . Cultural diffusion appears as a friendly merchant traveller, a timeless Marco Polo, innocently roaming the world, gently picking up a few ideas in one place and harmlessly depositing them in another. (Hoogvelt, 1971, p. 18)

Education inevitably has power implications, but it is perverse to regard it as an instrument of oppression in 'developing' countries. Only when it was given an agricultural or applied 'African' bias did Africans see it quite explicitly in this light (Musgrove, 1952). In the main, as Foster (1965) makes clear, they got what they wanted: an education that was abstract, literary, and non-applied.

Reference has already been made to Lerner's (1958) account of the satisfaction of men who moved into modernity in the Middle East. Since he made his study there has been some reaction, notably in Iran. This is exactly as Sprott foretold some years ago: although urban-industrial society will eventually cover the world, he thought, there will be some reaction from time to time, notably in Islamic countries, from those who have a vested interest in preserving the *status quo* (Sprott, 1967). But wherever there has been careful monitoring of the individuals embracing modernity the picture is in line with Lerner's. Inkeles gave a 'Psychosomatic Symptoms Test' to his modernized subjects and found no evidence that modernization is associated with personal maladjustment. The indications were the opposite (Inkeles and Smith, 1974, pp. 263–264).

The team of psychologists from the Johns Hopkins University were looking in 1954–1955 for evidence of frustration and hostility among the more highly 'acculturated' people of East Africa. They found surprisingly little. Their study, which used a variety of projective tests, was carried out with pupils in secondary schools in Buganda and in the remote and primitive North Nyanza Province of Kenya. The acculturated were delighted with their lot, showed no resentment against authority (whether black or white), and eagerly looked forward to further modernization. The only frustration they seemed to have arose from the educational process itself.

The level of personal frustration was low and there were few aggressive themes in TAT stories. There was no sense under the then colonial regime of education as oppression by an alien power:

> In line with the generally eager acceptance of acculturation as desirable is the fact that nearly half of the Ss expressed positive attitudes towards Europeans who, as representatives of the 'new' culture tend to be in a dominating acculturating role. The contribution of Europeans most consciously valued was the civilizing, educating influence which they had brought to East Africa. (Ainsworth and Ainsworth, 1962)

It would really be surprising if it were otherwise. Although the authors do not make this point, the subjects of this study were all volunteers for modernity. They were voluntarily in attendance at fee-paying schools. A central theme of this chapter is that some primitive people do not volunteer. The former come preponderantly from settled villages devoted to agriculture in which neighbourhood and family ties are very strong; the latter are typically semi-nomadic pastoralists. It is the cultivators who have personal problems arising from extreme interdependence who seem to have most to gain from change.

Gellner is undoubtedly correct in seeing the rapid global diffusion of scientific industrial civilization as 'the main event of our time'. He sees it as not only irresistible but properly so, because it is highly effective in satisfying needs: 'The cognitive and technical superiority of one form of life is so manifest, and so loaded with implications for the satisfaction of wants and needs—and, for better or worse, for power—that it simply cannot be questioned' (Gellner, 1968).

Nevertheless, pastoralists by implication question it and in practice resist it. It is cultivators who turn to modernity and show a capcity to do so perceptively, critically, and selectively. They are able to develop what Daniel Lerner sees as the essential and defining skill of the modernizing personality—empathy. In the isolated tight-knit community empathy is neither common nor necessary. Empathy is a product of cities. In the village everyone else is much like yourself: no effort is needed to imagine yourself in his shoes.

But it is in the very tensions of settled village life that a creative potential lies. African art and the tsetse-fly have always been coterminus, as Livingstone noted (Westermann, 1949, p. 39). Where there is no tsetse-fly cattle and pastoral people flourish and art does not. The message that comes out of Africa is this: high art, witchcraft, the tsetse-fly, and a taste for schools and modernity go together. An interest in education and associated change is most likely to be found under conditions which Gluckman (1940) described as 'temporary equilibrium'. For the modern mind, as Berger says, has no final resting place.

## REFERENCES

Ainsworth, L. H., and Ainsworth, Mary D. (1962), 'Acculturation in East Africa', *Journal of Social Psychology*, **57**.

Barry, H., Child, I. L., and Bacon, M. K. (1959), 'Relation of child training to a subsistence economy', *American Anthropologist*, **61**.

Bascom, W. R., and Herskovits, M. J. (1959), *Continuity and Change in African Cultures*, University of Chicago Press, Chicago.

Beattie, John (1964), *Other Cultures*, Cohen & West, London.

Belal, Abdul Aziz (1979), 'Culture and development: An approach to underdevelopment', *Culture*, **6**.

Berger, P. L., Berger, B., and Kellner, Hansfried (1974), *The Homeless Mind*, Penguin, Harmondsworth, Middx.

Bolton, C., Bolton, L., Gross, L., Koel, A., Michelson, C., Munroe, R. L., and Munroe, R. H. (1976), 'Pastoralism and personality: An Andean replication', *Ethos*, **4**.

Colson, E. (1953), 'Social control and vengeance in plateau Tonga society', *Africa*, **23**.

Doob, L. W. (1960), *Becoming More Civilized. A Psychological Exploration*, Yale University Press, New Haven, Conn.

Edgerton, R. B. (1971), *The Individual in Cultural Adaptation*, University of California Press, Berkeley.

Evans-Pritchard, E. E. (1940), *The Nuer*, Clarendon Press, Oxford.

Fischer, C. S. (1971), 'A research note on urbanism and tolerance', *American Journal of Sociology*, **76**.

Fortes, Meyer (1936), 'Culture contact as a dynamic process', *Africa*, **9**.

Fortes, Meyer (1938), *Social and Psychological Aspects of Education in Taleland*, Oxford University Press, London.

Fortes, Meyer (1945), *The Dynamics of Clanship among the Tallensi*, Oxford University Press, London.

Foster, Philip J. (1965), *Education and Social Change in Ghana*, Routledge & Kegan Paul, London.

Foster, Philip J. (1977), 'The vocational school fallacy in vocational planning', in J. Karabel and A. H. Halsey, *Power and Ideology in Education*, Oxford University Press, New York.

Gellner, E. (1968), 'The new idealism—cause and meaning in the social sciences', in I. Lakatos and A. Musgrave (eds), *Problems in the Philosophy of Science. Proceedings of the International Colloquium, London 1965*, Vol. 13, North Holland Press, London.

Ginsburg, Norton (1966), 'The city and modernization', in M. Weiner (ed.), *Modernization*, Basic, New York.

Gluckman, M. (1940), 'Analysis of a social situation in modern Zululand', *Bantu Studies*, **14**.

Gluckman, M. (1949), 'An analysis of the sociological theories of Bronislaw Malinowski', *Rhodes-Livingstone Paper*, no. 16, Oxford University Press.

Goldthorpe, J. E. (1955), 'An African elite', *British Journal of Sociology*, **6**.

Goldthorpe, J. E. (1975), *The Sociology of the Third World*, Cambridge University Press, Cambridge.

Gouldner, A. W. (1971), *The Coming Crisis of Western Sociology*, Heinemann, London.

Gugler, Josef (1969), 'On the theory of rural–urban migration', in J. A. Jackson (ed.), *Migration*, Cambridge University Press, Cambridge.

Hoernlé, A. W. (1931), 'An outline of the native conception of education', *Africa*, **4**.

Hoogvelt, A. (1971), *The Sociology of Developing Societies*, Macmillan, London.

Hunter, Monica (1934), 'Methods of study of culture contact', *Africa*, **7**.

Huntingford, G. W. B. (1950), *Nandi Work and Culture*, HMSO, London.

Inkeles, Alex, and Smith, David H. (1974), *Becoming Modern*, Heinemann, London.

Klingelhofer, E. L. (1971), 'What Tanzanian secondary school students plan to teach their children', *Journal of Cross-Cultural Psychology*, **2**.

Kohn, Melvin L. (1969), *Class and Conformity. A Study in Values*, Dorsey Press, Homewood, Ill.

Kuper, Adam (1975), *Anthropologists and Anthropology: The British School 1922–1972*, Penguin, Harmondsworth, Middx.

Leach, E. R. (1973), 'The study of man in relation to science and technology', *Journal of the Royal Society of Arts*, **71**.

Lerner, Daniel (1958), *The Passing of Traditional Society*, Free Press, New York.

Le Vine, Robert A. (1973), 'Patterns of personality in Africa', *Ethos*, **1**.

Le Vine, Robert A. (1974), 'Parental goals: A cross-cultural view', *Teachers College Record*, **76**.

Lloyd, Barbara (1966), 'Education and family life in the development of class identification among the Yoruba', in P. C. Lloyd (1966).

Lloyd, P. C. (1966), *The New Elites of Tropical Africa*, Oxford University Press, London.

MacGregor, G. (1946), *Warriors without Weapons*, University of Chicago Press, Chicago.

Mahlobo, G. W. K., and Krige, E. J. (1934), 'Transition from childhood to adulthood among the Zulus', *Bantu Studies*, **8**.

Mair, L. P. (1934), 'The study of culture contact as a practical problem', *Africa*, **7**.

Malinowski, B. (1943), 'The pan-African problem of culture contact', *American Journal of Sociology*, **48**.

Malinowski, B. (1945), *The Dynamics of Culture Change*, Yale University Press, New Haven, Conn.

Maquet, J. J. (1964), 'Objectivity in anthropology', *Current Anthropology*, **5**.

Marris, Peter (1959), 'Social change and social class', *Listener*, 5 November.

Mead, M. (ed.) (1953), *Cultural Patterns and Technical Change*, New American Library, New York.

Mitchell, Clyde (1956), 'Labour migration and the tribe', *Listener*, 25 October.

Munroe, R. L., and Munroe, R. H. (1972), 'Obedience among children in an East African society', *Journal of Cross-Cultural Psychology*, **3**.

Musgrove, F. (1952), 'A Uganda secondary school as a field of culture change', *Africa*, **22**.

Musgrove, F. (1953), 'Education and the culture concept', *Africa*, **23**.

Musgrove, F. (1955), 'History teaching within a conflict of cultures', *History*, **140**.

Musgrove, F. (1977), *Margins of the Mind*, Methuen, London.

Nettl, J. P., and Robertson, R. (1966), 'Industrialization, development or modernization', *British Journal of Sociology*, **17**.

Oberg, Kalervo (1938), 'Kinship organization of the Banyankole', *Africa*, **11**.

Park, R. E. (1928), 'Human migration and the marginal man', *American Journal of Sociology*, **33**.

Park, R. E., and Burgess, E. W. (1925), *The City*, University of Chicago Press, Chicago.

Peristiany, J. G. (1954), 'Pokot sanctions and structure', *Africa*, **24**.

Raum, O. F. (1938), 'Some aspects of indigenous education among the Chaga', *Journal of the Royal Anthropological Institute*, **68**.

Read, Margaret (1936), 'Tradition and prestige among the Ngoni', *Africa*, **9**.

Read, Margaret (1938a), *Native Standards of Living and African Culture Change*, Oxford University Press, London.

Read, Margaret (1938b), 'The moral code of the Ngoni and their former military state', *Africa*, **11**.

Read, Margaret (1959), *Children of Their Fathers*, Methuen, London.

Rodney, Walter (1972), *How Europe Underdeveloped Africa*, Bogle-L'Ouverture, London.

Rostow, W. W. (1960), *The Stages of Economic Growth. A Non-Communist Manifesto*, Cambridge University Press, Cambridge.

Sprott, W. J. H. (1967), 'Society: What is it and how does it change?', in *The Educational Implications of Social and Economic Change*, The Schools Council Working Paper no. 12, HMSO, London.

Synge, P. M. (1938), *Mountains of the Moon*, Lindsay Drummond, London.

Westermann, Diedrich (1949), *The African Today and Tomorrow*, Oxford University Press, London.

White, C. M. N. (1953), 'Conservatism and modern adaptation in Luvale female puberty rites', *Africa*, **23**.

Wilson, Monica (1956), 'To whom do they pray?', *Listener*, 1 November.

Winter, Edmund H. (1955), *Bwamba Economy: The Development of a Primitive Subsistence Economy in Uganda*, Government Printer, Kampala.

Wirth, Louis (1938), 'Urbanism as a way of life', *American Journal of Sociology*, **76**.

# CHAPTER 6

# *Culture, Relativism, and the Curriculum*

An entirely admirable consequence of the sympathetic study of 'other cultures' has been this: that when working-class and black children go to school in England they may not be made to feel ashamed of their origins. Their social background, interests, customs, and even their speech are not always disregarded and disvalued by their teachers. Sometimes the school curriculum will be based in some degree upon these 'other cultures'. These liberal changes should not be overstated: they will not be found in all our schools and they probably do not apply to gypsies. Fifty-two per cent of teachers in multicultural schools a few years ago thought that the curriculum should include work on the culture of immigrant children—but 20 per cent firmly did not (Brittan, 1976). Upper-class and middle-class culture has been pushed just a little from its central place in the school curriculum.

These liberal developments have had unfortunate as well as admirable consequences. In 'multicultural' schools in England teaching about their culture may be a profound embarrassment to Indian and West Indian children, a form of 'exposure' which actually increases racial tension (Jeffcoate, 1981). But more importantly, when the school in England is based principally on the non-mainstream culture of its pupils (whether Sikhs in Bolton, Jews in Manchester, or dockland children in Liverpool) the effect is segregation (or even secession) and the child is effectively confined to the world in which he was born. Ironically, such 'relevant' curricula may be thought particularly appropriate for children who are not very clever or come from poor homes. This is a denial of the essential purpose of schools. The family, as T. S. Eliot (1948, p. 43) reminded us, transmits cultures; it is the job of schools to transcend them.

These well-meaning shifts towards 'relevance' are anthropologically inspired (Midwinter, 1972a). They often have an air of desperation. Compensatory, 'head start' programmes in the 1960s tried without much success to get children from other cultures and subcultures 'in'; anthropology now provides a justification for leaving them out.

Compensatory education aimed at what then seemed self-evident: assimilation. It offered middle-class 'enrichment' to make good cultural deficits. It is now said that these deficits are a myth: there are no deficits but only differences. The 'social pathology model' of educational backwardness misconceived the problem.

The term 'culture' is at the heart of the debate. Students of art and literature talk of culture; anthropologists talk of cultures. Culture (in the singular) is ab-

114

solutist, cultures (in the plural) are relativist. This concept of culture as developed by anthropologists has been extensively used by educational theorists and itself suggests a relativist approach to the curriculum. No culture is morally superior to others (although, of course, some are backed by more power). But this apparently liberal doctrine can in practice be highly offensive and deeply damaging. My students in Africa in the 1950s saw this quite clearly: to go to school to learn their own culture was not only an absurdity and an irrelevance; it reinforced their subjection. They got witchcraft and Lunyankole at home; the whole point of school was to get science and English and possibly Greek.

The argument of this chapter is quite simply this: that 'other cultures' are often worthy of respect and support, but everyone must acquire a mastery of mainstream culture. Personal dignity, social efficiency, and above all justice require nothing less.

## 1. THE CONCEPT OF CULTURE

A culture is the customs of a group of people. The culture of one group may include polygamy, female circumcision, and ancestor worship; of another pigeon racing, monogamy, and infant baptism. 'Culture' has been massively 'reified': it has been treated as a thing, separate from individuals but with power, influence, and even rights over them. It is outside people and does something to them—for instance makes them do well or badly at school or become delinquents. One of the instruments through which it is said to exercise power and influence is the school curriculum (Bourdieu, 1977).

A society is people, a culture is their customs which are usually highly interdependent and mutually supportive. They form a fairly coherent pattern. Customs usually entail rules and prohibitions and imply and embody values: thus the bride-price in Africa is often prescribed and rule-regulated and implies a high valuation of women (wives for whom no bride-price has been paid, for instance in a Christian marriage, may upbraid their husbands for holding them cheap). Social psychologists who study the influence of 'culture' on, say, academic attainment or delinquent activity, usually equate culture with values. They do not study their subjects' customs but the values to which they subscribe. (Lower-class 'short-term hedonism' has been a strong favourite.) There are problems in this (reductionist) methodology which are usually ignored. There are dangerous assumptions about the link between behaviour and values.

There has probably been no more popular concept than 'culture' in twentieth-century social science. It has been all-pervasive and has seemed to explain everything. The first textbooks on the sociology of education were written largely in terms of 'culture' (Waller, 1932; Ottaway, 1953). It once seemed to throw remarkable illumination on juvenile delinquency (Sprott, 1955; Cohen, 1955). In 1950 Stuart Chase referred to it as 'the foundation stone of the social sciences' (Chase, 1950, p. 67); David Kaplan was much more alive to its amorphous character but wrote in 1965: 'I think it is fair to say that most anthropologists, at least in the United States, look upon culture as their master concept' (Kaplan, 1965). Even its 'sponginess' was seen by some as making it 'enormously useful' (Gerth and Mills, 1954, p. xxii). Classes have sometimes been interpreted as cultures (Gordon, 1947–1948; Sugarman, 1970); and today Marxists have given the concept of culture a new lease of life by interpreting the behaviour of youth, for example, in terms of 'class cultures' (Mungham and Pearson, 1976, p. 24; Hall and Jefferson, 1976, p. 13).

It has been said that a great intellectual jump occurred when 'customs' came to be understood as 'culture' (Peattie, 1965). Certainly the study of 'culture' turned attention to systematic interconnections in social life. The first definition of culture in this all-embracing way was made more than a century ago by Edward B. Tylor in his book, *Primitive Culture*. (The fact that this title was not a contradiction in terms was an immense step forward.) Tylor wrote:

> Culture or Civilization, taken in its wide ethnographic sense, is that complex whole which includes knowledge, belief, art, morals, law, custom, and any other capabilities and habits acquired by man as a member of society (Tylor, 1871, p. 1)

Tylor's immense step forward did not quite take him to the neutral, non-normative idea of culture that prevails today. (He never used 'culture' in the plural.) He nowhere adopted the relativist position that no culture is better or worse than any other. He ordered and ranked societies with confidence. His intention, he said, was to show both the uniformities and stages of culture and he would give 'especial consideration to the civilization of the lower tribes as related to the civilization of the higher'. He claimed that few would dispute an ascending order from Australian Aborigines to Tahitians, Aztecs, Chinese, and Italians. But by arguing that savages had a real culture, albeit a lower one, he moved towards a concept of culture in the modern anthropological sense (Stocking, 1963).

The subjective aspects of cultures have been emphasized in recent years: anthropologists may approach them from the 'inside' and try to see them as their members see them, using the same categories of thought and perception. A culture may be described as members' constructed or negotiated 'meanings'. The utility of a culture—what it does and achieves—is played down (Sahlins, 1976); its symbolic nature—what it says—is given emphasis (Schneider, 1968). Culture has thus been in some measure divorced from biological and material needs: it is the symbolic order through which men impose meaning on the world. It is not a way of life but a code or system of messages: cultures are epistemic communities (Scholte, 1970).

These are the conceptual refinements of recent years. But the way in which 'culture' has been generally understood over the past century is more commonsensically, in the tradition of Tylor, as a way of life. It is not a superior (or inferior) way of life: 'It refers', as Ralph Linton (1947, p. 20) says, 'to the total way of life of a society', and not simply to the parts which may be regarded as 'higher':

This totality also includes such mundane activities as washing dishes or driving a motor-car, and for the purposes of cultural studies these stand quite on a par with 'the finer things of life'. . . . Every society has a culture, no matter how simple this culture may be, and every human being is cultured.

Clyde Kluckhohn said precisely the same: a culture was a total way of life of a people and 'Each specific culture constitutes a kind of blue-print for all of life's activities' (Kluckhohn, 1950, p. 23).

That is the difficulty: it means too much. It is easily merged with any other concept that has some reference to the collective life. It is certainly very close to Bagehot's 'cake of custom' and Sumner's 'folkways'; but it is sometimes seen as being virtually the same as Kuhn's 'paradigms', Popper's 'frameworks' and (notably in the early writing of Peter Winch) Wittgenstein's 'forms of life'—although Wittgenstein, for all his claim that 'the limits of my language are the limits of my world', was probably referring to what is typical and basic in human activities, what is transcultural rather than cultural (Hunter, 1968; Sherry, 1972). It has been conflated with Levy-Bruhl's 'collective representations' and also, with particular reference to education, with Durkheim's 'social facts' and Rousseau's 'General Will'. Its flexibility diminishes its usefulness but ensures its longevity.

British anthropologists with the notable exception of Malinowski have generally been very suspicious of it. American anthropologists have embraced it. Malinowski made extensive use of the notion of culture to refer to 'an instrumental reality, an apparatus for the satisfaction of fundamental needs . . .' (Malinowski, 1945, p. 44). Culture was all the social institutions and arrangements necessary for meeting primary biological and secondary social needs: again an all-embracing (and non-normative) idea which included all that is required to sustain a people's way of life.

Evans-Pritchard had scant regard for the concept of culture which he said was irrelevant to the work of social anthropologists (Evans-Pritchard, 1951, pp. 16–19, 92); Radcliffe-Brown was scathing about culture (and Malinowski). 'Culture', he said, was a vague abstraction and studies of 'culture contact' were 'simply a way of avoiding reality'. The reality was concrete and complex: it was not 'cultures' that interacted but 'individuals and groups within an established social structure which is itself in process of change' (Radcliffe-Brown, 1952, p. 202).

The inadequacies of the concept of culture are now manifest. What is remarkable is its resilience. It has some utility as a descriptive category, but very limited value as an explanatory concept or as a 'variable' in empirical analysis. Coleman (1961) in America and Lacey (1970) in England are among myriads of social scientists who have said it explains academic failure at school. They are wrong. Lacey did not bother to show that working-class children were in fact failing or that their 'culture' was linked to their performance; Coleman said that the adolescent culture depressed academic performance but found no evidence that this was generally so, although a weak connection was found in the small minority (6 per cent) of highest achievers—they might have done even better if they had attached more importance to getting good grades (Coleman, 1961, pp. 261–262). A replication of Coleman's study has refuted his cultural hypothesis (Kandel and Lesser, 1972). The work of Lacey and Coleman is still generally regarded as 'proof' that subcultures have a crucial effect on how well or badly children do at school.

Subcultures seemed to offer a nonpathological explanation of school failure and delinquency: the process of becoming a failure or a delinquent was not essentially different from joining the Boy Scouts. Albert K. Cohen's (1955) subcultural interpretation of delinquency excited attention some 30 years ago. It has been severely criticized for its argument that the delinquent subculture is a reaction to and an inversion of the dominant middle-class culture. Working-class boys do not much care about middle-class culture anyway (Kitsuse and Dietrick, 1959), and the starkness of the opposition is exaggerated (Matza, 1964, p. 37). Delinquency is normal and supports the social order, as Durkheim (1938, pp. 67–73) and others (Mack, 1964) have maintained. Delinquency, says Matza, is so precarious that it can only survive with subterranean support from the middle class. But none of the critics attacked the value of the culture concept itself. It has survived intact. As Cohen (1966, p. 108) has been pleased to point out: 'My interpretation of the meaning of delinquency has been severely criticized. However, the critics have not taken similar exception to the more general theory of subcultures, of which the explanation of delinquency is a special application.'

If we get back to the original notion of culture as customs we have a useful approach to social behaviour. The trouble has been that people's values (their culture) have been 'measured' in survey research, and these measures have been correlated with observed (or more usually self-reported) behaviour. The correlations are either zero, unimpressive, or fudged. This is so even in 'youth culture' research (Murdock and Phelps, 1972). Even 'measured' deferred gratification—allegedly central to the middle-class subculture—has a very weak connection with social class: 73 per cent of American middle-class children say they are in favour of saving, but so are the vast majority (68 per cent) of working-class children (Schneider and Lysgaard, 1953). One English study showed a higher proportion of working-class boys (72 per cent) than middle-class boys (63 per cent) in favour of saving, but Oppenheim (1955) insisted that his study supported the class and deferred-gratification thesis.

The concept of culture has become pretentious in theory and trivialized in practice. Yet there is little doubt that the local custom of playing billiards most nights at the Miners' Institute conflicts with the scholastic custom of spending two or three hours every night on homework; and that the working-class customs of relatively early and uxori-local marriage conflict with the requirements of a middle-class career. But it is less from its application in empirical research than from its theoretical elaboration that the concept of culture continues to influence education. Cultures are seen as tremendously powerful. But they do not only have might: they have right.

## 2. WHAT IS, OUGHT TO BE?

Culture has been given an enormous importance, independence, and autonomy as a distinct segment of reality. A long line of eminent American anthropologists have contributed to this end over a period of 60 years—including Kroeber, Lowie, Murdock, and Leslie White. The presentation of culture as a mighty, independent 'thing', external to individuals but impinging powerfully upon them, led Radcliffe-Brown (1957, p. 30) to protest that to 'say of culture patterns that they act upon an individual . . . is as absurd as to hold a quadratic equation capable of committing a murder'. Elsewhere he attacked the view that culture was something that did things to people (Radcliffe-Brown, 1949). Douglas Haring (1949) protested likewise: 'Culture never does anything to anyone.' But it is the exaggerated, reified notion of culture which they attacked that has given it an irresistible claim to representation in the school curriculum. Subcultures and 'other cultures' make exactly the same claim: they have full rights of representation, too.

Radcliffe-Brown was overreacting to the pretensions of culturologists. Culture certainly does something to people: it constrains them. As Clyde Kluckhohn (1950, p. 33) said: 'Culture regulates our lives at every turn. From the moment we are born until we die there is . . . constant pressure upon us to follow certain types of behaviour that other men have created for us.' In the simple sense that we are born into a family and neighbourhood with particular customs (including language) we are involved in these 'folkways' willy-nilly. (It was this constraining character of culture that Ruth Benedict passionately attacked in *Patterns of Culture*: she said it was neither necessary nor desirable.) But it is a highly reified, abstract, autonomous, and suprapersonal notion of culture that Radcliffe-Brown and Douglas Haring are contesting. It is this strong notion that has given all cultures and subcultures their powerful claim upon the educator's attention.

For more than half a century social scientists have been reacting to Kroeber's characterization of culture in 1917 as 'the superorganic'. They said he made culture (or civilization) into something mystical which was above the sum of individuals; and they contested his claim that it could not be explained in psychological terms.

Kroeber had made much of the fact that inventions and discoveries were commonly made independently but concurrently by a number of widely scattered individuals: 'Anaesthetics, both ether and nitrous oxide, were discovered in 1845 and 1846, by no less than four men in one country.' He concluded that there was 'a majestic order pervading civilization' and that the social was *sui generis*, not to be reduced to individuals' mental states. The 'social substance' was quite distinct from mind and body and 'transcends them utterly' (Kroeber, 1917).

Half a century of protest followed. Sapir (1917) attacked first. But this majestic, transcendental view of culture found powerful allies and was in any event scarcely distinguishable from what Durkheim had said about 'social facts' more than 20 years earlier. Kroeber's 'superorganic' was treated as simply another term for Durkheim's 'social facts'. But when Murdock wrote about 'the science of culture' in 1932, strongly supporting Kroeber's view, he made no mention of Durkheim although he appears at times to be merely paraphrasing his work. Like Durkheim he argued that culture was external to individuals and obligatory and could not be 'reduced' to psychological states:

> Moreover, the individual is not a free agent with respect to culture. He is born and reared in a certain cultural environment, which impinges upon him at every moment of his life. . . . He has no choice but to conform to the folkways current in his group. Culture is superindividual, also, in the fact that its constituent folkways have in every case a history of their own, a history of their origin and diffusion which is quite independent of the lives and qualities of individuals. (Murdock, 1932)

Durkheim in a famous dictum had said that every time a social phenomenon is directly explained by a psychological phenomenon we can be sure that it is false (Durkheim, 1938, p. 104). Likewise Murdock, who argued that psychology could not possibly explain the evolution of radio or the diffusion of the use of tobacco. Cultural phenomena, said Murdock, operated in a 'distinct realm' and 'The fact that culture is superindividual lifts it beyond the sphere of psychology'.

Murdock later recanted. He did so very publicly in the Huxley Memorial Lecture of 1971. He had already rebuked British anthropologists for their 'widespread indifference to psychology' in an earlier publication (Murdock, 1951); he now dismissed culture altogether as a 'reified abstraction' which could not explain human behaviour and made an impassioned plea for the use of psychology by social scientists (Murdock, 1971). But Leslie A. White has remained faithful to Kroeber (and Durkheim). He never tired of reprimanding Boas for failure to rise to the sublime vision of culture proposed by Kroeber (White, 1946). He approved of Lowie's (1936) contention that culture was a thing *sui generis* and explicitly linked Kroeber's 'superorganic' with Durkheim's social facts. 'Culture must be explained in terms of culture.' No psychologist could tell us why one people prohibits marriage between cousins and another requires it. 'The culturologist is well aware that culture does not and cannot exist without human beings. . . . But as the culturologist demonstrates, culture may be treated as if it had a life of its own' (White, 1947). Less polarized positions were later taken by American anthropologists (for example, Kaplan, 1965); but after 30 years under attack Kroeber felt vindicated: if culture were not 'really' external and autonomous we must certainly treat it as if it were (Kroeber, 1948).

Durkheim had talked of 'social facts' in two distinct senses: on the one hand, as customs, rules, and traditions (for instance religious and professional practices); on the other, as social 'currents'—in effect public opinion—which influenced rates of social participation as in marriage rates, divorce rates, birth rates, and suicide rates. Social facts in this second sense were none other than 'collective representations', the collective mind.

In both senses social facts were general in character, external to individuals, and coercive: they existed before the individual was born, they were ready-made for his use, they would be there after he was dead. They could not be explained in psychological terms because they existed outside and apart from individual minds. The system of currency was such a social fact; but the suicide rate was no less 'external', with 'the same objectivity and the same ascendancy over the individual'. Durkheim's social facts had the same majesty, potency, and irresistibility as Kroeber's 'superorganic':

> These types of conduct or thought are not only external to the individual but are, moreover, endowed with coercive power, by virtue of which they impose themselves upon him, independent of his individual will. (Durkheim, 1938, p. 2)

It is curious that British anthropologists have been enormously influenced by Durkheim's nonpsychological notion of 'social facts' (Evans-Pritchard, 1951, pp. 52–53; Needham, 1962, pp. 50, 126) and yet have been hostile to the concept of culture from which it is virtually indistinguishable. Fred Clarke treated them as equivalent in a series of highly influential publications in the 1930s and 1940s. His concern was the school curriculum in England (and in Wales). On the authority of the culture concept, powerfully reinforced with Durkheim's concept of social facts (conflated with Rousseau's concept of the General Will), Clark argued that whatever is must be.

He did not phrase it precisely like that; and he was careful to leave himself a loophole (in the shape of individual conscience). But 'One cannot be genuinely human unless one has become the bearer of a culture' (Clark, 1948, p. 29) and education in its widest sense must produce 'a determinate citizen type' (Clarke, 1948, p. 9), for 'whatever else education may mean, it must mean primarily the self-perpetuation of an accepted culture—a culture which is the life of a determinate society' (Clarke, 1936, p. 249).

A philosopher of education has argued recently (in a discussion of the problem of cultural relativism and the curriculum) that 'it is not a legitimate purpose of general education to confirm anyone in a particular way of life' (Walkling, 1980). This is precisely the opposite view to that which Clarke consistently maintained. 'It is the first business of education', Clarke asserted, 'to induce conformity in terms of the culture in which the child will grow up.' This was not only right but inevitable: it was useless to complain of 'indoctrination': 'A child cannot even learn his mother-tongue without being indoctrinated' (Clarke, 1948, p. 29). And learning his mother-tongue—calling an animal 'dog' rather than 'chien' or 'hund'—was a matter of external authority and in no way a matter of personal choice (Clarke, 1936, p. 263).

Clarke was the chairman of the advisory committee which produced a report entitled *The Curriculum and the Community in Wales* (Welsh Department, 1952). The results are entirely predictable. 'All education', we are assured, 'implies community and some degree of conformity.' The Welsh grammar school is severely rebuked for 'driving a wedge between curriculum and community, between school and life'. Since most Welsh people would henceforth probably remain in Wales, there was no longer any need 'to impair the cultural integrity of Welsh grammar school education'. The curriculum of all schools should fully reflect the Welsh culture. This applied especially to the new secondary modern schools since 'the vast majority' of their pupils 'will spend their lives in Wales'.

A culture was in the first place no more than a set of customs. It has gained in importance: it has now acquired rights. One theorist of multicultural education has recently regretted the outcome: 'Cultural autonomy, seen as a fundamental human right, can be used to sustain a conception of static cultures and constant minority group membership' (McLean, 1980).

Nowell-Smith (1971) said this doctrine was pernicious. It undermined both wisdom and courage. It implied that 'individuals ought always to do what the mores of their society dictate'. What is, ought to be. This was cultural relativism—a highly confused doctrine based on 'certain logical errors generated by semantic ambiguities'. But it was not merely highly confused; it was thoroughly immoral.

And it is utterly impracticable, for it is preposterous to say that a culture *qua* culture qualifies for a place in the school curriculum. There is not only a Muslim culture in Britain, there is a drug culture; there is not only a West Indian culture, there is a delinquent culture; there is not only a lower-working class culture, there is a homosexual culture. There are youth cultures, street cultures, regional cultures, religious cultures. Some say there is a 'culture of poverty' and there may be distinctive 'age cultures', too.

It is, perhaps, 'whole' cultures rather than subcultures that have rights: cultures with a linguistic base and at least a latent claim to political recognition? This has never been explicitly stated, and it would exclude the working class and English Catholics in spite of the distinctive 'linguistic code' of the former and the history of oppression and sacrifice of both. But it would include the gypsies and Jews in Britain, also Sikhs, Muslims, West Indians, and Hindus as well as the Welsh. Steven Lukes (1981) says cultures have rights *qua* cultures and instances the Kurds in Turkey, Iraq, and Iran: 'they have rights to cultural survival and genuine autonomy'. But whether we are talking about whole cultures or subcultures, the problem of relative merits remains. Lukes does not say the Kurdish culture should be preserved because it has value but because it exists.

## 3. THE REPUGNANCE OF RELATIVISM

If you say that one culture is better than another you will nowadays be attacked for being racist or at best ethnocentric. The proposition that no culture is better than another is cultural relativism. It is the basis of most contemporary discussion of the multicultural curriculum.

The anthropological concept of culture invites relativism although it does not require it. It is a neutral term, non-evaluative, non-judgemental: it does not contain within itself any basis for ranking one culture higher or lower, more valuable or less worthwhile, than another. But that does not preclude the ordering of cultures by some external standard or measuring rod. The search for such external standards is difficult and their validation perhaps logically impossible. But to deny the possibility of valuing one culture over another is morally repugnant.

Whatever the problems in logic, it is impossible to rate the culture of Nazi Germany above, or equal to, the culture of Periclean Athens; or the culture of Spain at the height of the Inquisition the equal of even Edwardian England. I may rate an oriental despot neither better nor worse than a constitutional monarch: he is the product of his society and should be seen in context; but I cannot rate oriental despotism as the equal of Western democracy. A Batoro witchdoctor may be neither 'better' nor 'worse' than a Western scientist; but witchcraft, even in context, is inferior to science.

The experience of Nazi Germany dealt a severe blow to cultural relativism—from which it has now completely recovered. But English and American anthropologists who were alive and involved in the Second World War were cured of any serious inclination to cultural relativism. Morris Ginsberg's Huxley Memorial Lecture of 1953 opened with a reference to Nazi atrocities: he challenged relativists to say 'whether it can really be the case that there is no rational way of deciding between the ethics of a Roosevelt and the ethics of Hitler'. He suggested various criteria for judging a culture, like the degree to which it permits self-criticism; and he claimed that there are 'unmistakable differences of level'; but he found no logical basis for differentiation, merely asserting that 'it is the higher that decides that they are higher. But this I fear cannot be helped' (Ginsberg, 1953). He has been suitably taken to task for saying so (Hanson, 1975, p. 31). Ginsberg's case is not really based on logic but on a gut reaction against denying any difference between goodness and evil.

Relativism has come more easily to a younger generation of sociologists and anthropologists with fainter memories, if any, of Hitler's Germany. For Robert Redfield, also writing in 1953, the memories were still fresh:

> It was easy to look with equal benevolence upon all sorts of value systems so long as the values were those of unimportant little people remote from our own concerns. But the equal benevolence is harder to maintain when one is asked to anthropologize the Nazis. (Redfield, 1953, p. 146)

Relativism is also repugnant because it negates the idea of progress: one culture cannot be valued against another or against itself at a different point in time. And yet, as Gellner (1968) points out, cultures are constantly doing what in relativist theory is impossible: judging, valuing, and perhaps repudiating their former selves. This is a learning process in which modern societies with their developed historical sense and exact historical scholarship are constantly engaged. Modern England has judged and repudiated its sixteenth-century belief in witchcraft and the Divine Right of Kings. Whole societies come to the conclusion that what they formerly believed was based on error. In its strongest form, the doctrine of relativism says that no external judgement can be made of a society's beliefs. In fact societies commonly judge their former selves, change their behaviour accordingly, and make what can properly be called progress. Their new selves are not simply different; they are superior.

Even Thomas Kuhn conceded that later science was superior to earlier science, that scientific advance was unidirectional and irreversible. Just as cultural relativists emphasize the difficulty, perhaps the impropriety, and even the impossibility of comparing cultures, so Kuhn talked of the 'incommensurability' of scientific 'paradigms' (Kuhn, 1962, p. 103). Nevertheless, he was clear that one scientific theory and framwork of assumptions and ideas was not as good as any other: later ones were better. Kuhn was very sensitive to the charge of relativism and its implicit negation of the idea of progress. 'In that sense', said Kuhn, 'I am not a relativist' (Kuhn, 1970, p. 264).

But the basis of Gellner's case against relativism, like Ginsberg's, is not logical argument but moral outrage:

> It is intuitively repellent to pretend that the Zande belief in witchcraft is as valid as our rejection of it, and to suppose it such is a philosophical affectation which cannot be maintained outside the study. (Gellner, 1968)

## 4. THE IMPORTANCE OF KUHN AND WINCH

The case of relativism received an enormous boost between 1958 and 1964. Relativism, always implicit in Tylor's concept of culture, had hitherto been mainly ethical or moral relativism; a much stronger form now found powerful advocates: epistemological relativism. It was not only morals and customs that could not be compared: it was ways of thinking and forms of belief.

In 1958 Winch published his book, *The idea of a Social Science*; in 1962 Kuhn published *The Structure of Scientific Revolutions*, and in 1964 Winch published a famous paper called 'Understanding a primitive society' in the *American Philosophical Quarterly*. I have discussed these publications elsewhere and referred to the books as 'the two key books of our generation' (Musgrove, 1978b).

They have had enormous influence. It is not only morals that may be 'relative', to be judged, if at all, in context; but rationality, logic, and science itself are apparently relative, too. They must be seen from the 'inside' and understood as their practitioners understand them. But the difficulty with a form of rationality or logic that is different from one's own is how to understand it at all.

Epistemological relativism leads to the conclusion that magic in its own particular context is as good as physics and just as intellectually unassailable. 'Judged from the standpoint of sociology no behaviour is, properly speaking, irrational', says one supporter of this 'inside', *Verstehen* position. He goes on: 'The term "magic" is best expunged from our sociological vocabulary altogether' (Peel, 1969). Enclosed in one's own logic and rationality the upshot is collective solipsism; and cognitive sovereignty is conferred on every tiny parish in the world of the mind.

The criteria of logic, maintained Winch, were 'not a direct gift of God' and were only intelligible in the context of particular 'ways of living and modes of social life' (Winch, 1958, p. 100). He recognized that Evans-Pritchard had been at unusual pains to take an 'inside' view of Zande sorcery, but took him severely to task for concluding nevertheless that Zande beliefs were mistaken. Evans-Pritchard had imposed irrelevant European criteria on Zande thought. 'What we are concerned with are different criteria of rationality' (Winch, 1964). It was not the Zande who were guilty of misunderstanding, but Evans-Pritchard: 'The European is in fact committing a category-mistake.'

Kuhn's studies in the history of Western science lead to a broadly similar view: but what are incommensurable in this case are not cultures but 'paradigms'. For Karl Popper science was judged from the 'outside', by eternal standards of logic, by the repeatability or falsifiability of results, the assembling of evidence to support or reject hypotheses; for Kuhn science was judged from the 'inside', in terms of the taken-for-granted rules and assumptions that prevailed at a particular time—within the currently accepted 'paradigm'.

Kuhn saw marked discontinuities in scientific advance which was apparently not orderly, logical, and cumulative, but extra-scientific, even extra-rational, proceeding through a form of conversion, a new revelation which led to a 'paradigm-shift'. Such shifts—as from Newton's to Einstein's physics—occurred every two or three hundred years and arose from revolutions which were almost mystical in character and not governed by rules of reason. Kuhn's interpretation of science furthers the cause of relativism in two distinct ways: by emphasizing the gulf between paradigms which makes them virtually incomprehensible to one another; and by underscoring the irrational aspects of Western science which greatly weakens its claim to superiority over primitive beliefs.

Both Kuhn and Winch have been criticized for erecting self-enclosed worlds (which Popper referred to as 'frameworks') which are non-comparable and incapable of understanding one another. Both said that understanding from the outside was not actually impossible but very difficult. Winch (1964) said that we could extend our understanding 'to make room for' primitive categories of thought. Hollis (1972) is not alone in finding this method unconvincing: 'Winch's idea that we can add their concept of intelligibility to ours and so form a new concept of intelligibility is misguided. The only new concept of intelligibility which could result in this way is a contradiction.'

126

There are precisely similar difficulties with Kuhn. He had argued that what emerged from a scientific revolution 'is not only incompatible but often actually incommensurable with what has gone before' (Kuhn, 1962, p. 103). Popper attacked the 'myth of the framework' which he claimed was a logical and philosophical mistake and said that Kuhn was exaggerating a difficulty into an impossibility. He maintained that Kuhn's logic was mistaken and that 'the relativistic thesis that the framework cannot be critically discussed . . . does not stand up to criticism'. The different frameworks were not mutually untranslatable languages. It was difficult for people brought up in different frameworks to communicate, 'But nothing is more fruitful than such a discussion; than the culture clash which has stimulated some of the greatest intellectual revolutions' (Popper, 1970, p. 57).

Kuhn replied to his critics. He said that he did not really feel like a relativist and conceded that later scientific paradigms were better than earlier ones; but as between historical pairs, he insisted, there was no basis for saying that one was nearer the truth. He continued to emphasize the difficulty of one paradigm understanding another—for instance the conception (and classification) of chemical substances before and after Dalton; he allowed the possibility of 'translating' the other's theory into one's own language, but to the end this process had the character of religious conversion: 'That sort of change is, however'—he said quite explicitly—'conversion, and the techniques which induce it might well be described as therapeutic, if only because, when they succeed, one learns one had been sick before' (Kuhn, 1970, p. 277).

## 5. TRANSCENDENTAL YARDSTICKS

The anti-relativists have sought transcendental criteria and yardsticks against which all cultures (paradigms, frameworks, and forms of life) could be measured, valued, and placed in order. When he wrote his book *Civilization* in the 1920s Clive Bell's measure was 'good states of mind'. His book was a scathing attack on anthropologically inspired relativism. He used Westermarck's extensive anthropological data (as published in his *Origin and Development of Moral Ideas*) to attack Westermarck's relativist position. He placed fifth-century Athens, Renaissance Italy, and eighteenth-century France before the Revolution at the top of his hierarchy of civilizations. His measuring stick—as arbitrary, in the last analysis, as any other—was taken (without acknowledgement) from the Cambridge philosopher, G. E. Moore, whose work—especially his *Principia Ethica*—greatly influenced all the 'Bloomsbury Group'. Of highest value were things and activities which were good in themselves, valued for their own sake, and not for their possible utility. The only good things as ends were good states of mind. Civilizations could be ranked according to the weight they placed on things which were good in themselves (Bell, 1938). African societies came at the bottom.

From the late 1920s, as Freud's work became more widely known, psychoanalytical theory seemed to offer the possibility of transcultural criteria for evaluating whole societies. Freud himself discussed the possibility and recognized the difficulties: neurotic individuals were judged against a normal background, but what was a normal background for judging a civilization? (Freud, 1953, p. 142).

Others have been undeterred by such problems. Freeman (1965) says that the anus-plugging ritual in the initiation of Chaga men would be neurotic and perhaps psychotic in any culture. It is based on serious misperceptions of reality. Accurate perception of the real world, argues Freeman, is necessary for mental health and provides 'an empirical scientific principle . . . which enables those who employ it to transcend the doctrine of cultural relativism'. Obeyesekere (1966) has no difficulty in exposing Freeman's error: culture itself so influences perception that while intra-cultural comparisons are perfectly in order, inter-cultural comparisons are not.

Ruth Benedict was a passionate anti-relativist whose transcultural standards were drawn from psychiatry. It is curious that the famous book which she published in 1934, *Patterns of Culture*, is commonly seen, even by sophisticated anthropologists, as the testament of cultural relativism (Jarvie, 1975). It is not—although it concludes by using the great diversity of cultures as an argument for reducing the pressures of any one of them on its members.

It is individuals that Ruth Benedict is reluctant to judge (or constrain), not cultures: indeed, her judgement of the Puritan culture of eighteenth-century New England (and of twentieth-century business-class America) is savage and uncompromising. The Puritan divines of New England had a sense of guilt which 'is found in a slightly saner society only in institutions for mental diseases'. Their context does not excuse them. 'From the point of view of a comparative psychiatry they fall in the category of the abnormal' (Benedict, 1961, p. 199). Most, perhaps all, cultures were so uncertain of themselves that they placed undue pressure on individuals to conform: 'Tradition is as neurotic as any patient: its overgrown fear of deviation from its fortuitous standards conforms to all the usual definitions of the psychopathic' (Benedict, 1961, p. 196).

But Ruth Benedict had not surmounted the problem that Freud had already pointed out. Like many another she had plucked her measuring rod from the fashionable intellectual tools to hand. It is as arbitrary as any other. The reaching out for transcultural criteria goes on. Winch himself, who (like Kuhn) denies that he is a relativist, pursues universals. He has endorsed T. S. Eliot's trinity of birth, copulation, and death: 'the very notion of human life is limited by these conceptions' (Winch, 1964). He has also postulated the 'norm of truth-telling' as an absolute, inescapable from a society's language: it is not a convention, like a rule of the road, which a society chooses to adopt or reject (Winch, 1960). Birth, copulation, death, and the norm of truth telling are universal facts. It is not clear in what way they are or can be standards.

In the field of epistemology the anti-relativist case should be easier. Steven Lukes (1967) argues plausibly that there is at least one transcultural criterion of rationality—the law of non-contradiction. But even the staunchest of anti-relativists has to admit that we are 'not yet in possession of a clear and rationally defensible alternative to relativism' (Jarvie, 1975). Gellner argues not from logic but from 'the real world', which simply does not have 'those self-contained units which could be their own standards of intelligibility and reality (and everything else)'. Some consideration of the world as it really is, which Winch always contrives to avoid, offers—and Gellner puts it no higher than this—'a kind of solution' (Gellner, 1968).

The paradigm or culture to which Gellner refers and which he accords undoubted supremacy over all others is 'the scientific-industrial form of life'. If a doctrine conflicts with this superiority, 'then it really is out'. Gellner's case rests on the self-evident cognitive superiority of modern scientific-industrial societies. This cognitive superiority does not necessarily mean superiority in other spheres of life, but it will tend to do so. It will usually help to increase a society's wealth which in turn has a long-run effect of reducing inequality. There is probably simply more human decency around. (It is, moreover, the only culture that castigates itself for being ethnocentric and indulges in cultural relativism.) Gellner's position is not logically unassailable; but it fits in with my own experience of working at 'cognitive development' in a developing country and it is the position I hold:

> The philosophical significance of the scientific-industrial 'form of life', whose rapid global diffusion is the main event of our time, is that for all practical purposes it does provide us with a solution of the problem of relativism—though a highly unsymmetrical one. (Gellner, 1968)

Gellner doubts whether the problem of relativism has a formal solution; but the technical and cognitive effectiveness of scientific-industrial civilization makes its basic characteristics not really optional. And there is no doubt that its sheer efficiency in explaining cause and effect puts it far ahead of any other culture, and to pretend otherwise is condescension of the worst kind: universal benevolence which relaxes standards of judgement for people different from ourselves.

## 6. THE CURRICULUM AND ETHNIC MINORITIES IN CONTEMPORARY BRITAIN

But I would not argue for a wholly assimilationist educational policy in a multicultural society. The business of the school is not to transmit any group's culture intact; but if it is to engage the minds and imaginations of its pupils it will at least start from where they are. And 'where they are' is where much that was formerly self-evident and taken for granted in their lives is now at least implicitly challenged and made problematical. It is where culture contact and conflict raise questions which nobody had before thought to ask. But on the question of Western mathematics (as opposed, say, to 'oral', memory-based computation) and Western science (as opposed, say, to African witchcraft) there is simply no issue at all. The school must be blatantly, straightforwardly, and assertively 'assimilationist'.

The ideas of cultural relativism have been applied systematically to the school curriculum since 1970. In that year Stephen and Joan Baratz (1970) published a highly influential article on the subject in the *Harvard Educational Review*. Three years later Nell Keddie (1973) edited a widely read and often reprinted collection of 'relativist' papers in *Tinker, Tailor . . . The Myth of Cultural Deprivation*. The Open University made such views widely available to teachers in the 1970s in a number of publications on the sociology of education (Cosin *et al.*, 1977; Giles and Woolfe, 1977). The basic proposition is that differences are not deficits. But the great power of the white middle class, it is said, has enabled them to define cultural differences as deficits because their culture is the yardstick of success.

Relativism in the curriculum was a reaction against the disappointing results of 'Headstart' programmes and 'compensatory education' in the 1960s. An opposite reaction to the same record of failure is associated with the name of Arthur Jensen (1969). Jensen said that the children in question were stupid; the relativists said they had remarkable but generally unrecognized powers.

The relativists argued that the problem of cultural deprivation and educational backwardness had been misconceived. It was because social scientists used a 'social pathology model' that they defined differences as deficiencies. But apparently inferior and defective cultures like the North American Negro culture had great strengths which linguists in particular were now making clear: 'the social pathology model', said Stephen and Joan Baratz, 'has led social science to establish programs to prevent deficits which simply are not there'.

They argued for a proper recognition of these other cultures in the school curriculum; but their final recommendations—as Edwards and Hargreaves (1977) point out—are virtually identical with those of 'deficit theorists'. Their aim is not to keep Negroes 'out' in a (revalued) culture of their own, but to get them effectively 'in'. For this to happen—as Edwards and Hargreaves also point out—Negroes may need to learn skills which enable them to become effective members: 'No judgment need be made as to the "superiority" of the other group.' In any event, Stephen and Joan Baratz are clear that North American Negroes must be brought into mainstream culture, but unlike deficit theorists they do not tell us how to do it. They say that first we must have a great research programme to discover how Negroes are different (but not pathological):

> Then and only then can programs be created that utilize the child's differences as a means of furthering his acculturation to the mainstream while maintaining his individual identity and cultural heritage.

This is unexceptionable. Clearly it is a pluralist rather than an assimilationist solution, but the mainstream Western culture stands at its centre; and it is based on a recognition of differences and their utilization and not their denial. That is precisely the recommendation of this book.

Modern Britain, it is now widely argued, is a multicultural society and cultural diversity should be reflected in the school curriculum and valued by teachers: 'Underpinning the prescriptive force of this general position is cultural relativism' (Zec, 1980). But a thorough-going relativism which says that one culture is just as good as another leads finally to a 'well-intentioned apartheid' (Zec, 1980) and a denial of any real value in 'other cultures' at all: 'Respect for other cultures is only possible for a non-relativist; for some-one who from where he stands sees something in another culture and values it' (Zec, 1980).

Less strong and coherent forms of relativism in fact influence the present-day curriculum. A generally benevolent attitude to minority cultures leads to an attempt to enhance the black child's 'self-concept': in other words, schools must give the members of minority cultures a proper pride in themselves and their 'inheritance'. This will also help them to do well in their school studies. There is no evidence that multicultural school curricula have either consequence; what evidence we have rather suggests the opposite. I am not arguing that minority cultures should find no place in the curriculum: on the contrary, they should be firmly in place. It is the way we relate minority and mainstream cultures to each other in the curriculum and the child's experience that is at the heart of the educational and social problem. It is within an unending dialectic of integration–particularism that an answer lies.

At one extreme, our schools may attempt to assimilate other cultures to the English way of life; at the other, they may in practice perpetuate other cultures, sustaining their separateness and even their isolation. Cultural relativism, it is convincingly argued, tends to lead to the latter, encouraging teachers to transmit cultures rather than to transform them. 'Transmissionism' is the handing on of whatever exists and it is likely to 'produce people armed against cross-cultural sympathy and tolerance' (Walkling, 1980). 'Transformationism', on the other hand, encourages a critical awareness of one's own culture and its competitors. Cultural relativism and the 'transmissionism' it supports have been seen as a major threat to a truly multicultural society: 'Extreme relativism or transmissionism in a curriculum implies a sort of cultural protectionism' (Walkling, 1980).

In practice, even to relativists all minority cultures are not equally relative. West Indian, Hindu, and Muslim cultures may be worthy of transmission through the school curriculum; but gypsy culture is not. Some local education authorities have established gypsy schools to prepare children for 'normal', mainstream schools. (Walsall was notable for its development of gypsy schools in the early 1970s.) The schools have been staffed by volunteer teachers who are sympathetic to the 'gypsy problem', but their aim has been to make gypsies 'normal'. The schools are bridges to normal society, although in the event very few gypsy children appear to cross them—principally because normal schools do not, after all, actually want them and they can be excluded with a clear conscience because they have 'schools of their own' (Worrall, 1977).

The outcome is neither assimilation nor the perpetuation of a distinctive culture but the creation of a somewhat demoralized subproletariat. The gypsy schools that were conceived as preparatory tend in practice to be terminal. At least one student of these schools deplores the initial attempt at assimilation as much as the eventual failure to achieve it (Worrall, 1977). And yet it is difficult to see what a 'truly' gypsy education would be, which respected and nourished the traditional culture. The main ingredients of 'gypsy culture' are three: a migratory way of life; self-employment; and criteria of cleanliness somewhat different from our own. Modern urban-industrial civilization requires people who are sedentary, employees, and clean. A curriculum for gypsies might conceivably aim at producing efficient nomadic entrepreneurs. Cultural relativists have nowhere proposed it.

The cultures of Hindus, Muslims, and even West Indians are perhaps more easily identified and catered for in the school curriculum. They have history, music, art and crafts, a cuisine, religious beliefs and practices, perhaps dance and personal dress and adornment which readily furnish curricular materials. Strenuous and often imaginative efforts have sometimes been made to introduce such elements into a new multicultural curriculum.

The separatist potential of these curricula is not as a rule fully realized for the simple reason that the curricula do not work: the West Indians resist or are simply bored (the African past, even the Caribbean past, is not in any strong sense 'their' culture); and for Hindus and Muslims it is really an irrelevance if not an impertinence—they get their traditional culture more authentically at home: it has not been 'got up' by an alien with a weak grasp of what it is really about. The real separatist—even secessionist—curricula are what Muslims increasingly provide for themselves in private schools.

Much has been made of the salvationist Rastafarian movement as an expression of the separatist culture of the West Indian in Britain and his quest for a distinctive identity. All brethren are reincarnations of ancestral slaves who thus maintain their position on the fringes of society without any sense of cultural loss (Hebdige, 1976, p. 152). In fact, the strong resentment of West Indians against English schools has not been because they were deprived of their traditional culture but because they were given it. The only way they could gain the effective access to English culture which they wanted was by setting up private Saturday, community schools of their own. Whereas Muslims set up private schools to stay out, West Indians set them up to get in.

Maureen Stone, herself a West Indian (who received her university education in India), has given us an excellent and technically expert study of West Indians' experience of English schools (Stone, 1981). Some children attended schools with specially designed multicultural curricula; others did not. Some attended 'hard-grind' Saturday schools which West Indian communities in London have established for themselves to provide instruction in basic skills of literacy and numeracy. The children attending the 'enriched', culturally adapted schools—which taught Caribbean history, literature, art, and music—were actually more hostile to school and to teachers than the children who attended the 'no frills' Saturday schools:

It is interesting that in spite of the suggestion that community groups encourage anti-school feelings, it is in fact the MRE [Multi-racial Education] group which shows the greatest amount of negative feelings and supplies the largest number of children who can find nothing to like about school. (Stone, 1981, p. 217)

West Indian children in Britain generally know very little about their background in the Caribbean (and further back still in Africa). It is therefore recommended by some that they be taught 'Black Studies' so that they will learn to be 'secure in and magnanimously proud of their cultural heritage' (Bagley and Coard, 1975). This will make them more involved in school learning and improve their self-concepts. Maureen Stone found no evidence that it did either. Children who were involved in MRE projects had no higher self-evaluation than those who were not (Stone, 1981, p. 231).

The West Indians in Britain want schools which will teach them marketable skills so that they can effectively join and hold their own in the host society. When they get Black Studies instead, and schools which turn in on the West Indian community, they set up their own weekend schools. Maureen Stone is deeply contemptuous of 'the romantic ideal of "community" which relates back to the Cambridge [village] colleges of the 1930s' (Stone, 1981, p. 237). West Indians do not want schools to relate them to their communities: they want schools to get them out. Culturally relevant curricula are profoundly irrelevant curricula: 'Saturday schools were necessary because weekday schools were shortchanging the kids' (Stone, 1981, p. 174).

The culturally adapted school is for teachers: it makes them feel good. They are liberal and progressive and doing something for blacks. In fact, their posture is often offensively patronizing. Maureen Stone is deeply contemptuous of steel bands and emphasis on 'relationships' at the expense of literacy:

> I want to suggest that MRE is conceptually unsound, that its theoretical and practical implications have not been worked out . . . while at the same time creating for teachers, both radical and liberal, the illusion that they are doing something special for a particularly disadvantaged group. (Stone, 1981, p. 100)

'All pupils', says Robert Jeffcoate (1976) 'should know the history and achievements of their own culture and what is distinctive about it.' But he reproves Muslim families for sending their children for after-school Koranic instruction and an uncritical exposition of Islamic culture. He is opposed to culturally adapted curricula which fossilize minority cultures: he approves of the transformational role of schools. And he knows that basing the curriculum on the culture of an ethnic minority can be very counterproductive: his experience as a Schools Council research officer in multicultural schools led him to the conclusion that such experiments could antagonize white children while 'embarrassing or upsetting the minority children whose culture was suddenly experiencing such public exposure' (Jeffcoate, 1981).

In any event, a project on Indian history and culture simply bypassed the world that the Sikh pupils were actually in. Jeffcoate agrees with those teachers who criticized the project leader because she 'seemed to have taken no account of Indian migration into Britain, the transformation of the borough into a multicultural community, the new evolving forms of British–Indian culture, nor, above all, what her white pupils knew and felt about all three' (Jeffcoate, 1981). She had disregarded the significant social world of her pupils, both black and white—what Malinowski would have called the 'third cultural reality'.

In Bradford the Muslims take what instrumental knowledge and skills they can get from English schools, but after ten years of schooling they are even more certain than when they began that theirs is a superior culture. They do not need a specially oriented or culturally adapted school curriculum to bolster their self-esteem or to reinforce an already overweening ethnocentrism. As they become richer the Muslims establish their own private schools (for instance in Bolton) so that their culture may remain inviolate. Equal rights and respect for all cultures is socially divisive and deeply destructive.

The Muslims in Bradford are not 'in between cultures', say Kitwood and Borrill (1980): they are firmly and unequivocally embedded in their own. There is a great and unbridged culture gap between the religious, group-oriented Muslim culture and the secular, individualistic culture of the host society. The Muslims are deeply contemptuous of the moral laxity of the English (and their failure to protect and segregate young girls). The introduction of Asian culture into the curriculum they see as absurd, although it might have some value in informing the unenlightened English.

Kitwood and Borrill concluded from their research in Bradford that the main effect of schooling for young Asians was 'not to facilitate general "social mixing" but to promote their solidarity'. Their contempt for Englishmen simply increased. Schooling enabled them to make close comparisons between British culture and their own: 'Their conclusion is that the latter is essentially superior.' They have no intention of being assimilated. Family and religion support them in their resistance to modernity. They remain wholly untouched by the outlook of cultural relativism.

## 7. THE DIALECTIC OF INTEGRATION–PARTICULARISM

One of the jobs of schooling is to open windows onto wider worlds. The culture concept closes them. There has often been a spirited and surprisingly successful opposition to the application of the culture concept to the school curriculum in many of the 'other cultures' of this book. They have refused to be confirmed by schooling in their traditional identities. Their culture has relevance in the curriculum only at its points of maximum tension with modernity. It is from this dialectical relationship of cultures in contact and conflict that a new synthesis, a third cultural reality, is built.

Successful resistance to 'cultural adaptations' is surprising because the adaptations were called for by the ruling class: and the ruling class was defeated. Thus from 1930 to 1950, officers of the Sudan Education Service tried systematically to keep education and teacher training at their experimental base at Bakht er Ruda close to the soil and traditional village life. After 20 years of determined effort they had failed. Their students insisted on receiving an academic education and opening a window on the West.

The new educational complex was established at Bakht er Ruda precisely because it was distant from Khartoum and an urban and Western way of life. European teachers—officers in the Sudan Education Service—were determined to abate the academic zeal of their pupils: their aim was 'to discover ways of diverting the interest of our pupils from academic learning to the practical affairs of rural life, giving them some knowledge and skill in rural pursuits and inspiring them with a spirit of service to the village community' (Griffiths, 1953, p. 15).

The pupils steadfastly resisted: they wanted studies which were abstract, literary, and non-applied and which looked out from the confines of village life to a wider world. 'Why were we not succeeding?' lamented the senior colonial education officer. His answer was this:

> In so far as education was not looked on as a means of qualifying for a job, it was thought of as literary, and leading to a knowledge of the great literary and religious heritage of the Arabs and a turning towards a knowledge of the modern world. (Griffiths, 1953, p. 22)

It was a matter for profound regret that 'To turn inwards to one's own rural environment' was unacceptable. The only 'applied' subject that succeeded was art, and this was precisely because there was no tradition of artistic achievement in the native culture to tie it to: 'He [the art teacher] made no attempt to restrict artistic activity to inadequate local tradition. He linked the students' efforts with European as well as Islamic art.'

A policy of 'cultural adaptation' in African schools had been recommended since the early 1920s when the influential Phelps-Stokes reports on West and East African education were published (Jones, 1922 and 1925). These were not everywhere approved and adopted by colonial governments, but their influence was powerful and pervasive. The inquiries were proposed not by the Colonial Office or individual colonial governments but by the American Baptist Foreign Missionary Society, and were financed by the American Phelps-Stokes Fund.

The American influence was singularly unfortunate: what had been done for North American Negroes was thought to be broadly suitable for tribal Africans. Philip Foster observes in his authoritative study of African education: 'it is clear that their recommendations were based on the wholesale transfer of concepts and practices developed with respect to Negro education in the southern United States' (Foster, 1965, p. 157). The culture concept was invoked throughout the reports and the key recommendation was 'cultural adaptation'.

Foster considers these reports deeply reactionary although they 'have been frequently seen as extraordinarily progressive documents' (Foster, 1965, p. 162). A decade earlier I had queried on social and educational grounds the heavily 'applied' and 'relevant' curricula that these reports recommended. Even arithmetic had to be made socially and morally meaningful and should be concerned not only with problems of hygiene and biology but 'with the volume of beer drunk and the computation of hours spent in moonlight orgies and dancing—with which the Commission showed a singular preoccupation' (Musgrove, 1952).

In the Gold Coast especially, official policy in the 1920s and 1930s was based on the Phelps-Stokes report. It was ineffective. Africans at all levels refused to accept it. In the Legislative Council in the 1930s 'it was recognized that African indifference to such forms of education was the principal obstacle' (Foster, 1965, p. 150). The Legislative Council did not simply recognize this fact; it approved and supported it. For the council itself now had African members, and they held no brief for a culturally adapted curriculum. (And when the University College of the Gold Coast was established after the war at Achimota its first principal was not an agriculturalist but a distinguished scholar of Greek.) My own conclusion from teaching African boys was this: that their culture was relevant at the points where it was in headlong conflict with modernity. These were the points on which curriculum development should be based.

I arrived at this conclusion pragmatically, noting the points at which my teaching became alive and fully engaged the interest and intellect of my pupils. I plotted these points of maximum tension (and vitality) and have described their curricular implications with special reference to the teaching of history (Musgrove, 1955).

My pupils grew up in their villages to tales of tribal migrations and conquests led by great heroes in which they were remarkably well versed; they had little inclination to study further what they already knew from oral tradition in great circumstantial detail. But the history of the British Empire prescribed by the Cambridge Oversea School Certificate had little reality for them. There were no obvious reasons why they should know about Wolfe at Quebec.

And yet the history of Britain and her Empire came alive in my hands for 'extraneous' reasons. Clive's achievements in India were really a bore, but corruption, with which he was charged and for which Hastings was impeached, was not. This was a matter of immediate and direct relevance to my pupils—the problem of obligations and rewards, of nepotism and gifts, of incorruptible chiefs and public servants. They were not outraged by 'gifts': they approved of them. Tribal concepts of honesty and propriety were sharply opposed to the new public morality invented for nineteenth-century England by Bentham, Chadwick, and the Webbs. It was on this deep conflict, and not on the splendours of the British Raj, that worthwhile and even exciting history lessons were, almost by accident, built.

I detailed a number of similar points of culture conflict on which a 'transformational' history syllabus must stand: the work ethic; concepts of liberty, wealth, and equality; notions of causality in human affairs. These apparently abstract issues arose from the packed detail of a history syllabus which presented an alien world.

My pupils were outraged by liberal historians who quietly assumed that movements towards greater equality were movements of 'progress'. As I wrote at the time:

> To my Bantu pupils it is patently untrue that all men are equal. . . . A Mubito from the clan which suplies the Bakama of Toro and Bunyoro, by the age of fifteen or so is becoming conscious of his superior station and this is recognized by his fellow pupils. The Babito are respected as superior people, yet this superiority is due solely to birth. . . . The social history lesson which deals with the distribution of wealth [in England] and its more equitable redistribution through taxation arouses storms of protest. Death duties, excess profits taxes and the like are seen as a gross infringement of a man's right to enjoy the superior social position in which he finds himself (Musgrove, 1955).

Early British colonies in North America were no less a bore than Clive in India; but the 'starving period' of early colonizers raised questions about the nature of wealth and capital deeply at odds with tribal ideas of the rich man as the hospitable man—who gives rather than saves. But above all, perhaps, excitement ran high over the nature of historical explanation. My pupils wanted full details to convince them of the reason for any event: the highly generalized accounts of social movements which satisfy English schoolboys and undergraduates did not satisfy them. I commented as follows:

> They want the full details, they wish to see how it really works, they want to understand fully the complexity of events and forces which bear upon the particular moment to produce the particular event. A detailed study of, say, the anti-slavery movement would give them insight into the machinery of history. They would gain an understanding of causality in human affairs at variance with their traditional philosophy of causality, witchcraft. A new culture tension would thus arise, but it is from these tensions, understood by studying the forces which created them, that a synthesis will come and a new African civilization arise. (Musgrove, 1955)

## 8. CONCLUSION

Today 'culture' is not so often presented as something that does things to people or even as something that has a right to exist because it exists. In the work of Schneider (1968) and of Sahlins (1976) it is the symbolic rather than the utilitarian character of culture that is emphasized. Culture refers to the way people give meaning to their world, 'and it does so according to a definite symbolic scheme which is never the only possible one' (Sahlins, 1976, p. viii). Culture-as-symbols which actually 'does' nothing has been sharply criticized as an emasculated and even a foolish concept (Hanson, 1975, p. 101; Feinberg, 1979); but the concept itself has certainly done things to people over the past 50 years. It has greatly influenced social scientists in general and educationalists in particular. And much of what it has done to them has been disastrous.

The disaster is on various fronts. First of all, it has been used in empirical research and it claims to explain behaviour—such as working-class or 'youth culture' underachievement at school—when in fact it does not (Musgrove, 1978a, 1965); in the second place, it has provided a justification for severely limiting the life of the mind. It legitimates enclosing people in their 'communities' when their full development as rational and self-directing human beings demands that they should get out; it is used to perpetuate ways of thinking and feeling which are inadequate and inefficient in the modern world; and it is used to justify a cultural 'pluralism' which rejects any real form of synthesis and may be deeply socially divisive.

The first business of schools is to educate children but this cannot be divorced from its social consequences: inevitably 'ethnic educational systems are more than educational structures' as Chazan (1978) has observed, 'and they require more than educational criteria for their analysis'. In a highly intelligent, perceptive, and well-informed examination of Jewish education in Britain, Chazan focuses on the contemporary Jewish posture towards modernity.

The *yeshivot*—private Jewish schools with a wholly Jewish curriculum—take a strong separatist stance, but only a tiny minority (less than 1 per cent) of Jewish children attend them. Some 50 per cent of Jewish children attend part-time supplementary schools which have a compensatory function; and about a fifth of all Jewish children attend Jewish day schools which have 'Jewish' and 'modern' curricula in parallel. No attempt is made to integrate these curricula; nevertheless, the response of the Jewish day school to the dialectic of integration—particularism is not seen by Chazan as separatist but pluralistic.

Chazan argues that 'survivalism' for its own sake—what I have called 'what is, ought to be'—is dysfunctional: the traditional culture should survive only where some contemporary problem refers to it and provides some 'motivating tension' that gives it point. That was precisely my argument out of my African experience. Sympathetic to Jewish traditions and identity, Chazan nevertheless argues that 'A blind survivalist ethnicity is a doubtful commodity for second and third generation ethnics in open, pluralistic societies'.

The Jewish posture is not a perfect model for all ethnic groups in modern societies—the exclusiveness of the Jewish day school and the dualism of its curriculum makes it less than that. But it points in the general direction of a realistic position for any ethnic minority. It is not only a matter of school curriculum and organization: the Jews have refused total cultural assimilation but, faced with modernity, they have weakened some of the traditional agencies of Jewish socialization—family, neighbourhood, and religious observance. 'The Jews have knowingly, and in some cases willingly, accepted these changes, since modernity and integration have been important to them' (Chazan, 1978). They have probably not changed far enough; but this is the road that Muslims in Britain, for instance, must take. Appropriate school curricula are not enough: family, community, and religion must relax their hold. Well-intentioned community development (by English community developers)—perhaps underpinned by the concept of culture—will reinforce all three. It is a recipe for multicultural disaster.

The school curriculum must be transformational. There can be no tincture of compromise over a core curriculum of Western science, Western mathematics, Western logic, and a Western language. But there is an extensive interface of culture contact and conflict which offers focal issues for curriculum development.

Reaching back into the immigrants' own culture of (often distant) origins and ignoring the point they are at is done principally 'to enhance self-concepts'—to make them proud of themselves and their origins. The problem may be that some (for instance the Sikhs) are already too proud; and others (for instance West Indians) have very little to be proud about. Steel bands are not enough to set in the balance against slavery, one-parent families, and voodoo. In any event these are in the past and another country and they are largely irrelevant (and boring). The live issue is where cultures now conflict—for instance over child discipline. It is the West Indian's sense of superiority (as a firm manager of young children) and contempt and despair at the 'softness' of English teachers that provide live issues regarding social attitudes which qualify for a place in the school curriculum. For the Muslims it is the protected (and secluded) position of girls in any society which claims to be civilized and the barbarity of their hosts in being indifferent to it (and perhaps failing to provide single-sex schools).

There are many more such live issues, although these points of tension have not yet been adequately mapped—and they will change markedly from generation to generation. There are economic issues which are the very stuff of a live (and transformational) curriculum—the way shops in entire neighbourhoods are now in Asian hands. These are not issues to be avoided but confronted: this is where involvement is at its greatest and where background cultures have most to offer in explanation. But the background culture is often a dead culture: Islamic fatalism and submission do not prepare us for such entrepreneurial zeal. What we are concerned with is a third cultural reality with its own dynamic and its own determination. This is the culture that should be reflected in the schools.

The concept of culture has been used to legitimate the 'freezing' of primitive people in their primitive state; Midwinter has used it to legitimate the freezing of Liverpool's slum population in theirs. He invokes a simplistic, even facile version of cultural relativism. He points to the skills of various primitive people in context—the skill of Australian Aboriginals in rubbing sticks together to make fire, the Eskimo's sophisticated understanding of the properties of snow, and the Bantu's cleverness in categorizing and tallying cattle. 'What is less apparent is the subcultural relativity that exists in our own society. . . .' This apparently justified keeping the child's conceptual development within the 'relevant' context of his city, street, and gang. School should not 'bombard' him with new concepts 'which are foreign, remote, bizarre, irrelevant and unrealistic in terms of his background' (Midwinter, 1972b).

Mays was almost betrayed into a similar posture through his application of the culture concept in his studies in the 1950s of the Crown Street district of Liverpool's dockland. This was one of the first uses of the concept of culture in England in empirical educational research. Culture was tied very closely to community and Mays took a somewhat sentimental view of both. He saw the school as not simply another local amenity but tied to local life like the pub in a highly personal way. But in spite of his sympathy for working-class cultures and communities he recognized that schools must provide a way out (Mays, 1962, p. 103).

In his preface to Mays's book Simey's position was unambiguous: recognizing the merits of working-class cultures justified neither perpetuating them nor locking young people into them: 'To preserve the culture of a slum deliberately would be to segregate a number of human beings into a kind of folk museum: an intolerable suggestion.' It is precisely this intolerable suggestion that the culture concept has made tolerable. The doctrine of cultural relativism is its vindication.

## REFERENCES

Bagley, C., and Coard, B. (1975), 'Cultural knowledge and rejection of ethnic identity in West Indian children in London', in G. K. Varma and C. Bagley, Race and Education Across Cultures, Heinemann, London.
Baratz, S. Stephen, and Baratz, Joan C. (1970), 'Early childhood intervention: The social science base of institutional racism', Harvard Educational Review, 40.
Bell, Clive (1938), Civilization, Penguin, Harmondsworth, Middlx.
Benedict, Ruth (1961), Patterns of Culture, Routledge & Kegan Paul, London.
Bourdieu, P. (1977), 'Cultural reproduction and social reproduction', in J. Karabel and A. H. Halsey, Power and Ideology in Education, Oxford University Press, New York.
Brittan, E. M. (1976), 'Multicultural education: Teacher opinion on aspects of school life: Changes in curriculum and school organization', Educational Research, 18.
Chase, Stuart (1950), The Proper Study of Mankind, Phoenix House, London.
Chazan, B. (1978), 'Models of ethnic education: The case of Jewish education in Great Britain', British Journal of Educational Studies, 26.
Clarke, Fred (1936), 'The conflict of philosophies', Year Book of Education, Evans, London.
Clarke, Fred (1948), Freedom in the Educative Society, University of London Press, London.
Cohen, A. K. (1955), Delinquent Boys, Free Press, Glencoe, Ill.

140

Cohen, A. K. (1966), *Deviance and Control*, Prentice-Hall, Englewood Cliffs, N.J.

Coleman, James S. (1961), *The Adolescent Society*, Free Press, New York.

Cosin, R. B., Dale, I. R., Esland, G. M., Mackinnon, D., and Swift, D. F. (1977), *School and Society. A Sociological Reader*, Routledge & Kegan Paul, London.

Durkheim, É. (1938), *The Rules of Sociological Method*, Free Press, New York.

Edwards, A. D., and Hargreaves, D. H. (1977), 'The social scientific base of academic radicalism', in R. B. Cosin *et al.*, *School and Society*, Routledge & Kegan Paul, London.

Eliot, T. S. (1948), *Notes Towards the Definition of Culture*, Faber, London.

Evans-Pritchard, E. E. (1951), *Social Anthropology*, Routledge & Kegan Paul, London.

Feinberg, R. (1979), 'Schneider's symbolic culture theory: An appraisal', *Current Anthropology*, **20**.

Foster, Philip J. (1965), *Education and Social Change in Ghana*, Routledge & Kegan Paul, London.

Freeman, Derek (1965), 'Anthropology, psychiatry, and the doctrine of cultural relativism', *Man*, **65**.

Freud, S. (1953), *Civilization and its Discontents*, Hogarth Press, London.

Gellner, E. (1968), 'The new idealism—cause and meaning in the social sciences', in I. Lakatos and A. Musgrave, *Problems in the Philosophy of Science. Proceedings of the International Colloquium, London 1965*, vol. 13, North Holland Press, London.

Gerth, H., and Mills, C. W. (1954), *Character and Social Structure*, Oxford University Press, London.

Giles, Ken, and Woolfe, Ray (1977), *Deprivation, Disadvantage and Compensation*, Open University Press, Milton Keynes.

Ginsberg, M. (1953), 'On the diversity of morals', *Journal of the Royal Anthropological Institute*, **83**.

Gordon, Milton M. (1947–1948), '*Kitty Foyle* and the concept of class culture', *American Journal of Sociology*, **53**.

Griffiths, V. L. (1953), *An Experiment in Education. An Account of an Attempt to Improve the Lower Stages of Boys' Education in the Moslem Anglo-Egyptian Sudan 1930–1950*, Longmans, London.

Hall, Stuart, and Jefferson, Tony (1976), *Resistance Through Rituals*, Hutchinson, London.

Hanson, F. Allan, (1975), *Meaning in Culture*, Routledge & Kegan Paul, London.

Haring, Douglas G. (1949), 'Is "culture" definable?', *American Sociological Review*, **14**.

Hebdige, Dick (1976), 'Reggae, rastas, and rudies', in S. Hall and T. Jefferson, *Resistance Through Rituals*, Hutchinson, London.

Hollis, Martin (1972), 'Witchcraft and winchcraft,' *Philosophy of the Social Sciences*, **2**.

Hunter, J. F. M. (1968), ' "Forms of life" in Wittgenstein's *Philosophical Investigations*', *American Philosophical Quarterly*, **5**.

Jarvie, I. C . (1975), 'Cultural relativism again', *Philosophy of Social Sciences*, **5**.

Jeffcoate, Robert (1976), 'Curriculum planning in multiracial education', *Educational Research*, **18**.

Jeffcoate, Robert (1981), 'Evaluating the multicultural curriculum: Students' perspectives', *Journal of Curriculum Studies*, **13**.

Jensen, A. R. (1969), 'How much can we boost IQ and scholastic achievement?' *Harvard Educational Review*, **39**.

Jones, Jesse (1922), *Education in Africa: A Study of West, South and Equatorial Africa by the African Educational Commission*, Phelps-Stoke Fund, New York.

Jones, Jesse (1925), *Education in East Africa*, Phelps-Stoke Fund, New York.

Kandel, D. B., and Lesser, G. S. (1972), *Youth in Two Worlds. United States and Denmark*, Jossey-Bass, San Francisco.

Kaplan, David (1965), 'The superorganic: Science or metaphysics?', *American Anthropologist*, **67**.

Keddie, Nell (1973), *Tinker, Tailor . . . The Myth of Cultural Deprivation*, Penguin, Harmondsworth, Middx.

Kitsuse, J. I., and Dietrick, D. C. (1959), 'Delinquent boys: A critique', *American Sociological Review*, **24**.

Kitwood, T., and Borrill, C. (1980), 'The significance of schooling for an ethnic minority', *Oxford Review of Education*, **6**.

Kluckhohn, Clyde (1950), *Mirror for Man*, Harrap, London.

Kroeber, A. L. (1917), 'The superorganic', *American Anthropologist*, **17**.

Kroeber, A. L. (1948), 'White's view of culture', *American Anthropologist*, **56**.

Kuhn, Thomas S. (1962), *The Structure of Scientific Revolutions*, University of Chicago Press, Chicago.

Kuhn, Thomas S. (1970), 'Reflections on my critics', in I. Lakatos and A. Musgrave, *Criticism and the Growth of Knowledge*, Cambridge University Press, Cambridge.

Lacey, C. (1970), *Hightown Grammar*, Manchester University Press, Manchester.

Linton, Ralph (1947), *The Cultural Background of Personality*, Routledge & Kegan Paul, London.

Lukes, Steven (1967), 'Some problems about rationality', *Archives of European Sociology*, **8**.

Lukes, Steven (1981), 'Oppressed of the oppressed', *The Times Higher Education Supplement*, 19 June.

Lowie, Robert (1936), 'Cultural anthropology: A science', *American Journal of Sociology*, **42**.

Mack, J. (1964), 'Full-time miscreants, neighbourhoods, and criminal networks', *British Journal of Sociology*, **15**.

McLean, Martin (1980), 'Cultural autonomy and the education of ethnic minority groups', *British Journal of Educational Studies*, **28**.

Malinowski, B. (1945), *The Dynamics of Culture Change*, Yale University Press, New Haven, Conn.

Matza, David (1964), *Delinquency and Drift*, Wiley, New York.

Mays, J. B. (1962), *Education and the Urban Child*, Liverpool University Press, Liverpool.

Midwinter, E. (1972a), *Social Environment and the Urban School*, Ward Lock, London.

Midwinter, E. (1972b), 'Teaching with the urban environment', in J. Raynor and J. Harden, *Equality and City Schools. Readings in Urban Education*, vol. 2, Routledge & Kegan Paul, London.

Mungham, G., and Pearson, G. (1976), *Working Class Youth Culture*, Routledge & Kegan Paul, London.

Murdock, Graham, and Phelps, Guy (1972), 'Youth culture and the school revisited', *British Journal of Sociology*, **23**.

Murdock, G. P. (1932), 'The sciences of culture', *American Anthropologist*, **34**.

Murdock, G. P. (1951), 'British social anthropology', *American Anthropologist*, **53**.

Murdock, G. P. (1971), 'Anthropology's mythology', *Proceedings of the Royal Anthropological Institute*.

Musgrove, F. (1952), 'What sort of facts?', *African Affairs*, **51**.

Musgrove, F. (1955), 'History teaching within a conflict of cultures', *History*, **140**.

Musgrove, F. (1965), 'Samples from English cultures' (review), *British Journal of Educational Psychology*, **35**.

Musgrove, F. (1978a), 'Curriculum, culture and ideology', *Journal of Curriculum Studies*, **10**.

Musgrove, F. (1978b), 'The domesticated university', *Universities Quarterly*, **32**.

Needham, R. (1962), *Structure and Sentiment*, University of Chicago Press, Chicago.

142

Nowell-Smith, P. H. (1971), 'Cultural relativism', *Philosophy of Social Sciences*, **1**.
Obeyesekere, C. (1966), 'Methodological and philosophical relativism', *Man*, **1** (n.s.).
Oppenheim, A. N. (1955), 'Social status and clique formation among grammar school boys', *British Journal of Sociology*, **6**.
Ottaway, A. K. C. (1953), *Education and Society*, Routledge & Kegan Paul, London.
Peattie, Lisa R. (1965), 'Anthropology and the search for values', *Journal of Applied Behavioral Sciences*, **1**.
Peel, J. D. Y. (1969), 'Understanding alien belief-systems', *British Journal of Sociology*, **20**.
Popper, Karl (1970), 'Normal science and its dangers', in I. Lakatos and A. Musgrave, *Criticism and the Growth of Knowledge*, Cambridge University Press, Cambridge.
Radcliffe-Brown, A. R. (1949), 'White's view of a science of culture', *American Anthropologist*, **51**.
Radcliffe-Brown, A. R. (1952), *Structure and Function in Primitive Society,* Routledge & Kegan Paul, London.
Radcliffe-Brown, A. R. (1957), *A Natural Science of Sociology*, Free Press, Glencoe, Ill.
Redfield, Robert (1953), *The Primitive World and its Transformations*, Cornell University Press, Ithaca, New York.
Sahlins, Marshall (1976), *Culture and Practical Reason*, University of Chicago Press, Chicago.
Sapir, E. (1917), 'Do we need a superorganic?', *American Anthropologist*, **19**.
Schneider, D. M. (1968), *American Kinship: A Cultural Account*, Prentice-Hall, Englewood Cliffs, N.J.
Schneider, Louis, and Lysgaard, Sverve (1953), 'The deferred gratification pattern: A preliminary study', *American Sociological Review*, **18**.
Scholte, Bob (1970), 'Epistemic paradigms', in E. N. Hayes and Tanya Hayes, *Claude Lévi-Strauss*, MIT Press, Cambridge, Mass.
Sherry, P. (1972), 'Is religion a "form of life"?', *American Philosophical Quarterly*, **5**.
Sprott, W. J. H. (1955), 'Delinquescent worlds', *Listener*, 9 June.
Stocking, G. W. (1963), 'Matthew Arnold, E. B. Tylor and the uses of invention', *American Anthropologist*, **65**.
Stone, Maureen (1981), *The Education of the Black Child in Britain,* Fontana, London.
Sugarman, B. (1970) 'Social class, values and behaviour in school', in M. Craft, *Family, Class and Education*, Longmans, London.
Tylor, Edward B. (1871), *Primitive Culture. Researches into the Development of Mythology, Philosophy, Religion, Language, Art and Custom*, vol. 1, John Murray, London.
Walkling, Philip H. (1980), 'The idea of a multicultural curriculum', *Journal of the Philosophy of Education*, **14**.
Waller, Willard (1932), *The Sociology of Teaching*, Wiley, New York.
Welsh Department, Ministry of Education (1952), *The Curriculum and the Community in Wales*, HMSO, London.
White, Leslie A. (1946), 'Configurations of culture growth', *American Anthropologist*, **48**.
White, Leslie A. (1947), 'Culturological vs. psychological interpretations of human behavior', *American Sociological Review*, **12**.
Winch, Peter (1958), *The Idea of a Social Science*, Routledge & Kegan Paul, London.
Winch, Peter (1960), 'Nature and convention', *Proceedings of the Aristotelian Society*, **20**.
Winch, Peter (1964), 'Understanding a primitive society', *American Philosophical Quarterly*, **1**.

Worrall, R. V. (1977), 'Gypsies, education and society. Case studies in conflict', unpublished MEd. thesis, University of Birmingham.

Zec, Paul (1980), 'Multicultural education: What kind of relativism is possible?', *Journal of Philosophy of Education*, **14**.

# CHAPTER 7

# Age, Rituals, and Symbols: Education and the Social Order

Throughout this book I have compared primitive and modern peoples in order to tell teachers something of value and relevance about ourselves. Finally, I shall compare some of the uses of age, rituals, and symbols by primitive and modern societies for the ordering of social life. I shall do this not to suggest some particular teaching method or curriculum design, but to offer to teachers some overall perspective on their work.

I take age, rituals, and symbols because their importance to the social order is commonly overlooked or de-emphasized in modern societies. Social class is given a position of central importance. But education is deeply implicated in the uses of age and symbols to create and sustain social order. If teachers are to grasp the significance of their work they should understand the way they are involved in age-grading arrangements and the power that schools have as social statements. For institutions do not only do things, they say things: they are rhetorical devices. Social structures are not simply networks of institutions; they are networks of messages.

Thus compulsory schooling from 5 to 16 communicates three truths: that the young are dependent, redundant, and have 'gone public'; they have been moved out of the private world of kinsmen into the public sphere. These three truths are communicated afresh every day through the ritual of legally enforced school attendance; they are dramatized twice daily in ceremonial registration.

A study of primitive life alerts us to the importance of other influences than 'class' on the social order (which is simply how people ordinarily and customarily behave towards one another). Sociologists say that the basis of the social order is class; anthropologists say that primitive societies do not have social classes—though today they may have Westernized elites (Lloyd, 1966). Age and descent, symbols and ritual, have a key role in studies of their social structures. The argument of this chapter is that they are by no means unimportant in ours.

There are, of course, important differences. In primitive societies the rules of marriage are probably more important for social order than they are with us. The 'incest taboo' divides all societies into two (slightly unequal) halves: in one there are those we can marry, in the other there are those we cannot. (The halves are slightly 'unequal' because the latter are sacred, the former profane.) There is a fundamental opposition between sisters and wives. These polarities are of diminished importance in modern societies. But other distinctions emerge which are hardly found in the primitive world—for instance the strong

144

opposition that now exists betwen private and public. This is now probably stronger than the opposition between gentlemen and players.

But age, ritual, and symbols remain important for creating and sustaining social order. It is true that age in the simple sense of seniority yields in large measure to merit in career advancement (although it remains embedded in incremental salary scales); but age is now finely calibrated and is the key to interlocking social timetables and individual changes of role. Correct timing and accurate synchronizing of major transitions in life are of infinitely greater importance and complexity than in preindustrial and primitive worlds.

Ritual and symbols remain important, too. They are now more secular and civic but they remain potent. In education, says Bernstein, they are 'major mechanisms for the internalization and revivifying of social order' (Bernstein, 1975, p. 56). We may scale down our ceremonial (and abolish badges, school colours, and Speech Day); we must not imagine that we have seriously impaired the symbolic order of the school.

The uses of age, symbols, and ritual will be examined with special reference to the way generation succeeds generation. There are always dangers of personal stress and social dislocation in this takeover and process of social renewal. The 'age-set' societies of Africa are said to handle these problems 'better' than we do—at least in the sense of promoting 'smoother' transitions. It is a central argument of this chapter that this view is false.

I shall first discuss the significance of age for social structure and then the nature of ritual and symbolism in our schools. Finally, I shall illustrate the continuing importance of age and ritual by referring to studies I made (with Roger Middleton) in the late 1970s of rites of passage and the meaning of age in contrasted groups in English society (Musgrove and Middleton, 1981). It is in *rites de passage* that age and symbols can be seen working together to bring shape and order to social life.

## 1. YOUTH IN AGE-SET AND MODERN SOCIETIES

Age can make a contribution to social order in two ways: on the one hand, it provides empirical categories and indices for regulating behaviour (thus people can vote at 18); on the other, empirical categories can be converted—as Lévi-Strauss has taught us—into logical categories for thinking about society and making sense of it. Thus old and young are empirical categories, but we may also use 'old' and 'young' to think with. They constitute a binary opposition like other empirical contrasts which are *bonnes à penser*: left and right, men and women, black and white, cooked and raw, sisters and wives. Just like these assorted polarities, age contrasts may be used as part of 'the conceptual apparatus with which societies order their world and create a social order' (La Fontaine, 1978, p. 18).

That is no concern of mine here. This section is about the use of empirical categories and indices to regulate social relationships. Particular attention will be given to primitive age-set societies compared with modern industrial societies like America and Britain.

Some 40 years ago the American Sociological Society devoted its annual conference in New York to the subject of age, sex, and social structure; 36 years later at Swansea the British Anthropological Association did the same. This at least indicates the continuing importance of age as an aspect of social structure. But both conferences suggested a diminished importance of age in modern compared with primitive societies. It was not used in precise and determinate ways as it was, apparently, among nonliterate folk. 'In our society', said Talcott Parsons, 'age grading does not to any great extent, except for the educational system, involve formal age categorization.' Age lines for most purposes were 'not rigidly specific but approximate'. But Talcott Parsons conceded that 'this does not necessarily lessen their structural significance (Parsons, 1942).

What is now quite clear is the extraordinary sloppiness and imprecision of age-grading in primitive societies and the remarkable precision and meticulous articulation of age as a social regulator in ours. This is partly because of legally prescribed and enforced age definition and cut-off points. But within these frameworks accurate timing of personal trajectories and 'multirelational synchronization' are distinguishing features of modernity, as Peter Berger has eloquently and convincingly claimed. The timetabling and sequencing of life today entails 'a process of planning which attains a calculus-like complexity' (Berger *et al.*, 1974, p. 69). The longer life of modern man, as well as the wider range of choices available to him, makes the rational handling of chronology more and not less important (Stub, 1969). By comparison, primitive societies commonly work with enormous margins of error and a temporal untidiness and lack of fit which are not only a source of social disorder and inefficiency but of high levels of personal frustration and stress.

In our educational system, as Talcott Parsons conceded in 1941, age-grading is a basic structural fact. It has increasingly overridden other bases of educational classification, including academic ability and attainment. This is one startling difference between preindustrial and modern schools: thus in seventeenth-century France it was quite common that 'young men between nineteen and twenty-four sat with children between eleven and thirteen (Ariès, 1973, p. 214). The class was the structural unit of the school, but in the seventeenth century 'the connection between age and class still remained very vague and loose'. Today the connection is tight indeed. Julius Roth (1963) has examined the 'timetables' of men in modern societies and emphasized the way in which schooling involves a rigid and unvarying temporal progression whereby pupils are promoted and graduated 'on time' regardless of performance. And some 50 years later they will also be retired 'on time' with similar disregard for their abilities and capabilities.

We have used age, it is said, to create a social category, youth, which inhabits a no-man's-land on the fringes of society. In this limbo there are no clear rules or guidelines. The young have an ever extended 'student role' which is socially uninvolved and without serious relationship to action: 'It is a relatively passive role, always in preparation for action, but never acting' (Coleman, 1972). The distinguishing features of this marginal world are its lack of structure, its normlessness, and 'anomie'.

The picture of primitive age-set societies that we have been given for 50 years is utterly different (and often explicitly 'superior'). In 1936 Evans-Pritchard gave us a classic account of Nuer age-sets in *Sudan Notes and Records*. It is a picture of a highly efficient mechanism for promoting harmonious relationships between young and old and among the young themselves; indeed, it appears to bind together all the members of an otherwise loosely knit society into a well-integrated whole.

In a society without an explicit political structure the age-sets, along with the kinship system, determined 'everybody's attitude towards everybody else' and regulated such important matters as marriage. Thus no man could marry the daughter of a member of his age-set (and so find himself in a subordinate position as his son-in-law). But above all the age-set system provided, in a highly egalitarian society, a form of legitimate authority which everyone obeyed. Evans-Pritchard illustrated the importance of this in the day-to-day relationships in the cattle camp, and the way 'their smooth working is partly a result of the social stratification by age'. Older men were obeyed without question in spite of the 'extraordinary pride of the Nuer, the object of ceaseless astonishment to Europeans'. The real measure of the effectiveness of the age-set system was that it actually led fiercely proud and independent young men to obey someone—their seniors.

It also brought unity to a scattered people, transcending kinship ties and promoting a sense of national identity:

> Age-sets are organized tribally and are one of the institutions common to all members of the same tribe and may, therefore, be supposed to act as a unifying agency in the loose political life which we have seen characterizes Nuer tribes. (Evans-Pritchard, 1936)

Age-sets emerge as a supremely important and efficient mechanism for regulating the relationships between aspiring young men and their established seniors and for ensuring the cohesion of the tribe.

The integrative and adaptive role of age-sets was the powerful message that came from the functionalists over the next 20 years. Eisenstadt gave perhaps the best organized statement of this view in the 1950s (Eisenstadt, 1954, 1956). He opposed age-grades and age groups to kinship groups and argued that the former performed socially integrative functions when the latter did not.

Eisenstadt made a comparative study of more than 50 traditional African societies. The key terms in which he describes age-set societies are 'integration', 'solidarity', 'continuity', and 'stability'. The emphasis is on the age-set's society-wide embrace, 'its criteria of membership are universalistic in that they apply to the community as a whole'. Like Evans-Pritchard, Eisenstadt saw age-sets as ensuring social harmony and cohesion:

The personal, particularistic relations of the family and kinship unit are replaced by impersonal, universalistic relations with any member of the society. (Eisenstadt, 1954)

'Rites of passage', of which initiation into age-sets (often through circumcision) may be an important example, have often been seen in a similarly 'integrative' light. Van Gennep said that they occurred so that status transitions could be 'regulated and guarded so that society as a whole will suffer no discomfort or injury' (van Gennep, 1960, p. 3). Even debased and emasculated rites in Africa (White, 1953) and in England (Pickering, 1974) have been interpreted as having important integrative functions. But the best recent studies of age-grade systems powerfully indicate that they promote tension and social dislocation and that societies 'cohere' not because but in spite of them.

## 2. THE DYSFUNCTIONS OF AGE-SET SYSTEMS

The 'moran' of the Samburu tribe of East Africa are the young men who have been circumcised and initiated into the warrior age-set usually around the age of 15. Young boys (and women of all ages) 'dote on the notion of moranhood' (Spencer, 1970, p. 154). But these young men will not marry until they are about 30 and will not become junior elders until they are about 35. For 20 years they live in a social limbo, their position is highly marginal, they are associated not with the centre but with the fringe of society and the bush. They are not without glamour; but they endure a protracted period of dependency in a 'firestick' relationship with tribal elders. The age-set system keeps them in a state of humiliating irresponsibility until they are well past the mid-point of life which by our standards is relatively short.

This is the unmistakable picture that comes out of the anthropological studies of Paul Spencer. The Samburu (like the Arusha) are related to the Masai tribe: age is a principal means of regulating social relationships. The Samburu, the Arusha, and the Masai are societies 'whose hierarchy of age-grades provides the major dimension of social stratification in what are otherwise strongly egalitarian societies' (Spencer, 1976).

It is the source of demoralization and social disharmony. At 14 or 15 young men join a queue which extends over almost two decades. They are restive, resentful, and delinquent: 'The elders control all significant activities and treat the moran as juveniles, and the moran respond by indulging in various deviant though ultimately innocuous activities' (Spencer, 1976). The firestick relationship with elders is 'a repressive regime aimed at holding them during their twenties in an extended period of delayed adolescence. . . . In effect, during this period of queueing, they are held in a state of social suspension'.

The Arusha men marry earlier than the Samburu (usually around 20), but must wait for another dozen years before they become junior elders; and though they do not have to wait for wives they have to wait for land. Until their early thirties there is 'an element of delinquency among the moran entailing adultery, stock theft, disobedience and affrays'. There is great tension between the generations:

> At each level there is a certain resentment between adjacent age-sets: the older resent the aspirations of the younger and are reluctant to hand on their greater experience and knowledge: and the younger resent their permanent inferiority and the privileges withheld from them. (Spencer, 1976)

Otto Raum's account of Chaga age-grades and generational succession shows the build-up of intolerable tension before a new age-class is formed. The elders hold back the initiation of boys as long as they possibly can; the pressure from the boys increases until the elders finally yield. In the meantime the boys have been disturbed and delinquent: the Chaga recognize their rebellious behaviour which they call the '*kisusa* spirit'. When this can no longer be curbed, 'the demand for tribal initiation and the formation of a new age-class is raised before the chief'. The pressures might lead to young men being brought 'in' before society is really ready for them, for it was principally 'the clamour and restiveness of the adolescents which decided the older section of Chaga society to start the formal education of the initiation camp' (Raum, 1938).

A recent study of the ethnographic literature on 21 age-set societies in Africa makes abundantly clear the conflict and disorder generated by age-set systems. Conflict and disorder centre on three main problems: the timing of the transitions, the age-range of the age-sets, and the abruptness of changes in role. 'Despite the fact that life-course transitions in age-set societies are organized and ritualized, these transitions are neither simple nor smooth' (Foner and Kertzer, 1978).

The timing of transitions is normally indeterminate and a matter for decision by the elders. Setting the date is a centre of conflict and the delay engineered by the elders may be a matter of years rather than weeks. Among the Nandi the young are often so thwarted and provoked that they oppose the current warriors with force; among the Karamajong the senior age-set steps down only when it is too senile and decimated by disease to hold on.

The wide age-range within age-sets is also a source of personal frustration and social inefficiency. The interval between sets may be as much as 10 years (Nuer) or even 15 (Kipsigis and Nandi). Boys who just missed one age-class may be mature men in their late 20s before the next one is formed. In these circumstances it is not only individuals who are put under stress, but the working of social institutions and the tribal economy:

> The workings of the age systems can in these various ways bring hardship to some members of an age set and create problems for the society. The rules of the age system may disregard the needs of certain individuals; they may violate other social norms for what is age-appropriate behavior; or they may be at odds with societal require-

ments for qualified personnel such as warriors of fighting age. (Foner and Kertzer, 1978)

By contrast, precision timing and predictability of status transitions are a feature of modern industrial societies which are far more finely and firmly age-graded than they were a century ago. The timing of status changes was far more varied then than it is today: the point at which an individual left school, started work, left home, married, and set up his own home was not so clearly prescribed. In America as in France and Britain some youths might not go to school at all while others continued with an intermittent attendance into their 20s. The sequencing of status changes was also relatively indeterminate. Life was less linear: people made fresh starts; and the route into adult life was more meandering, leisurely, and arbitrary than it usually is today.

A century ago all was not lost if a girl had not married by the time she was 20 or at worst 21. Perhaps the most remarkable tightening of life-course schedules has been in respect of marriage for both women and men. In America in the nineteenth century the 'spread' of marriage among males covered a span of 20 years; today it is 7. Among women it has shrunk from 15 to 8 (Modell *et al.*, 1976).

Young people have a longer (and less broken) education than formerly, but they leave home earlier and complete the move to a household of their own in a far shorter time: American males have reduced the period of transition, since the late nineteenth century, by a third, from 22 years to 14. And they are more likely to take the various steps—leaving school, entering the workforce, getting married—bunched together at around the same age: 'In contrast to a century ago, young people today are more likely to be similar to one another in the age at which they leave home, enter marriage, and set up their own households' (Modell *et al.*, 1976).

The transitions are more complex, often multiple: going to college does not necessarily exclude marriage, and becoming a wife (and mother) does not necessarily exclude work. Complex and interlocking career decisions are made over a briefer period of time. The broad latitude that marked growing up a century ago has been replaced with a more prescribed and tightly defined schedule of life-course organization. And the penalties for wrong decisions and delay are almost certainly greater: it is far more difficult to recover lost ground.

The enormous stress on the individual is matched only by the increased harmony and efficiency of society. 'Growing up as a process has become briefer, more normful, bounded and consequential—and thereby more demanding on individual participants' (Modell *et al.*, 1976). But social conflict and incompetence are reduced: age norms delimit the field of contestants for desired positions to manageable numbers of well-prepared persons. The social order is more orderly, its synchronization smoother, its integration tighter and tidier, because of the greater importance of age in the social structure of modern industrial societies.

## 3. RITUAL AND CONSERVATISM

Like age, ritual and symbols are usually seen as less important in the regulation of life in modern than in primitive societies. To become modern is to become simple and more direct. There is a great deal of truth in this. But both ritual and symbols remain potent with us. Ritual is generally conservative, but symbols have a revolutionary potential: they are rather ambiguous, open to negotiation and, like the cross, may be invested with new and subversive meanings. Symbols may be used to bring in a new order as well as to preserve the old.

Ritual is heavily symbolic behaviour: it means 'more than it says', it stands for something beyond itself. It is highly emotionally charged in spite of its standardized and repetitive forms. But it is usually seen as Durkheim saw it—as powerfully reinforcing and stabilizing the *status quo*.

Ritual may be implicated in change in rather indirect ways and perhaps more so in the transformations of primitive societies than in the modern world. In 1965 John Beattie gave the Malinowski Memorial Lecture on ritual and social change, but mentioned change only at the end as an afterthought (Beattie, 1966). It would be difficult to locate it centrally in such an analysis. New rituals may be a response to social change in primitive societies, but they are not part of its cause: they are an aspect of millenarian movements like the Ghost Dance in some North American Indian tribes, cargo cults in the South Seas, and the Mau Mau revolt in Kenya. They are a response to an order that has already broken down and are an attempt to secure remedies: 'What they [the Melanesians and North American Indians] did was to stage a dramatic performance, or a series of such performances, and then to wait for what they wanted to come about' (Beattie, 1966).

With us, too, ritual is at best only very indirectly implicated in change. Protest movements may find strength and solidarity through ritual, but that is a very different matter from using ritual behaviour to bring about change. The ritual uses of motorbikes by the 'bike boys' of the 1960s have been perceptively described by Paul Willis (1978, pp. 11–61): 'The ensemble of bike, noise, clothes *on the move* gave a formidable expression of identity to the [motorbike] culture and powerfully developed many of its central values.' Other subversive postwar youth groups like the Teds, Mods, and Skinheads have been similarly interpreted as finding powerful support in 'a set of social rituals which underpin their collective identity' (Hall and Jefferson, 1976, p. 47). But the rituals themselves do not further subversion; they simply give strength and cohesion to people who do.

We do not expect ritual to 'bring something about' in the way that followers of cargo cults did. That is probably the crucial difference between ritual in modern and primitive societies: with us it is simply 'expressive', a language; with primitive people it has important instrumental purposes, too.

Beattie deemphasized this instrumentality of ritual in the primitive world. He said ritual is more like a sonnet or sonata than it is like a scientific experiment. But even Beattie conceded that 'ritual is often, indeed generally, held by its practitioners to be effective as well as expressive. The sorcerer *intends* to injure his enemy (not just to relieve his feelings); the rainmaker *intends* to make rain; the sacrificer *intends* to avert a spirit's wrath. And each thinks, or may think that what he does will bring about his desire' (Beattie, 1966). It is in modern societies that ritual is solely a form of communication. We do not expect Armistice Day rituals to bring back the dead.

This does not diminish its importance: it simply makes it important in different ways. But we do not need ritual either, said Gluckman, for marking off different social roles. This was why we have less of it. Our social roles are well defined and segregated and it is easy to know who is who; but in small-scale primitive societies there is more danger of confusion, there is a multiplicity of undifferentiated and overlapping roles which need ritual to separate them (Gluckman, 1962).

We have less ritual than primitive people, it is expressive and not instrumental, and it is arguably shallower, with less command over the personalities of the people involved. Bocock (1970) has maintained that our ritual is more civic than sacred, invites a shallower response, and allows people merely to watch rather than become actively and deeply involved. Pickering (1974) said we still have a great deal of ritual but it is trivial. Some 80 per cent of baptisms, 90 per cent of first marriages, virtually a 100 per cent of burials take place in church; but this quite abundant ritual, said Pickering, is nowadays empty, with little meaning for participants. It survives not for its religious significance but because it helps to bring kinsmen home from afar.

And yet there is substantial agreement among sociologists and anthropologists that ritual is of great importance in both modern and primitive societies for precisely the reasons that Durkheim (1915, p. 427) gave: all societies feel the need to uphold and reaffirm at regular intervals the collective ideas which make their unity and personality. Today televison makes royal weddings, and even Royal Ascot, extremely potent symbols of social solidarity. The televised coronation in 1953 was an act of communion in which our nation renewed its devotion to common moral values and reestablished its contact with the sacred (Shils and Young, 1953).

Gluckman, it is true, has argued that ritual does not necessarily express and promote solidarity: on the contrary, it may express and celebrate social conflict. This is his famous 'ritual rebellion' thesis which he developed through a consideration of Zulu and Swazi agricultural ceremonies. At the time of harvest there is the problem of sharing plenty (or scarcity) and so there is potential conflict: a 'staged' overthrow of authority dramatizes a dangerous situation (Gluckman, 1954, p. 6). But even these rituals do not after all promote revolution and change but the opposite: ritual rebellion makes real rebellion superfluous and reaffirms the underlying social unity (Gluckman, 1959, pp. 109–136; 1963, p. 18). Beidelman (1966) says Gluckman has wholly misinterpreted the *Incwala* rites because he did not find out what the people involved thought they were doing. The rites are really, says Beidelman (who has not asked them either), rites of 'royal separation'. But even for Beidelman the rites are socially conservative and through them the traditional authority of Swazi kings is reinforced and enhanced.

The ritual of school life in England has been interpreted in similar terms. In a speculative essay on the subject Bernstein's favourite term is 'revivify'. The symbolic function of ritual, he says, is to relate the individual to the social order and revivify that order. It is true that ritual is only a 'restricted code' and its messages are not only highly predictable but also condensed, but it powerfully transmits the established order (Bernstein *et al.*, 1966, Bernstein, 1975).

Bernstein distinguishes between 'consensual' and 'differentiating' rituals in schools: the former bind pupils together, the latter set them apart. Consensual rituals are assemblies and ceremonies, totems, scrolls, and plaques, as well as the rituals of punishment and reward; differentiating rituals separate children according to age, sex, and perhaps ability. But both types of ritual, says Bernstein, 'are major mechanisms for the internalizing of social order'. They are means of social control, 'they revivify the social order within the individual', they deepen his respect for authority. They have socialized him into conformity and acceptance of the *status quo*.

There is no conception in Bernstein that school ritual is 'for' anyone but the pupils. But the contribution of ritual to social order is not only, or even mainly, through the 'socialization' of the people directly involved. Clearly this could not be so in the case of infant baptism and burying the dead. Ritual is essentially a public language which speaks (solemnly and authoritatively) to spectators, audiences, and congregations. For the reinforcement of social order it is the audience that must 'get the message' which may often be lost on the individuals immediately and directly concerned.

That is the central point of Leach's seminal paper on 'magical hair'. There is a gap between the personal meaning of ritual and the social statement that it makes. Rituals in which hair is close-cropped signal discipline and tight social control: the audience knows this but the shorn novice may not. 'We have no grounds for assuming', says Leach, 'that the actors in public rituals are in a psychological condition which corresponds to the symbolism of their performance.' Nor is this particularly important; but it is crucial that the symbolism should not be lost on the congregation: 'In the kinds of rituals which an anthropologist ordinarily observes, the meaning of the performance, in the eyes of the assembled congregation, is seldom in doubt' (Leach, 1958).

A true grasp of schools and their rituals for social order comes from understanding their message for society at large. It is their public posture that counts. However meaningless they may be for their pupils they have an important message for everyone else. The Latin curriculum may have bemused most pupils; but it was a powerful signal that this was a non-domestic sphere (Ong, 1959). The vernacular is for families; Latin is another world.

## 4. SYMBOLS AND SOCIAL STATES

Schools are rich in symbols and school systems themselves constitute a symbolic order: they not only 'do' something, they 'say' something. The connections between schools, symbols, and the social order will be considered within three quite different perspectives: the first is a 'structural' perspective (derived from Émile Durkheim), the second is a 'structuralist' perspective (derived from Claude Lévi-Strauss), and the third is a 'symbolic interactionist' perspective (derived from Max Weber and G. H. Mead). A structural view of symbols sees them as models of the underlying social order; on a structuralist view symbols 'tell us' not about the structure of society but of the human mind; and a symbolic interactionist view sees symbols as less determined by structures of any kind: meanings are bestowed on symbols by people who use them in everyday life, they are open to negotiation and renegotiation, and the social order is an ongoing accomplishment of members.

Durkheim's structural interpretation of symbols drew heavily on the ethnographic data available in the early years of this century, especially the published work on Australian Aboriginals and North American Indian tribes. The way he related their symbols to the social order is the subject of his book, *The Elementary Forms of the Religious Life* (first published in 1912) and the notable work he wrote with Marcel Mauss, *Primitive Classification* (first published in 1903). These works have had an incalculable influence on English anthropologists, especially Evans-Pritchard, Mary Douglas, and Rodney Needham. Their influence on Basil Bernstein and on reinterpretations in recent years of the school curriculum is no less incalculable. The structural perspectives of Durkheim, rooted in a highly imperfect ethnography, are the theoretical basis and legitimation of today's 'open' schools and the 'integrated' curriculum.

The fragmentary writings of Durkheim's pupil, Robert Hertz (who died in battle in 1915), have also been remarkably potent. In Hertz's discussion of the symbolism of the right hand and the left, the doctrine of symbolic replication finds its purest expression (Hertz, 1973): the duality of society imposes itself on the human body, but the left is inferior to the right. It corresponds to the profane half of society which 'provides me with wives and human sacrificial victims, buries my dead and prepares my sacred ceremonies'. This is the theory which underpins the contemporary curriculum.

Its most straightforward, indeed classic, formulation is this: 'The first logical categories were social categories; the first classes of things were classes of men' (Durkheim and Mauss, 1963, p. 82). In other words, social groups preceded concepts and were their model. If this remarkable and inherently unlikely proposition is false—and it almost certainly is— the entire intellectual edifice of structuralism (and curriculum theory derived from it) falls to the ground.

It is the basis of Evans-Pritchard's analysis of Nuer time concepts (Evans-Pritchard, 1939) and spear symbolism (Evans-Pritchard, 1953), as it is of Needham's analysis of Banyoro symbolism of the right hand and the left (Needham, 1967); it is the basis of Middleton's analysis of the concepts of time and space in Lugbara myth (Middleton, 1954), of Leach's interpretation of the myth of the Virgin birth (Leach, 1969) and of Good King Wenceslas (Leach, 1966). It is likewise the basis of Bernstein's distinction between public and formal language (and restricted and elaborated codes) (Bernstein, 1959), collection and integrated curricula (Bernstein, 1971), and 'closed' and 'open' schools (Bernstein, 1967). It is the basis, too, of his celebrated discussion of the different décor of lavatories in relation to the purity and exclusiveness of social categories (Bernstein, 1975, pp. 153–156). It is the basis of Mary Douglas's discussion of social boundaries and the distinction between groups and grids (Douglas, 1973). It is the doctrine of the symbolic replication of the social state.

The theory revolves around boundaries. The boundary is the key symbol: orifices, exits and entrances, beginnings, endings, reversals, renewals—where one thing ends and another begins. Boundaries between spirit and matter, between one part of the year or of life and another, between subjects taught in schools, replicate the strength, sharpness, permeability of the boundaries between social groups.

I have discussed this doctrine elsewhere and pointed to its logical, conceptual, and empirical inadequacies (Musgrove, 1979, pp. 18–22, 29–30). Durkheim said that social organization was the origin and model for forms of thinking—that social hierarchy, for example, was the model for logical thought (Durkheim, 1915, p. 148). Rodney Needham (1963) has pointed to the weak empirical support for this view, and Swanson (1960) has failed to show any convincing connection between the 'shape' of concepts and the 'shape' of society; John Bowker (1973) has made the point that the theory can admit of no exceptions (but Durkheim and Mauss conceded many). The doctrine has been cogently attacked by Benoit-Smullyan (1966) and Raymond Firth (1975; 1973, pp. 13–14). The structuralist approach of Lévi-Strauss is potentially its greatest challenge: if one is correct the other is not. When Needham (1973, p. xxxi) reviewed the extensive work on the symbolism of the right and the left he finally concluded that it reflected not the social order, but 'constant tendencies of the human mind'.

There are, in short, serious doubts about an allegedly automatic corrrespondence between symbols and social states. No doubts strike Basil Bernstein (1967) when he claims a necessary correspondence between 'open' schools and 'open' societies. The organic solidarity of modern societies (as distinct from mechanical social solidarity in the past) is replicated not only in the integrated curriculum but in the new spatial layout of the school. This claim is based on a simple and ancient Durkheimian proposition that has never been proved.

Structuralist (as distinct from structural) perspectives seem to hold greater promise. They have been developed—though never coherently formulated—by Claude Lévi-Strauss. But they are suggestive and tantalizing and finally inconclusive. They direct our attention to 'transformations', and this is of particular interest to educationists; but the method is never explicit. The underlying model for symbols is not society but language; and the opposition between consonant and vowel is transposed into the opposition between the cooked and the raw (Lévi-Strauss, 1966).

This is the 'new' anthropology (Ardener, 1971). It has nothing in common with the 'new' sociology, which is subjective, interpretive, and phenomenological. Lévi-Strauss rejected any such phenomenological or 'extentialist' approach with contempt. Indeed, he rejected experience: this was no route to reality and truth (Lévi-Strauss, 1976, p. 71). It was the logical structure of human minds that must concern anyone who wished to understand the social order, and this was revealed in the analysis of myth. Durkheim goes from social order to symbols; for Lévi-Strauss it is the other way round.

Lévi-Strauss's analysis of myth has been savagely attacked: it is arbitrary; many other interpretations would be perfectly feasible (Cohen, 1969). One close examination of this treatment of myth concludes that he 'creates a set of problems so ill-defined as to be meaningless and provides a solution to match' (Thomas and Kronenfeld, 1976). And yet his work is powerfully evocative, providing new insights and suggesting new meanings to old problems.

The writing of Lévi-Strauss that is most directly relevant to education is his brilliantly evocative essay on cooking (Lévi-Strauss, 1966). In this he describes the 'culinary triangle' of the cooked, the rotted, and the raw. But behind this triangle are a number of simple but basic oppositions, pairs of contraries of the kind familiar in structuralist literature and revealed in the binary structure of myth: between nurture and nature, the boiled and the roasted, the economical and the prodigal, the plebeian and the aristocratic, and between endocuisine and exocusine. And Lévi-Strauss says that the cooking of a society is 'a language in which it unconsciously translates its structure—or else resigns itself, still unconsciously, to revealing its contradictions'.

The entire essay on cooking is easily 'reduced' or transposed to educational terms and makes a great deal of sense. The educational system is also a language in which a society unconsciously translates its structure or else resigns itself to revealing its contradictions. The educational system announces by its very existence pairs of contraries: the opposition between public and private, the exchange of kinsmen for colleagues, the transformation of nature to nurture, and of boys into men.

Some of the system's subsections are 'roasted' and by contrast others are 'boiled'. The roasted are schools which leave pupils somewhat exposed, unprotected, and make them tough and able to fend for themselves; the boiled are the schools which are carefully and protectively enclosed. Schools that are roasted are for men, for untamed adventurers and entrepreneurs; but schools that are boiled are for women or fastidious and sensitive boys. The boiled is endocuisine, for enclosed, intimate groups; the roasted is exocuisine, for open banquets and even uninvited guests. The roasted is Eton and Harrow; the boiled is Bedales and Dartington Hall.

The formal structure of our educational system is a powerful message based on pairs of contraries and supported by myth. Anstey's *Vice Versa* (1882) is perhaps the most elegantly structured myth: it involves role reversal when Mr Bultitude changes places with his schoolboy son and is abused and debased; and it dramatizes starkly the opposition between home and school. One kinsman is literally exchanged for another and removed from the domestic realm. The 'message' of modern schooling for society is clear. 'Island' stories have also dramatized discontinuities with family life and have provided myths for constructing binary worlds (Rebbitt, 1975).

We can have sex without marriage, food without cooking, communication without language, and growing up without schooling. Marriage, cooking, language, and schooling are not simply instrumental and functional, they are profoundly symbolic: they announce that we have moved from nature to nurture, that we are men and not beasts.

Schooling as a 'language' may be distorted and fail to translate society's structure. Reformers may force it to say things it does not mean. If the school is made to give the message that the distinctions between school and home, kinsmen and colleagues, public and private, young and old, have been virtually eliminated it will be made to lie. Attempts to give symbols new meaning without change in the underlying structures to which they refer leads to confusion and contradictory messages which lose their credibility. The lies that schools may be forced to tell come out clearly in the interactionist studies of symbols referred to in the next section. This in itself suggests that symbolic interactionism is not enough: there are underlying social realities which cannot be changed merely by manipulating the symbols. Manipulating or even renegotiating the symbols may be merely a new name for cosmetics.

## 5. LANGUAGES THAT LIE

The third perspective is that of 'symbolic interactionism'. It is far more commonsensical than the other two; it does not invoke 'deep structures' of any kind, but suggests how people use symbols in their daily affairs to order and make sense of their world. It accords symbols a greater degree of autonomy but perhaps ascribes to them more power than they have.

Most of the writing on the symbolic world of the school is highly speculative: the authors have not investigated symbols, their nature and use. Only Kate Evans has done so. Her important studies are presented in an interactionist perspective (Evans, 1971, 1974, 1979).

In the 38 schools which she studied in the late 1960s, symbols were extensively used and were of crucial importance for the ordering of time. The marking, ordering, recording, registration, and division of time was the central preoccupation of all the schools. Registration rituals took a great deal of time and effort; attendance statistics were displayed; clocks, calendars, and timetables were prominent. Ancient schools drew attention to the date of their foundation. Time divisions were inflexible and electric bells made them public, outside of individual discretion. There were marked social-class and regional differences in the number of clocks: they were most abundant in girls' grammar schools in the south, comparatively sparse in unselective schools in the north. Clocks helped pupils to manage and appropriate time. They were especially important in the sixth form where there was more free time to be managed and ordered (Evans, 1971, pp. 105–133). The schools were clearly and explicitly implicated in the tight time schedules of the wider society and pupils were sensitized to their requirements.

The symbolic order of the school accurately informed pupils about the significance of tight time schedules in the modern world; it also signalled accurately what social status and condition they could expect. Academically distinguished schools for high status pupils confirmed them in their social position; they said in effect: 'You are high status children and this school ensures that you will be high status men and women.' There was a strong emphasis on 'bounds', on the separation of the elite from the mass; staff were expected to be on close personal terms with pupils; the schools often had quadrangles and life turned inwards to these sacred areas, away from the everyday world outside. The school magazine was humourless and written in formal prose. The celebration of war deaths was important: symbols of sacrifice, loyalty, and honour were placed before the young.

Meritocratic 'status-striving' schools for mainly working-class boys and girls emphasized cleanliness and polish, door-mats and litter-bins; there were cold, unscarred vinyl and formica surfaces and an aggressive sterility of tactile space. There was respect for the privacy and spatial segregation of the staff. The dividing line between the sixth form and the rest of the school was sharp and fiercely defended; ties were worn by the sixth form and black blazers with badges which showed impregnable fortresses and rapacious beasts. All the symbols were of disciplined striving. School emblems were frequently hybrid monsters, symbols of transformation and change.

It is in their architectural symbolism that postwar schools have been made to lie. Bernstein said that 'open' schools tell us about the open society; Kate Evans knows that they tell us about the intentions of architects. Teachers may be left with an architectural message that few or none of them believe. They may circumvent the architectural rhetoric in various ways; some are forced to dissimulate.

Of course, some spaces can be modified by the current inhabitant: headmasters rearrange their office furniture; movable screens and partitions are part of the stagecraft of everyday life. Kate Evans knows this, too, and has given us highly perceptive accounts of the way headmasters manage the margins around their desks and position their chairs to proclaim their authority. The arrangement of furniture and the positioning of secretaries give off powerful messages about the boundaries that are sacred and must be maintained and those that are open to negotiation. But 'reception areas' contain invasion and belie the openness that has been claimed. The language of the objects in the headmaster's room is in fact bureaucratic, at odds with the child-centred vocabulary that he speaks (Evans, 1974).

Open-plan primary schools in postwar Britain did not 'replicate' a new-found organic social solidarity—organic solidarity has been with us, says Durkheim, since cities emerged in the thirteenth century; they reflected a deliberate (and conceivably quite mistaken) interpretation of the nation's mood by the Development Group in the Architects and Building Branch of the Ministry of

Education in 1949. These architects reached their own view of what was happening in schools and society and took it upon themselves to reinforce what they thought were the anti-hierarchical tendencies of the day. They concluded that 'various barriers and divisions within schools were lessening and tried to produce a school architecture which reflected this trend' (Evans, 1979).

This was as arrogant as it was inept, and teachers have been trying to correct the architectural rhetoric they were given ever since. It is true that some teachers have tried to live up to the architects' view of what they should be doing, but many have found the message socially false and professionally inadequate. The shell of the school gives one message; the way teachers use the space inside gives another.

Kate Evans found from the observations and inquiries in open-plan schools that there was an unending struggle 'to compensate for the dissolution of spatial boundaries by an intensified structuring and specification of the temporal, aesthetic, and knowledge orders'. In spite of official moves towards 'openness', 'The dominant theme from the external frontier of the school is a message of structured exclusion'. The 'message' of teachers was the very opposite of the message of architects:

> I found in my research study that . . . the move to an open-plan building produced the introduction of a timetable, subject specialization at the top of the school, and a considerable amount of streaming. Thus the very barriers which the educational architects claimed were dissolving . . . were in fact reinforced and in some cases instigated in response to the new forms. (Evans, 1979)

Negotiating new meanings for symbols is unavailing if the underlying social realities are unchanged.

## 6. AGE AND RITES IN THREE SOCIAL GROUPS

Age and ritual come together to shape social order in 'rites of passage'. This is clear enough in primitive societies and was described in a classic study by Arnold van Gennep (1960). In the late 1970s I tried to discover whether this is still true for us. With Roger Middleton I explored the meaning of age and major transitions in life for a group of retired Methodist ministers in their seventies, a team of professional footballers in their twenties, and a group of teachers in their thirties taking part-time higher degrees. (There were 24 'subjects' in all.) The three groups were chosen because of the marked differences in their life-cycle schedules and in the overall phasing of their lives (Musgrove and Middleton, 1981).

The parsons, footballers, and teachers were asked to talk about their life and its turning points. They were simply asked: 'Looking back on your life, would you pick out any particular stages or turning points?' (with prompts, if necessary, for adolescence and marriage). In relation to the influence of age they were asked five questions: 'Do you think there is a proper time for doing particular things, like getting married?'; 'Would you be bothered at the thought of people markedly different in age getting married?'; 'Would it bother you working for someone younger than yourself?'; 'Do you feel that age should be respected?'; and 'Do you feel strongly that you "belong with" people of about your own age?'

This was a *Verstehen* study of rites made 'from the inside'; it was less an attempt to understand them as public messages than as private meanings. Experience of a turning point was classified as a 'rite' on the basis of its symbolic character for the individual concerned—if it was emotionally highly charged and clearly 'stood for something' other than and beyond itself. Rites were not preclassified. In this very open exploration of the meanings of 'actors' there was no attempt to test precise hypotheses. Nevertheless, the views of notable social scientists were inevitably in mind, for instance those of Ralph Linton. In 1942 he had emphasized discontinuities in the life cycle of men and women in modern industrial societies. For Linton marriage marked the major discontinuity and constituted the most important *rite de passage*. Rites of passage had generally degenerated, he said, but 'it is significant that puberty ceremonies have deteriorated more than marriage ceremonies. Marriage still marks a very definite and abrupt status transition' (Linton, 1942). I was particularly interested to see whether marriage (rather than adolescence) was the major rite of passage for the subjects of this study.

Neither the experience of adolescence nor first leaving home carried any special meaning which lent it ritual significance; but the three women among the 24 interviewees—all graduate teachers—referred to a 'delayed adolescence' in their early twenties. It had been postponed from their studious and docile teenage years.

Leaving home for the first time, at whatever age (it had occurred within the range 15 to 24 years), was generally an easy and natural transition which was not seen as a special marker or divide. Only three experienced it as especially difficult, and only one of these as in any way symbolic. It had been difficult for two of the professional footballers who had left home in their northern villages at the age of 15. One went as a 'juvenile' to Arsenal, the other to Blackpool. Both were miserably homesick: 'I was so unhappy it was unbelievable. I used to cry nearly every night. Away from home, you know . . . because I wanted to be back with my family. And my dad said, "If you come back home, I'll break your neck." You know, that's how they talk round Barnsley. . . . And it was cold. I used to go to bed at half-past-six. I'd just stay there and cry.'

For a 40-year-old teacher, a late entrant to the profession, leaving home for the first time, at the age of 23, had high symbolic value. He was working in his home town in a clerical post and decided to become a lumberjack in Canada:

> I was totally dissatisfied with myself. I was shy and retiring; I felt myself just utterly boring.

He found liminality:

I wanted to get to a state where I had no security whatsoever. And I found this in Canada, where I'd nowhere to sleep, no money, no friends. And, you know, I felt I'd achieved something. I ended up with my basic self and I felt I could go on from there.

He went on to be a 'debarker' and learned to run across the logs as they came out of the mouth of the lake. His return to England was a rite of incorporation and transformation: 'After I'd done that lumberjacking I felt really big.'

But typically, leaving home had no special meaning. Teachers had found the transition from home to college easy: 'I didn't notice any emotional break, really, I thoroughly enjoyed Keele,' said a 31-year-old teacher of working-class origin. 'I left home to go to college when I was twenty', said a Methodist minister whose father had been an office manager; 'I thoroughly enjoyed it. I was the type who would have enjoyed Public School. I was a very keen football player and cricketer and tennis player.'

No one saw his adolescence as a particular stage in life. 'I was always happy at home with my mum and dad,' said one footballer; 'My mum never put a curfew on me,' said another; 'She thinks I'm a big boy and can look after myself,' said another. 'I had a very happy home life,' said a teacher; 'we didn't really have any major conflicts. Well, there were differences, of course. Smoking and drinking, that sort of thing. But adolescence was not the traumatic experience for me that it may be for others.'

Two footballers attributed an unremarkable adolescence to the total indifference of their mothers. 'My mother has never been particularly interested in anything I've done,' said one. 'It sounds terrible, but it isn't really. She just left it all up to me.' The other footballer, from a northern mining town, was more critical:

All my mother does is cook the meals, you know. They're not bothered what happens. As long as they get their money on payday, they don't care two hoots. As long as they get their money, that's it, women around where I come from. It's a real working class area. Sounds daft, but it's true.

For the three women teachers, adolescence was merely deferred. One geography teacher, now in her mid-thirties, is married to an Anglican parson and had a turbulent time in her twenties. But her teenage years were tranquil:

I came from a very working-class background, but the sort of working-class area where children are encouraged to get on. . . . I missed out on adolescent development because I didn't have any sort of conflict with my parents. No conflict of any sort. They encouraged me. I was a bookwormish little lady. It was terrible. I probably had an adolescence in my twenties, I suspect. . . .

Her first conflict with the adult world was at the end of her university course when she wanted to marry a man of 23 who was preparing for the Church. The bishop objected. ('It's too young for the image, you know. We had a terrible to-do.') They were finally allowed to marry on condition that her husband deferred his training for a year.

After her bookish schoolgirl years she now went wild. ('But not really wild. You can't be really wild as a curate's wife. But I probably pushed a lot more and reacted a lot more than I would now.') She became very outspoken and intolerant: 'I suspect I had a late adolescence in that sense . . . maybe because I was a very bookish child and didn't have many relationships beyond a good, stable family. I was reading at three. That cuts you off, doesn't it?' If she had gone on to take a PhD she would still be cut off now: 'I suspect I'd still be the adolescent that I was at twenty.'

The daughter of a sernior university lecturer told a similar story. A physics teacher now in her thirties, married with two young children, she recalled her schoolgirl years at home as a very happy time: 'I can't remember any difficulties at all. I wasn't the sort of person to be going out a great deal. Guides and church youth club were my only activities. . . . We were a very close family. We didn't go out a tremendous amount. We just enjoyed ourselves in the family, really.'

Men and her time at the university changed all that: 'I probably had adolescent problems when I went to university rather than in adolescence. I'm sure I did. That's because I started having boyfriends. I never had boyfriends before.' The big conflict was over the one she eventually married. ('My parents strongly disapproved.') He failed his degree and has had no regular work in the ensuing decade. 'He's just pipping his exams all the time.' In the meantime he has fathered two children, his wife has become senior physics mistress and is now taking a parttime higher degree. 'I sometimes think it's a shame my husband's not working: he's so much cleverer than me.' But she says she has little sense of stages in her life: 'It's all been such a gradual, happy sort of transition. I've never been an unhappy person. Most of my conflict has been since I've been married.'

The third woman teacher was 30 and unmarried. Her father was an engineer and she had no conflicts at home. She attended a girls' grammar school and had no contact with boys. But she also considers that she experienced an adolescent phase after 18: 'I really don't think that adolescence was a particular phase. The phase came when I was released from it and went away to University. That was a real phase, a real turning point. You know, freedom and a tremendous change in my life. There I was allowed to be me, and I couldn't believe it. I knew men for the first time, men who were just friends. I was deliriously happy about that.' She had actually rebelled at 18 by applying to read for a degree in theology instead of English. ('I crossed out English on my application form without telling anyone. That was the first time I'd ever taken a step out of line. But then I had to tell them. Everyone freaked, you know . . . all their faces dropped.') She has never looked back since.

Ralph Linton's emphasis on marriage as a rite of passage in modern societies gained no support in this study. For the Methodist ministers who had married 50 years previously in the 1920s, it was supremely important, partly because it was geared to ordination. But for the teachers and footballers, who had married in the 1960s and 1970s, it was not an important signal of status change. It was the mortgage rather than marriage that marked the transition to adulthood and independence. But though marriage itself signalled little change, a first child deeply modified social relationships, marked a major change of social state, and transformed the whole of life. This significance of a first child was far greater for the young footballers and teachers and made a far greater impact on their lives than had been the case with the Methodist ministers 50 years before. The relative importance of a first child and marriage appeared to have been reversed.

The teachers had scarcely noticed getting married apart from the fact that they were appreciably better off. A 33-year-old teacher had married two years previously, but 'I don't regard that as traumatic either. I'd been going around with this girl long enough, and you can't string them along for ever, can you?' But he now enjoyed a richer and easier life:

> One thing I've noticed is how much better off I've been over the past couple of years. My wife's also a teacher and there's only the two of us. It's not bad, really: you can buy what you want and you can go on holiday, go abroad and that sort of thing. I quite like doing that. . . . But that's the great difference between now and nine or ten years ago.

He remembers graduation as an important day in his life, and concedes: 'Well, I suppose my wedding day was, really. But I'm not sure that I think of it like that. I think my wife would: she would think it was great. But I've never really . . . it sounds awful to say it . . . but I've never really regarded it as . . . perhaps because, as I say, I'd known my fiancée for so long.'

The footballers had married (somewhat younger) almost by accident, scarcely noticing that they did so. 'I married at eighteen. I didn't want to go to Liverpool by myself, and I was courting, so. . . . It all sounds daft.' Another remarked: 'When she said, "Let's get married" I thought, "Why not?" But if she hadn't mentioned it I most probably would have gone on the same.' He was 20 at the time.

A mortgage for a house marked the real transition from youth to adult status. It had no connotation of debt and disgrace: it was a mark of dignity and honour. For a teacher in his late thirties a stately and dignified progression through life was marked by a series of mortgages of increasing magnitude. The young footballers—who lived cautious, highly prudential, non-hedonistic and carefully calculated lives—saw a mortgage as a major landmark. The oldest footballer, now over 30, who has had a very successful career, finds less significance in his medals than his mortgage which is now paid off:

> My house is paid for. Most people pay mortgages till they're what? Till they're sixty, don't they? Till their dying day. But mine was paid off when I was twenty-eight. Paid for.

He is contemptuous of the miners in his home town for failing to recognize the social significance of a mortgage:

> All they've done with their life is go to the pit and have a few pints. And I say, 'How much are you paying for your house-rent? Seven or eight quid? Why don't you get a mortgage?' 'What?' they say. You know, they just don't understand. 'Why don't you get a mortgage? Instead of going out every night and spending all that on ale, save it and get a bit of a downposit.' But, you know, you can't tell them. But you couldn't tell me. It's just experience and living with different and better people.

A 22-year-old unmarried footballer had just bought a semi. 'At the beginning of last year I had some money and I wanted to buy a house as an investment.' Inflation a well as status has influenced his decision: 'I didn't want my money to rot in a bank.' His friends were taking the same step in their early twenties: 'The lads were in fact buying houses at the time. They were buying semis, you know. Some were getting married. . . . And I have just in fact bought a semi myself.'

The woman teacher of religious education had not got a husband but she was getting a mortgage. At present she was again living at home:

> I shall get a mortgage and buy something, a small terraced. I've seen a mid-terraced house, a small mid-terraced. I'll move when the completion date's through in February. I'll tell my mother it's the travelling to work that gets me down, but it's the living at home that gets me down. My parents still have this little image of me, you know. And I can sort of feel the chisel as they're trying to fit me back into it. And I don't really fit. They're starting to try to put me back where I was.

A mortgage was a sure line of defence for her adult status and identity.

The Methodist ministers had, on average, waited seven years to marry and had finally done so around the age of 30. Marriage had to wait until they had finished three or four years at a theological college (which they tended to enter in their early twenties) and three years' probationary service before being ordained. 'Seven year for Raehel', is what they used to say. Marriage followed hard on the heels of ordination and one reinforced the significance of the other. As an 80-year-old interviewee recalled (he had married at 32 after a 12 year courtship): 'It was ordination on Tuesday, co-ordination on Thursday, and sub-ordination ever since.'

This was part of the firm temporal and organizational scaffolding within which the ministers were to live their orderly and linear (though geographically chaotic) lives. Ordination (followed by a manse without a mortgage) was a rite of segregation which cut them off from normal, secular life. Retirement 40 years later was a rite not of separation but of incorporation which reunited them with society. They regretted only that at this stage they were unable to afford a mortgage which would have confirmed beyond reasonable doubt their re-entry into the world.

All the ministers approved in retrospect of the old rule regarding marriage and none had resented it at the time. A 70-year-old man, whose father had worked in the Tyneside shipyards, married at 28 after many years of courtship:

> There was a very stern rule: it was clearly understood that a man accepted for the ministry did not marry until he was ordained. . . . If a chap married on probation . . . oh, by Jove! If they didn't throw him out they generally placed a penalty of extra probation on him. The Wesleyan church, going back to the pre-union days, was very strict indeed. If a man married on probation and children were born before he was ordained, they were not allowed to come under the connexional children's fund. And they were actually referred to in Wesleyan circles as 'connexional illegitimates'.

He strongly disapproved of married theological students today; neither of his own children—a man of 38 and a woman of 41—was married, and he did not feel that this was a matter for regret.

A former Durham miner recalled:

> I was ordained at Bradford in 1937. After which famous event we were wed. We'd waited for seven years. I was thirty and she was thirty-one. For seven years we wrote letters and we wrote letters and we wrote letters. We didn't live in the same place, you see. We lived seventeen miles apart.

But the old system was recalled with approval: 'It was an extremely good system, really. It was the discipline that. . . . It was hard, but I think it was a good thing.'

The lives of Methodist ministers were lived within finely coordinated and superimposed inner, organizational, and transcendental timetables. Conversion, being 'called' to the ministry, the 7-year rule for marriage, the 20-year rule for a superintendency, the 4–5-year rule for moving to another living, all embraced within an overriding divine plan, provided a firm scaffolding for life. The ministers remained unswervingly on course, and none experienced anything resembling the 'mid-life crisis' that is nowadays suggested in the psychoanalytical literature. 'I think I could sum it up by saying that my experiences throughout the years have invariably confirmed the convictions I had when I first recognized that I had a call to the ministry. Of course, the thing's unfolded . . . but it's confirmed what I believed at the start.'

Another retired minister claimed that nothing had ever changed his thinking. He was 'called' at 11, converted at 19, worked in a shop till he was 25 when he left home for college. When he was asked to look back over his long life and recall the main milestones and turning points he answered wholly in terms of landmarks in organizational history:

> I think it's quite extraordinary. You see, I was trustees' secretary in my twenties, and I arranged the jubilee of the church, the fifteenth anniversary of the church. It was a special effort: we built a new organ chamber. . . . And then fifty years afterwards I was invited to take the centenary service. I was trustees' secretary from 1922 to 1925 and, as I say, I arranged the jubilee; and then I went back three years ago and took the centenary.

His life found its symmetry and meaning in the great, recurrent festivals and celebrations of his church. Its rites of passage were his rites of passage: 'The church', he concluded, 'is still the best organization. No man is an island.'

But the organization, its rituals and obligations, were simply an expression of the divine will. Even the frequent moves from living to living expressed a divine order. A sharp distinction was made between simply accepting the offer of a living, and being sent by God. As one retired minister and his wife recalled their lives in terms of moves, this divine architecture was laid bare:

> 'It's amazing how things work out for the good. When I come to think of it, most of my appointments have been given me. I don't think . . . have I ever accepted? I accepted Elland. But most of them I've been sent.'
> 'You accepted a few, but Southend definitely was. . . .'
> 'I was sent to Southend.'
> 'And definitely Hatfield.'
> 'I wasn't invited there. They weren't invitations. Now that's most remarkable. . . .'
> 'We *have* had invitations. . . .'
> 'Right at the beginning I was sent to Melton because a man broke down there. . . . In a sense I was asked to go to Manchester. . . .'
> 'Because you were down for Warminster, really, weren't you?'
> 'But I was invited to Northampton.'
> 'Yes, and you were invited to Ipswich.'
> 'But I wasn't really invited to Barking. It was arranged there.'
> 'Things were done in high places. There was a switch. But Chelmsford. . . .'

And so a lifetime was ordered and found its meaning in a scheme of binary opposition in which transitions were defined as 'sent' or 'invited', sacred or profane. Forty years of life were reconstructed, stretched between these polarities, somewhat asymmetrical, with the balance tipped towards the divine.

The final transition, retirement, was movement from the sacred to the profane: a rite of reincorporation which restored normality. One minister's wife observed: 'I think ministers and their wives miss out on normality. It's a very lonely life. Now we've come back here in retirement, they don't look on us so much as the parson. We learn more of the little undercurrents now.' Her husband concurred:

> That's very true. They treat us now as if for the first time in our lives we're normal human beings . . . except that now and then one of them will remember . . . and it's all spoiled temporarily. . . .

The timetable of professional footballers' lives was finely calibrated. They advanced from juveniles and apprentices to professional status through nicely graduated steps. Their lives, like the Methodist ministers', were highly structured; but their careers, unlike the ministers', were drastically foreshortened. Successive transfer fees accelerated the passage of time. Throughout their twenties they were engaged in urgent future planning. The teachers in their thirties taking degrees were testing the openness of life: afraid that closure had already occurred.

Closure for footballers arrives early, perhaps before 30, and certainly not much after:

> When I was twenty-eight the manager said, 'Right, that's it: you're twenty-eight now, I can't give you a rise now.' And they start looking for someone to replace you. In the old days you used to get players playing till they were thirty-four or thirty-five. Not now. You see now, when they're thirty, they're virtually shattered. Especially in midfield, running around for six or seven years. And they say, 'Oh, he's no good. He's twenty-nine now.' And they do look old at that age now, people in football.

After 30 it is a bonus. 'Not many people have a good ten years at the game.'

At 21 they are taking coaching badges or planning small businesses against the time when they are 30. A university graduate in psychology, still only 23, is planning to take a master's degree in clinical psychology. But he has also thought of doing a correspondence course in accountancy. He has an almost frantic sense of time passing:

> Time's passing and I'm not doing anything. I've got to make a decision within the next four years, I reckon, by the time I'm twenty-seven. When I think of age I see a line at thirty, and I can't see past it. I've got to have something done by thirty, you know. Forty fades off into the distance, and then fifty, and after that. . . .

The sense of accelerated time leads to intolerance of waste. A marriage going wrong at 24 has to be jettisoned quickly: 'I thought, "I'm missing everything. It's all going flashing past me. If I don't get hold of myself soon, my life's going to be finished and there'll be nothing to show." '

There was no such urgency among the teachers, but a sense that both their careers and mental lives had closed in. Without clear plans to change their lives and careers, they were tentatively testing the possibilities of openness. The rest of life was not, perhaps, finally decided and implicit in all that had gone before, age-related career stages were not immutable and preordained. One found reassurance in the biographical summaries at the end of research papers:

> Whenever I read journal articles I read the author's biography: when they got a degree, when they got a doctorate, what they did before. I'm always fascinated by people who, you know, worked somewhere then all of a sudden, at the age of thirty or thirty-four or seventy-three, took a degree or a Ph.D., that sort of thing. Because in that way I suppose I seem to think, 'Well, there's time for me yet to change my . . . options are still open.' That is how I look at things.

His own career to date had been perfectly linear: his father was an accountant; he took a degree at LSE; at 24 he acquired both a wife and a mortgage. In his early thirties he was fondly savouring models of indeterminacy.

Age certainly matters and shapes social relationships. This was the case not only for the two heavily 'age-graded' groups but for the teachers as well. The teacher married to a parson was particularly aware of its influence. She knew that there was an older generation that did not see things her way: 'There's definitely a generation where women don't go out to work. I've suffered from this. Especially clergy wives don't to out to work, despite the fact that they don't pay clergy enough to live on.' At school it is the youth and inexperience of senior people that is resented:

> There was a great deal of bitterness when Manchester was going comprehensive and they were reappointing everybody. This school I was at appointed a girl of twenty-five as head of Biology, with two years' teaching experience. The bitterness was incredible. And I felt that I really couldn't see how anyone could have proved themselves for that sort of position at that sort of age. When you can see that there's proven experience people are happy about it. It's when you see something happening that seems purely fortuitous. . . .

The footballers had strikingly conservative social attitudes—the older ones, nudging 30, regretted that collars and ties and suits were no longer required in the dining room and when travelling to any away match ('Even the boss wears a crew-neck pullover now'). They respected social position and occupational rank. ('Football opens things up social-wise. . . . The working-class person like me'—his father is a lorry-driver—'can meet directors like we've got here. They're talking about money all the time. . . . After the game we can go upstairs and have a drink with them, and that.') And they respected age, not only because of the experience it implied.

They disapproved of large age differences in marriage and so did the parsons. The latter disapproved very strongly of youthful marriage, too: 'It is one of the things that has trouble me very greatly . . . I have tried to dissuade them. . . .' (This parson's own daughter married at 37.) And they tended to think that respect should be automatically accorded to age:

> Yes, I think so. Oh, yes. I think that it's sensible for a young man, even if he's not in agreement with everything that the older man says, should show a certain willingness to believe that the older one has reached certain opinions, certain conclusions, as a result of genuine experience.

But the gulf between the generations, another parson thought, was virtually unbridgeable:

> You see, I think the generations are irreconcilably divided. My generation was totally different from my father's generation, and my children's generation is totally different from mine. I've felt that all my life. Of course they run into each other. But I'm quite sure that mentally and psychologically the generations are different. They are set apart.

## 7. CONCLUSION

The age of individuals and more generally the organization of the passage of time are still important for the social order of modern societies; ritual of a standardized public form almost certainly has less 'depth' and is purely expressive rather than instrumental, but it is not without significance for social unity; and key institutions like marriage and schooling are themselves powerful symbols: they not only do something, they 'say' something. Age, the division of time, ritual, and symbols shape the social order of modern as of primitive societies; formal ritual is less important, but age in many ways is more (and more efficiently 'used').

Educational systems do not support the social order simply by producing people with appropriate values, attitudes, knowledge, and skills, or even by 'reproducing' whatever class system prevails: they do so by signalling and reinforcing basic facts about modern social structures. They are like rules of incest in primitive societies, signalling and regulating the social exchange on which society rests. All schools are public schools: they 'say', in effect, that we exchange kinsmen for colleagues and override the social divisiveness of family and kin. The particular curriculum and its meaning (or otherwise) for pupils is largely irrelevant. The system itself is a symbol, a message. It says further that nature has been transformed into nurture, and that boys, in due course, will be transformed into men.

The importance of age and the divisions of time is the central issue of this chapter. Impressive historical research in America shows how today the schedules and sequences of life, especially in the four or five years before and after 20, must be finely integrated in a very tight programme of change; this is abundantly illustrated in the accounts of their lives by retired parsons, career footballers, and teachers which are given in the preceding section. It is the principal message that comes from research on the symbolism of schools: it is the dividing, registration, calibration, and management of time that are of central concern. But these are not simply empirical facts: they promote order because they emit powerful messages and have meaning beyond their immediate utility.

The small-scale social inquiry reported in the preceding section underlines the symbolic character of age distinctions and 'markers' in the life cycle. The markers and the symbols reported there had not been pre-selected: they are the meanings that the 'actors' themselves found in age and particular transitions in life. It would be easy to impose pre-selected criteria, like van Gennep's tripartite diachronic structure, on the changes experienced at different stages in life. The footballers experienced separation (leaving home perhaps as early as 15); liminality (a period as a 'juvenile' or apprentice); and incorporation (professional status); the parsons experienced rites of separation from the secular sphere on ordination; their entire careers as ministers were a form of liminality; retirement was a rite of re-aggregation. This kind of formal dissection is a pointless and unhelpful imposition on the experience of those involved. The truly meaningful and symbolic rites of passage were entirely unexpected and would not be picked up in such an analysis: mortgages were a complete surprise; and so, indeed, was a parson's retirement, not as a rite of separation but of incorporation.

The point of taking contrasted groups is to make comparisons which suggest the function of rites of passage, as distinct from their meanings for 'actors'. This study lends some support to the functionalism of both van Gennep and Gluckman. Rites of passage were both more objectively elaborate and subjectively meaningful for the Methodist ministers than for the other two groups. This is consistent with van Gennep's thesis regarding the special significance (and danger) of transitions between profane and sacred spheres; and with Gluckman's thesis regarding role ambiguity: a secularized world calls for an especially emphatic differentiation of the parson's role. (The 'dog-collar' has emerged only comparatively recently along with secularization.) But the comparisons in this study are also between different points in time. Marriage as a rite of passage does not simply differ in importance between different social groups: in the 1920s it was still perhaps the most important rite of passage in life; in the 1970s it was not.

But concepts of chronological age are important *bonnes à penser*: they are part of the conceptual apparatus which members employ to create social order. The meaning of temporal relationships and sequences may be open to renegotiation; but age remains an important aspect of social structure. Chronological age is still an important principle of social differentiation, especially, perhaps, in the bipolar opposition of youth and old age.

# REFERENCES

Ardener, Edwin (1971), 'The new anthropology and its critics', *Man*, **6**.

Ariès, Philippe (1973), *Centuries of Childhood*, Penguin, Harmondsworth, Middx.

Beattie, John (1966), 'Ritual and social change', *Man*, **1** (n.s.).

Beidelman, T. O. (1966), 'Swazi royal ritual', *Africa*, **36**.

Benoit-Smullyan, E. (1966), 'The sociologism of Émile Durkheim and his school', in Harry Elmer Barnes (ed.), *An Introduction to the History of Sociology*, University of Chicago Press, Chicago.

Berger, P. L., Berger, B., and Kellner, Hansfried (1974), *The Homeless Mind*, Penguin, Harmondsworth, Middx.

Bernstein, B. (1959), 'A public language: Some sociological implications of a linguistic form', *British Journal of Sociology*, **10**.

Bernstein, B. (1967), 'Open schools, open society?', *New Society*, 14 September.

Bernstein, B. (1971), 'On the classification and framing of educational knowledge', in M. F. D. Young (ed.), *Knowledge and Control*, Collier-Macmillan, London.

Bernstein, B. (1975), *Class, Codes and Control*, vol. 3, Routledge & Kegan Paul, London.

Bernstein, B., Elvin, H. L., and Peters, R. S. (1966), 'Ritual in education', *Philosophical Transactions of the Royal Society of London*, **251**.

Bocock, R. J. (1970). 'Ritual: Civic and religious', *British Journal of Sociology*, **21**.

Bowker, J. (1973), *The Sense of God*, Oxford University Press, London.

Cohen, Percy S. (1969), 'Theories of myth', *Man*, **4** (n.s.).

Coleman, James S. (1972), 'How do the young become adults?', *Review of Educational Research*, **42**.

Douglas, Mary (1973), *Natural Symbols*, Penguin, Harmondsworth, Middx.

Durkheim, É. (1915), *The Elementary Forms of the Religious Life*, Allen & Unwin, London.

Durkheim, É., and Mauss, M. (1963), *Primitive Classification*, translated by Rodney Needham, Cohen & West, London.

Eisenstadt, S. N. (1954), 'African age-groups: A comparative study', *Africa*, **24**.

Eisenstadt, S. N. (1956), *From Generation to Generation*, Routledge & Kegan Paul, London.

Evans, Kate (1971), 'The symbolic culture of the school', unpublished MA thesis, University of Manchester, Manchester.

Evans, Kate (1974), 'The head and his territory', *New Society*, 24 October.

Evans, Kate (1979), 'The physical form of the school', *British Journal of Educational Studies*, **27**.

Evans-Pritchard, E. E. (1936), 'The Nuer age-sets', *Sudan Notes and Records*, **19**.

Evans-Pritchard, E. E. (1939), 'Nuer time-reckoning', *Africa*, **12**.

Evans-Pritchard, E. E. (1953), 'Neur spear symbolism', *Anthropological Quarterly*, **1**.

Firth, R. (1973), *Symbols. Public and Private*, Allen & Unwin, London.

Firth, R. (1975), 'The right hand and the wrong', *The Times Literary Supplement*, 21 February.

Foner, Anne, and Kertzer, David (1978), 'Transitions over the life course: Lessons from age-set societies', *American Journal of Sociology*, **83**.

Gluckman, Max (1954), *Rituals of Rebellion in South-East Africa*, Manchester University Press, Manchester.

Gluckman, Max (1959), *Custom and Conflict in Africa*, Basil Blackwell, Oxford.

Gluckman, Max (1962), 'Les rites de passage', in Max Gluckman (ed.), *Essays in the Ritual of Social Relations*, Manchester University Press, Manchester.

Gluckman, Max (1963), *Order and Rebellion in Tribal Africa*, Cohen & West, London.

Hall, Stuart, and Jefferson, Tony (1976), *Resistance Through Rituals*, Hutchinson, London.

172

Hertz, Robert (1973), 'The pre-eminence of the right hand: A study in religious polarity', in Rodney Needham (ed.), *Right and Left*, University of Chicago Press, Chicago.

La Fontaine, J. S. (ed.) (1978), *Sex and Age as Principles of Social Differentiation*, Academic Press, London.

Leach, E. R. (1958), 'Magical hair', *Journal of the Royal Anthropological Institute*, **88**.

Leach, E. R. (1966), 'Two essays concerning the symbolic representation of time', in E. R. Leach, *Rethinking Anthropology*, Athlone Press, London.

Leach, E. R. (1969), 'Virgin birth', in E. R. Leach, *Genesis as Myth and Other Essays*, Cape, London.

Lévi-Strauss, Claude (1966), 'The culinary triangle', *New Society*, 22 December.

Lévi-Strauss, Claude (1976), *Tristes Tropiques*, Penguin, Harmondsworth, Middx.

Linton, Ralph (1942), 'Age and sex categories', *American Sociological Review*, **7**.

Lloyd, P. C. (1966), 'Introduction', in P. C. Lloyd (ed.), *The New Elites of Tropical Africa*, Oxford University Press, London.

Middleton, J. (1954), 'Some social aspects of Lugbara myth', *Africa*, **24**.

Modell, John, Furstenberg, Frank F., and Hershberg, Theodore (1976), 'Social change and life course development in historical perspective', *Journal of Family History*, **1**.

Musgrove, Frank (1979), *School and the Social Order*, Wiley, Chichester.

Musgrove, Frank, and Middleton, Roger (1981), 'Rites of passage and the meaning of age in three contrasted social groups: professional footballers, teachers and Methodist ministers', *British Journal of Sociology*, **32**.

Needham, Rodney (1963), 'Introduction', in É. Durkheim and M. Mauss, *Primitive Classification*, Cohen & West, London.

Needham, Rodney (1967), 'Right and left in Nyoro symbolic classification', *Africa*, **37**.

Needham, Rodney (ed.) (1973), *Right and Left. Essays in Dual Symbolic Classification*, University of Chicago Press, Chicago.

Ong, W. J. (1959), 'Latin language study as a Renaissance puberty rite', *Studies in Philology*, **56**.

Parsons, Talcott (1942), 'Age and sex in the social structure of the United States', *American Sociological Review*, **7**.

Pickering, W. S. F. (1974), 'The persistence of rites of passage: Towards an explanation', *British Journal of Sociology*, **25**.

Raum, O. F. (1938), 'Some aspects of indigenous education among the Chaga', *Journal of the Royal Anthropological Institute*, **68**.

Rebbitt, D. (1975), 'The image of education in English fiction written for children on school life 1854–1970', unpublished MEd. thesis, University of Manchester, Manchester.

Roth, Julius (1963), *Timetables*, Bobbs-Merrill, Indianapolis, Ind.

Shils, Edward, and Young, Michael (1953), 'The meaning of the coronation', *Sociological Review*, **1**.

Spencer, Paul (1970), 'The function of ritual in the socialization of the Samburu moran', in Philip Mayer (ed.), *Socialization*, Tavistock, London.

Spencer, Paul (1976), 'Opposing streams and the gerontocratic ladder: Two models of age organization in East Africa', *Man*, **11** (n.s.).

Stub, H. R. (1969), 'Education, the professions and long life', *British Journal of Sociology*, **20**.

Swanson, Guy E. (1960), *The Birth of the Gods*, University of Michigan Press, Ann Arbor, Mich.

Thomas, L. L., and Kronenfeld, J. Z. (1976), 'Asdiwal crumbles: A critique of Lévi-Straussian myth analysis', *American Ethnologist*, **3**.

van Gennep, Arnold (1960), *The Rites of Passage*, translated by M. B. Vizedom and G. L. Caffee, Routledge & Kegan Paul, London.

White, C. M. N. (1953), 'Conservatism and modern adaptation in Luvale female puberty ritual', *Africa*, **23**.

Willis, Paul (1978), *Profane Culture*, Routledge & Kegan Paul, London.

# CHAPTER 8

# *Conclusion*

## 1. THE CELEBRATION OF SCHOOLING

This book celebrates modernity. It applauds cities, literacy, cognitive skills, and schools; scientific rationality, mobility, and educated elites. It is cautious about culture, community, and kin; it applauds choice, openness, new opportunities; it welcomes the plurality of plural societies, but insists that a core curriculum of Western literacy, numeracy, logic, and science is simply not optional. It is the business of schools first and foremost to equip all children of whatever background with the most advanced skills of thinking. Enriched self-concepts are peripheral. Teaching and learning out of context is crucial (chapter 3).

Social anthropology has been used extensively by non-anthropologists in recent years to point up the strengths and virtues of people who are not middle-class whites in modern industrial countries. Anthropologists themselves have sometimes done this, and their professional concern to understand other cultures properly leads them to view with insight and sympathy people who are often radically different from themselves. But educationists—especially sociologists of education—have used anthropological studies to make an often shrill attack on the white middle class. The concept of 'culture' has been an important item in their armoury.

The attack was directed at schooling—and especially that provided by selective grammar schools—as an allegedly 'middle-class institution'. All this has been valuable in widening our conception of 'what counts as knowledge' and as valid intellectual processes and cognitive skills; but it is perverse and destructive when it leads to the virtual imprisonment of 'other cultures' in their own social—and indeed cognitive—worlds.

Literacy has been viewed with curious disfavour: it is supposedly the middle-class accomplishment *par excellence*. Anthropologists, who are experts in pre-literate cultures, have made notable contributions to this belittlement, often unintentionally, but sometimes quite deliberately (see chapter 2). It is certain that pupils in schools should talk far more than they do and that the skills of oracy should be fully recognized and developed. The need for quietness in mass education—and public libraries—has undoubtedly stunted the skills of clear and dexterous self-expression and quickness in thinking 'on your feet'. This, in fact, is the middle-class skill *par excellence*, which pays handsome dividends in important social encounters, in committees and boardrooms; and it is precisely this skill that schools discourage and thwart. Schooling is a poor preparation for people who must have a ready tongue if they are effectively to hold positions of power. There is a real need to redress the balance between oracy and literacy in our schools; but the skills of the latter are crucial and quite fundamental to modern thinking. Without them we revert to something very like Levy-Bruhl's famous 'prelogical mentality'.

Above all this book celebrates school. It does so for two principal reasons; for its efficiency in promoting cognitive development, and for getting children out of their families. Cross-cultural psychological research makes it quite clear that without schooling children in primitive societies reach turning points on the path of cognitive development and fail to turn: from colour to form as the basis of classification at the age of 4, to a grasp of the 'invariance' of physical properties at the age of 7, and from concrete to formal operations at the age of 12 or 13. They remain cognitively undeveloped and immature for the rest of their lives (chapter 3).

The experience of cities will do something to rectify this: it will take learning out of embedded contexts and promote powers and habits of abstract thought. (In Western industrial countries city-effect is today all-pervasive and there is no need to live in cities to experience it.) But city-effect is not enough: schooling is needed to push cognitive growth as far as it will go. In these circumstances, as I have argued above (chapter 3), 'all our schools must be elite schools. They must all be very good indeed in a straightforward intellectual sense, with everyone in them at intellectual full-stretch. Their job is to "top up", at the difficult end, on what urban culture has already achieved. In an urban culture even passably average schools are redundant'.

## 2. THE POST-KINSHIP SOCIETY

In primitive societies everyone regards himself as related to everyone else. The shift from the tribe based on blood ties to the state based on 'local contiguity' was, according to Sir Henry Maine, a fundamental subversion of feeling of a kind we properly call revolution (see chapter 4). The consequences of this shift for education have been sketched by Edmund Leach (1973):

> What is it about modern society which makes us feel that it is a symptom of progress that every member of the population is now subjected by law to an institutionalized, extra-domestic, process of indoctrination over almost the whole age span between five and 20? The contrast with my primitive stereotype is total. . . . In primitive society the context of learning always remains domestic. Both at work and in play the individual is continuously surrounded by recognized kinsfolk.

Leach is in error only in judging the primitive state of affairs 'good' and the modern 'bad'.

In preindustrial societies in the West as well as in primitive societies in Africa and Oceania, education was carried out principally within the framework of

kinship relationships. It was an extended-family affair. I have examined elsewhere the shift from kinship to schooling that occurred as England industrialized (Musgrove, 1960). England's preindustrial system of education was
not a school system: it was apprenticeship. And the preferred, approved, and
most common form of apprenticeship was to an uncle—as the detailed records
of a guild such as the Cutlers of Hallamshire, for example, abundantly show
(Leader, 1905).

Stone has computed that in preindustrial England some two-thirds of male
adolescents were not living at home. They were not at school either: in the main
they were living in somebody else's home. They were there perhaps as servants
but more commonly as apprentices. There was 'a mass exchange of adolescent
children', the reason for which, says Stone, is far from clear. He links it rather
glibly to the reduction of 'oedipal and other tensions' and the danger of incest
(Stone, 1979).

What Stone fails to point out is that the households in which 'exchanged'
youngsters were living were commonly those of kinsmen, generally uncles.
William Hutton's late-eighteenth-century apprenticeship to his uncle, a Nottin-
gham stockinger, is typical. It is typical, too, in the minimal learning involved
and the cruelty which made young William abscond (Hutton, 1817). It is not
quite true, as Laslett has said of 'the world we have lost' that 'every relationship
could be seen as a love-relationship'. But Laslett's point is that most people
were normally involved most of the time with kinsfolk. The 'exchange' system
of apprenticeship did not remove them from the world of relatives to a non-
domestic sphere. Most people spent the whole of their lives living and working
in small family groups—if not their family of origin, then that of a near kinsman
(Laslett, 1965, pp. 1–10).

This is very like traditional Africa. A boy will learn to be a rain maker if his
uncle is a rain maker. Privileged and prestigious trades are kept in families and
it is entirely proper and laudable that a man hands on his skills and position to
his sister's son. Teachers are kinsmen. Among the Yoruba of West Africa
calabash carving, weaving, drumming, and medicine making are traditionally
restricted to particular lineages, 'workers are almost always united by ties of
kinship, members of a lineage following the same craft and sharing a common
workplace' (Lloyd, 1953). Today this is breaking down partly because of the
sheer speed of change and the need to train more bicycle repairers, for example, than an apprenticeship system can handle. But the lineage meeting is also
the craft meeting and the craft head is the compound head, the oldest man of
the lineage. The work group is usually a small group of kinsmen:

It is not uncommon for a boy to go to his mother's brother to learn the
craft of his mother's patri-lineage, for it is felt that the boy will have
some craft blood in his veins. In the old days it was unlikely that a
craftsman would adopt and train a boy unrelated to him. (Lloyd,
1953)

In primitive societies social exchange, on which the social order rests, is promoted by rules of incest; in modern societies by schooling. Compulsory schooling ensures exchange between the public and private spheres of life. Non-kinship forms of education have been explained in terms of the needs (especially the 'authority relationships') of capitalism; Leach (1973) echoes this view. I have contested it (Musgrove, 1979, pp. 72–82). Schooling, whatever its content, has formal properties which underlie today's social order. It exchanges kinsmen for colleagues, just as the rules of incest exchange sisters for wives (chapter 7).

## 3. THE PROBLEMS OF PLURALISM

This book has been concerned with 'other cultures' both at home and abroad. The study of other cultures abroad throws light for teachers on general problems like the conditions under which memory is effectively organized (chapter 2), new learning takes place (chapter 5), and rational beliefs are developed and sustained (chapter 4). 'Other cultures' at home are of interest and concern for different reasons: teachers must cope directly with the practical problems to which they give rise. What kind of teaching and curriculum will be appropriate and effective in multicultural schools (chapter 6)?

The ambiguities and inadequacies of the concept of culture have been examined above (chapter 6). The difficulties with the concept of 'subculture' are even greater (Clarke, 1974). Thirty years ago we talked about a 'mass society' and were troubled by the dangers of over-conformity; today we are troubled by the opposite. In the past two decades the focus of sociologists has moved to internal diversity and conflict. We are all plural—perhaps even pluralist—societies now.

Internal diversity takes a variety of forms and a variety of terms is used to analyse and describe it. 'Class' is one. 'Culture', 'subculture', and 'contraculture' are others (Yinger, 1960). When we speak of differences based on social movements, especially those with a strong ideological content, we may speak of cults and subcults. In modern societies, we are told, we now have a surfeit of subcults (Toffler, 1970, pp. 251–267). But a 'minority culture' (like the Sikhs in Britain) is neither a subculture nor a subcult. It is not derivative from the mainstream culture: it has an independent origin. The Negro culture in America is today often seen in a similar light and its independent African origin stressed (Keil, 1966, p. 5). But both subcultures and minority cultures may now claim full representation in our social and cultural institutions from television studio audiences to the school curriculum.

As late as 1960 Daniel Bell could say that, Marxism apart, mass society theory 'is probably the most influential theory in the Western world today' (Bell, 1960, p. 21). The theory was helped by the spectacle of the interwar (and indeed postwar) totalitarian states and by the apparently homogenizing effects of modern technology (Ellul, 1965, p. 332). Even classes might disappear and leave the mass at the mercy of small and powerful elites (Aron, 1950). Philip Selznick (1951) gave us a horrific view of infinitely malleable mass man.

We now have an opposite picture. Even the great American melting pot quite clearly failed to melt. When 'pluralism' was discussed 20 years ago—for instance by Rex (1959) and M. G. Smith (1960)—it was a problem comfortably distant in South Africa, the West Indies, Indonesia, and Kenya. It was with a sense of really pushing the argument that Rex suggested that such 'conflict analysis' might with some profit be applied to societies 'like our own'.

Neither Britain nor America is a 'pluralist' society in the hard sense in which South Africa is (although the members of some minority cultures in Britain meet their 'hosts' nowhere except in the market place, and their womenfolk not even there). We do not, like South Africa, have pluralism in the sense of 'formal diversity in the basic system of compulsory institutions' which is held together by the political order (Smith, 1960). But we certainly have today a hard form of pluralism in the sense that roles and statutes are not interchangeable without doing violence to existing social practice: the roles of wives, judges, husbands, priests are interchangeable among the Greeks, Italians, and Irish in New York; they are not interchangeable among the Sikhs, West Indians, English and Muslims in Rochdale. Greeks, Italians, and Irish in New York do not constitute a plural society; West Indians, Sikhs, Jews, and English in Accrington do.

Among the dangers that beset the application of the concept of culture (and subculture) is this: that it leads to a new form of stereotyping. 'Race' is out, 'culture' is in. Its application in the field of education (or politics) leads to the reinforcement of an identity which it not only identifies but actually creates. And if this is done to rectify injustice, to give oppressed minorities not only self-respect but their rights, this may be seriously to misconceive the problem of today's Western plural societies.

Subcultures—but more especially contracultures and subcults—may indeed arise from deprivation and oppression. (Subcultures are just as likely to arise from simple isolation.) The Black Muslims in North America and the Rastafarians in Jamaica are good contemporary examples of response to deprivation and oppression (Watson, 1973). But it would be a grave error to regard all subcultures and minority cultures as either oppressed or suffering from a sense of inadequacy and inferiority—which we should shape our school curricula to rectify.

The curricula of television in both America and Britain have been extraordinarily effective in rectifying it. Sometimes the effect of minorities-oriented programmes has been allied to already powerful traditions of high self-esteem. The result is not that the 'other cultures' in our midst present a problem because they feel inferior and unworthy; but precisely because they do not.

In the cotton towns of northern Lancashire where I conducted research into multicultural education (1980–1982). the Sikhs wore their turbans with a self-confident set of the head—just as the Jews of north Manchester wear their broad-brimmed, set-back trilby hats. The problem–both social and educational–seemed not to be self-abasement and low self-regard: the problem was arrogance.

In Rochdale the Pakistanis have 'incapsulated' themselves to escape moral contamination by their hosts. Schools breach their domestic defences and bring them into the public sphere; but they hold aloof from British life where they can, not out of fear or even a sense of personal inadequacy, but contempt:

> The reason for not participating in the British way of life is that the Pakistanis had learnt from childhood that the Western ways were bad, to be despised and regarded as a sign of moral failure. . . . They reverted back to their 'Pakistani behaviour' as soon as they got the opportunity. . . . This whole situation increased Pakistani incapsulation and dependence on the kinship-friendship groups, ethnic institutions and facilities, which are available in the areas of their concentration. (Anwar, 1979, p. 216)

Pakistani nightshift workers in Rochdale textile mills were quite clear that theirs was a superior culture and that their children must be saved from the corrupting influence of the English school:

> One nightshift worker wanted to keep Western influences away from the younger children, 'giving them religious and Urdu instruction and telling them what is moral and immoral'. Another respondent suggested: 'I would like to see the children getting education but having no social mixing with British people at individual level.' (Anwar, 1979, p. 167).

Another Pakistani textile worker is reported as explaining how he gave lectures to his children to respect their elders while he was giving them religious and Urdu language lessons at home. He explained how important it was to do this from an early age, otherwise, 'they learn independence and other rude things at school and it is difficult to counter that influence at a later stage' (Anwar, 1979, p. 59).

Pakistani women are even more gravely threatened by the depravity of white civilization. In Rochdale the majority of Muslims still do not allow their wives and daughters to work or have contact with the outside world. A home-tutoring scheme in English language for Pakistani women met with only limited success: their menfolk feared that 'those English ladies [the tutors] might teach their women about liberty and other permissive ideas' (Anwar, 1979, p. 166). There are widespread fears that even arranged marriages may one day be questioned, and the general result is that 'desperate attempts are being made to keep young people within the family-kinship fold and culture'.

In my own research into Jewish (voluntary aided) day schools in Lancashire I found no such withdrawal as Anwar found among the Pakistanis in Rochdale. But there was certainly a sense of both moral and intellectual superiority. There were German-born teachers who had survived Dachau and Belsen and spoke, unprompted, of their experience with pride. Pupils were aware of the marked 'over-representation' of Jews in England's intellectual and professional elites. The diaspora was the Jewish contribution to the wellbeing of mankind. They had no wish to make their homes in Israel. They would remain in England precisely because they were superior to their hosts.

The sense of superiority of Jews, Pakistanis, and Sikhs is certainly not media-induced though it is probably media-reinforced. Raymond Aron realized many years ago that television was less likely to uphold, 'mass society' than to fragment it and reinforce the identities of its constituent parts. The 'movie-radio-television culture', said Aron, would promote diversity—although authentic peasant and proletarian cultures would probably disappear (Aron, 1972, pp. 130–136). Alex Haley's television serial 'Roots' (1980–1981) powerfully illustrates this thesis.

The new Negro consciousness has been powerfully reinforced and taken out of the ghetto by the mass media. There is a sense not of black impotence but of black power based on nation-wide contacts. Resources for demonstrations or riots can be very rapidly mobilized and deployed. This is as true of England as of America. Ethnic minorities, which even 20 years ago felt isolated, powerless, degraded, become 'bolder as the lines of communication are opened up' (Singer, 1973). Mass communications have strengthened and forged new identities for ethnic minorities. We have a 'media-induced pluralism' of an active, self-assertive, and very self-confident kind:

> TV makes minority groups lose their minority weakness and perceive their strength through numbers in other cities and . . . the black community becomes much like McLuhan's 'global village'; a process of electronic gemeinschaft has accomplished this. (Singer, 1973)

Of course, television is not the whole story; ethnic groups are richer, too (and increasingly, in Britain will use their wealth to insulate themselves still further from their hosts and set up their own private, fee-paying schools).

If educationalists see the problem of curriculum change and development in multicultural schools in the 1980s as fortifying abject self-images, they have almost certainly got the problem wrong.

## 4. A CONFLICT OF PEDAGOGIES

I have been impressed during my recent research into multicultural schools in the cotton towns of Lancashire as much by a highly specific 'conflict of pedagogies' as by a more general conflict of cultures. This conflict is most starkly expressed in the contrast between the (part-time) Koranic schools of Muslim communities and the open-plan primary schools of local education authorities. The immigrant communities want a mastery of modern as well as their traditional knowledge; the education authorities seem to refuse it.

But I am also impressed by the way this conflict recurs universally in widely different social contexts wherever European and 'other cultures' meet and interact. Even the most relativist of modern educationists assume that non-directive, discovery methods have a universal validity and should be imposed impartially on all cultures whatever their past traditions and current problems. What 'other cultures' actually want from us many would see as most worthy, distinguished, and indeed central in our educational tradition (though perhaps a little old-fashioned)—high moral teaching and good learning: a sense of values and a strenuous and disciplined pursuit of knowledge. And we persistently refuse to give it. The arguments are educational, the imperialism pedagogic. It is then that 'other cultures' turn back upon themselves.

This no doubt somewhat idealized version of the Western educational tradition is not withheld from the people of other cultures in order to keep them in subjection. Often it is withheld to protect them from an 'over-academic' education and the risk of being chronically unemployed. But today it is principally because we have shifted significantly towards more open, less formal and directive methods of teaching and learning. 'Other cultures' may, in important respects, be in conflict with Western culture; but above all they are in conflict with the ethos and culture of teacher training. Education officers and local authority advisers as well as teachers regretted in their discussions with me that Pakistani parents wanted their children to use textbooks. I though these must be Urdu textbooks. No, I was told with regret, they were physics textbooks. And the textbooks were refused because they would restrict the free exploration and discovery which lead to true scientific knowledge and understanding.

If they can get from us an education in the older, honoured tradition of high moral purpose and disciplined learning (which is not too obviously and directly 'applied'), the Jews of Manchester will desert their own King David School and go to Manchester Grammar. Academic values override ethnic loyalties. And the well-to-do Muslims in Bolton, who now send their children to a Muslim private school, would do likewise. It is not sufficient to see this demand as a response to the 'power structure': a bid for entry into positions of importance and prestige. Often it is abundantly clear—as I have amply documented in this book (chapters 2, 5, and 6)—that an 'academic' education may be a very serious handicap in life, and is seen as such, especially in developing countries with a simple technology and embryonic bureaucracy. This is not readily explained in simplistic functionalist terms.

Of course, Koranic schools still adhere to a stultifying method of teaching which relies on repetition and recitation of matter which is scarcely and perhaps not at all understood. There may still be a proper place for such skills and routines in ritual life, but not in the mainstream of a modern, secular world. Professional-class Pakistanis in Rochdale recognize that this ancient form of Koranic teaching is too rigid: a Pakistani doctor is reported as saying that he wants his children to maintain a sense of ethnic identity, but 'Children should get a proper interpretation of the Quran and not just recitation. That is what we are trying to arrange—to provide a full understanding of Islam for our children with the help of the community' (Anwar, 1979, p. 203).

One reason for leaving Pakistan for England may well be to get an English education for the children. But in the event there is bitter disappointment with English schools:

'I brought them [my children] here so that they could get a good education but schools do not seem to have any control. . . . I am seriously thinking of taking them back before they get too old.' (Anwar, 1979, p. 167)

There is a remarkably widespread reaction against English education because it apparently fails to live up to its own traditions. What we provide falls short of the real thing, at least in the idealized form in which it is envisaged from Botswana to Bengal. Even Australian Aboriginals, who in one instance have some control over a school, are primarily concerned to provide for themselves what white schools had signally failed to provide—an effective Western education.

Their white teachers had formerly simply shown them films. This was doubtless a strategy born of despair in the face of the sheer difficulty of teaching a very backward people. But the Aboriginals wanted an effective 'European' curriculum—perhaps partly for political motives in the sense that they wished to be able to hold their own with the whites. When they achieved control of their own school at Strelley in Western Australia their principal aim was not to fortify and transmit Aboriginal culture: it was to gain mastery of white culture. The curriculum made a gesture towards fishing and gathering pearls, but their essential concern was to become modern (Liberman, 1981).

As in Rochdale and Ramsbottom, so in New York: when ethnic-minority parents want their children to be given mastery of the key skills and concepts of white culture, they come up hard against the professional culture of teachers and are severely rebuked for not understanding the true nature of education. The parents of Negro and Puerto Rican children attending one city-centre school in New York 'asked that the school give emphasis to the basic reading and mathematical skills to the children at an early age. These suggestions were rejected by the teachers who implied that the parents held an antiquated view of education. The teachers argued that attention be placed on the "growth of the whole child" not on basic skills' (Rosen, 1977). And the growth of the whole child, as Fred Clarke never tired of saying, must first and foremost be growth within his 'own' culture.

## 5. CONCLUSION: THE THIRD CULTURAL REALITY

The multicultural city-centre school in New York explicitly rejected 'deficit theories' of ethnic-minority differences and operated instead an 'alternative competency model'. These alternative competencies were those of 'other cultures' and were held to be no less valid and valuable than the competencies of middle-class whites. The real difficulty, in practice, was to know just what they were.

The school ('Center') had an official view of the place of other cultures in the curriculum, and 'other cultures' were not only ethnic minorities but social classes as well:

> The basic goal of the multicultural institution is to bring together and maintain a variety of racial, ethnic and class identities at all levels of the institution. (Center's policy statement quoted, Rosen, 1977)

The multicultural programme of the school had been carefully worked out in sophisticated theoretical terms—among which the key concept was 'culture'—and was seen by the director and his staff as a model; the American anthropologist (Rosen) who spent eight months making an intensive study of it concluded that it was a disaster.

The alternative competency policy explicitly rejected the melting-pot concept which 'fostered the loss of individual differences and assimilation of all people into a dominant culture' and proposed instead that 'alternative lifestyles will be given equal value within the classroom'. Recognition would be given to the particular intellectual skills of the different culture groups. The culture concept was applied to pick these groups out (Negroes, Latinos, and Anglos) and to provide each with culturally appropriate educational experiences:

> For the teachers and staff at the Center, culture consists of a set of fixed and nearly immutable traits tied to particular categories of persons. These categories and their corresponding traits are used alternatively to identify, stereotype, and explain human behavior. Moreover the tripartite division of the Center's population is largely invented by the Center itself and glosses over the great cultural and economic variety in background of the Center population. (Rosen, 1977)

The anthropologist who made this study concluded that, whatever else might be in doubt about this programme, 'it is clear that to begin with only the concept of culture is a step in the wrong direction' (Rosen, 1977). He pointed out very much as Radcliffe-Brown had done (see above, Chapter 6) that people do not experience cultures: they experience one another. The school staff had in fact applied a highly reified concept of culture: it not only entrapped the child in his category (his culture) but gave him a largely artificial category anyway. These are precisely the dangers in the use of the concept that I have examined above (chapter 6). Cultures—and even subcultures—come to be seen as independent entities which do things to people and have rights.

The argument of this book (especially in chapters 5 and 6) is that the social life of multicutural, plural, and modernizing societies is best interpreted as Malinowski's 'third cultural reality'. I have argued that the school curriculum—apart from the core curriculum of logic and science which is transcultural—should be based not on parent or contributary cultures but on the unending dialectic of conflict and interaction between them. Such a curriculum is based on where the children actually are: where their interests and minds are currently engaged. It needs a thorough research programme to establish what these focal points of tension are—conducted with a full awareness that these are constantly changing and may vary quite radically in different communities. But the issues would probably include, at least in areas of Asian concentration: the question of arranged or free choice marriages; the Asian takeover of retail shops and skill in running them; different ethnic contributions to the nightshift and the unemployed; fate and submission compared with enterprise and initiative; family loyalties and parental rights; what constitutes proper discipline at home and at school. These are merely points of departure for examining differing value systems, histories and religions, social traditions and current power dispositions. Such studies both explore and help to create a third cultural reality.

Malinowski's concept of a third cultural reality, a *tertium quid* with its own determinism, has found surprisingly widespread approval among sociologists and anthropologists. Rex (1959) was generally critical of Malinowski but conceded that he 'did make a real contribution to our understanding of the workings of the culture contact process by recognizing that there were emergent patterns arising in the contact situation different from those of the parent cultures'. Curiously, when Malinowski discussed education in 'culture contact' situations, he advocated *de facto* segregation.

Malinowski was as much influenced by his experience as a Pole as by his work as an anthropologist:

> In Europe we members of oppressed or subject nationalities . . . do not desire anything like fusion with our conquerors and masters. Our strongest claim is for segregation in terms of full cultural autonomy which does not even need to imply political independence. (Malinowski, 1943)

Schools in Africa would be no more than skills centres; the traditions of ancestor worship and initiation ceremonies must be upheld, but this would be done at home.

This is an utterly disastrous inference from the culture concept; and it is exactly such separate development within multicultural societies that the concept of culture legitimates today. Our task in education today—as it always has been—is not to preserve or transmit particular cultures but to transcend them; and the curriculum of any school in a multicultural society will be rooted in the unending dialectic of integration–particularism.

## REFERENCES

Anwar, Muhammad (1979), *The Myth of the Return. Pakistanis in Britain*, Heinemann, London.
Aron, Raymond (1950), 'Social structure and the ruling class', *British Journal of Sociology*, **1**.
Aron, Raymond (1972), *Progress and Disillusion*, Penguin, Harmondsworth, Middx.
Bell, Daniel (1960), *The End of Ideology*, Free Press, New York.

Clarke, M. (1974;, 'On the concept of sub-culture', *British Journal of Sociology*, **25**.

Ellul, J. (1956), *The Technological Society*, Cape, London.

Hutton, William (1817), *The life of William Hutton*.

Keil, Charles (1966), *Urban Blues*, University of Chicago Press, Chicago.

Laslett, Peter (1965), *The World We have Lost*, Methuen, London.

Leach, Edmund (1973), 'Keep social anthropology out of the curriculum', *The Times Educational Supplement,* 2 February.

Leader, R. E. (1905), *History of the Cutlers of Hallamshire in the County of York*, Rawson & Brailsford, Sheffield.

Liberman, K. B. (1981), 'Aboriginal education: The school at Strelley, Western Australia', *Harvard Educational Review*, **51**.

Lloyd, Peter (1953), 'Craft organization in Yoruba towns', *Africa*, **23**.

Malinowski, B. (1943), 'The pan-African problem of culture contact', *American Journal of Sociology*, **48**.

Musgrove, F. (1960), 'The decline of the educative family', *Universities Quarterly*, **14**.

Musgrove, F. (1979), *School and the Social Order*, Wiley, Chichester.

Rex, J. (1959), 'The plural society in sociological theory', *British Journal of Sociology*, **10**.

Rosen, David M. (1977), 'Multicultural education: An anthropological perspective', *Anthropology and Education Quarterly*, **8**.

Selznick, Philip (1951), 'Institutional vulnerability in mass society', *American Journal of Sociology*, **56**.

Singer, B. D. (1973), 'Mass society, mass media and the transformation of minority identity', *British Journal of Sociology*, **24**.

Smith, M. G. (1960), 'Social and cultural pluralism', *Annals of the New York Academy of Sciences*, **83**.

Stone, L. (1979), *The Family, Sex and Marriage in England 1500–1800*, Penguin, Harmondsworth, Middx.

Toffler, Alvin (1970), *Future Shock*, Bodley Head, London.

Watson, Llewellyn G. (1973), 'Social structure and social movements: The Black Muslims and the Ras-Tafarians in Jamaica', *British Journal of Sociology*, **24**.

Yinger, Milton M. (1960), 'Contraculture and subculture', *American Sociological Review*, **25**.

# Index

185

186